Wisdom With Understanding is Better Than Rubies

Lurine Karon Greenberg
Fine Arts Collection

THE MASTER MUSICIANS

BYRD

SERIES EDITED BY R. LARRY TODD
FORMER SERIES EDITOR, THE LATE STANLEY SADIE

THE MASTER MUSICIANS

THE MASTER MUSICIANS

BYRD

KERRY McCARTHY

OXFORD

UNIVERSITY PRESS

OXFORD
UNIVERSITY PRESS

Oxford University Press is a department of the University of Oxford.
It furthers the University's objective of excellence in research,
scholarship, and education by publishing worldwide.

Oxford   New York

Auckland   Cape Town   Dar es Salaam   Hong Kong   Karachi
Kuala Lumpur   Madrid   Melbourne   Mexico City   Nairobi
New Delhi   Shanghai   Taipei   Toronto

With offices in

Argentina   Austria   Brazil   Chile   Czech Republic   France   Greece
Guatemala   Hungary   Italy   Japan   Poland   Portugal   Singapore
South Korea   Switzerland   Thailand   Turkey   Ukraine   Vietnam

Oxford is a registered trade mark of Oxford University Press
in the UK and certain other countries.

Published in the United States of America by
Oxford University Press
198 Madison Avenue, New York, NY 10016

Library of Congress Cataloging-in-Publication Data
McCarthy, Kerry Robin.
Byrd / Kerry McCarthy.
p.   cm. — (The master musicians)
Includes bibliographical references.
ISBN 978-0-19-538875-6 (hardcover : alk. paper)
1. Byrd, William, 1539 or 40-1623.   2. Composers—England—Biography.   I. Title.
ML410.B996M32   2012
780.92—dc23
[B]
2012030248

3 5 7 9 8 6 4 2

Printed in the United States of America
on acid-free paper

For Joseph Kerman

Never without reverence to be named of the musicians

Preface

WRITING THE LIFE OF A RENAISSANCE ARTIST IS USUALLY A MATTER of filling in the gaps between an impressive body of art and some rather sketchy biographical documentation. This may be most keenly felt in biographies of Shakespeare, where the distance between what we see in the artist's works and what we know of his life can seem almost unbridgeable at times. The situation with William Byrd is less desperate. He lived a long and (for a musician of his time) quite well-documented life. He left some primary sources that would be the envy of Shakespeare scholars—including a series of first-person essays on his own music and the process of creating it. He also left, as Shakespeare did, a large and incredibly varied collection of works.

Byrd's career lasted nearly six decades, and more than five hundred pieces by him have survived. He wrote in almost every genre of his day: Latin masses and motets, English sacred music, accompanied and unac-companied secular songs, and a wide variety of music for keyboard and strings. If every note of his vocal music had been lost, he would still be considered a first-rate composer on the strength of his instrumental works alone. His musical life reflected many of the cultural conflicts and paradoxes of the English Renaissance. He was a Catholic dissident who thrived in a Protestant nation, acting as a revered court composer in public and producing music for clandestine Catholic services in private. Although Byrd is often at his most attractive as a marginalized figure, it is also important not to lose sight of how deeply he was involved with the Elizabethan establishment. He was as well known in his day as any court poet or playwright, and just as close to the centers of power.

The image on the cover of this book, a monumental painting made in 1604, illustrates the point nicely. It shows the negotiations for a peace treaty, the so-called Somerset House Conference, ending the two-decade war that prompted the Spanish Armada and tore apart much of northern Europe. The Spanish and Flemish delegates are on the left side of the table; their English counterparts are on the right. These were the most powerful and influential people in England, and all five of them were linked to Byrd in various ways. Robert Cecil, earl of Salisbury, is at the head of the table with a letter in front of him. Byrd wrote a suite of keyboard pieces in his honor, some of the last works he ever published. Henry Howard, seated next to Cecil, was one of Byrd's major patrons, to whom he dedicated a large and elaborate collection of music (the first book of *Gradualia*) the year after this picture was painted. Charles Howard and Thomas Sackville, the two older men by the window, both came to Byrd's defense (as Cecil also did) in his interminable legal disputes. Charles Blount, the young man in the middle of the group, was the lover and eventually the controversial second husband of the courtier Penelope Rich, whose colorful life Byrd commemorated in numerous songs.

There were also connections with the other side of the table. The Flemish delegation was sent from the Brussels court of the Archdukes Albert and Isabella, where Byrd's former student and colleague Peter Philips was director of music. Byrd's own son Thomas had recently emigrated to Spain and spent several years in Valladolid studying for the Catholic priesthood (without success, as it turned out; he was expelled from the seminary and sent back to London, where he eventually resurfaced in the distinguished post of Gresham Lecturer in Music). Even the location of the meeting was familiar to Byrd. He kept a private apartment in London, "in the earl of Worcester's house in the Strand," only a few minutes' walk from the sunlit room where the treaty was being negotiated. At a distance of more than four hundred years, the atmosphere of luxury, gravity, and political tension is still palpable in this painting. That was the world in which Byrd's music was created and performed.

Byrd cultivated literary connections as well as political ones: in fact the two were often inseparable in Renaissance England. He set the words of numerous contemporary poets, including Philip Sidney, Walter Raleigh, Edward de Vere, and a host of characters less familiar to modern readers. Some of Sidney's poetry appeared in musical settings by Byrd long before it was ever collected and published. Edmund Spenser's wedding ode *Prothalamion*, with the haunting refrain borrowed by T. S. Eliot—*Sweet Thames, run softly, till I end my song*—was written for the marriage of William Petre, one of Byrd's young patrons and a close friend of his family, to whom the composer dedicated a beautiful set of keyboard works. (Despite the personal connection with the Petre family, this was anything but provincial music. It eventually made its way into a clutch of European manuscripts, from which it would influence Sweelinck and his pupils well into the seventeenth century. It is no exaggeration to call Byrd, in mature pieces such as these, one of the first real Baroque keyboard composers.)

Byrd remained in touch with the court and with his fellow musicians until the end of his working life. His last published works, like his first, were printed in collaborative volumes alongside other people's music. He was now the revered senior partner, and a younger contemporary such as Thomas Morley, who had moved on to a lighter, more fashionable Italian style, was still eager to praise Byrd for his "deep skill" in music. That is a remarkably accurate two-word description of his talent. There was no shortage of skill in early English music —the furious virtuosity of John Bull's keyboard style, the dazzling word-painting of a Weelkes madrigal— but Byrd exercised his skill with a depth that rewards almost endless listening and study. "The oftener you shall hear it," as he himself said, "the better cause of liking you will discover." It would be an awfully arrogant statement if it were not so true.

Despite the wealth of biographical information that has come to the surface, much of it quite recently, we still know Byrd best of all through the music he wrote. It is difficult to look at his music without looking at his life; it is almost impossible to do the opposite. For that reason, I have decided to break with convention by treating life and works together in a single broad narrative. This is not an exact science because so many of Byrd's works, even those he published himself, cannot be given precise dates. There are also a number of historical gaps (such as the first two decades of his life) that have to be bridged with some mixture of context, speculation, and imaginative effort. I have done my best to fill them in without departing from known facts or resorting to wishful thinking.

A brief note on names and faces: "William Byrd" was not an uncommon name in Renaissance England, and a number of unrelated people have been confused with our Byrd at various times. One of them was a lawyer who witnessed Shakespeare's will in 1616. Another was a successful cloth trader who backed voyages to the New World. Yet another was singing in the choir of Westminster Abbey in the early 1540s: it is tempting to make some connection, but there is none. There is also no known link between the composer and the notorious eighteenth-century Colonel William Byrd of Virginia, although the two men did share the same fortunate habit of signing the title pages of books and pamphlets they owned. There is no evidence that the well-known engraved portrait of "Byrd" (or its companion engraving of "Tallis") is anything but a fanciful eighteenth-century artist's rendition of an Elizabethan gentleman. With that in mind, I have resisted the temptation to put it on the cover or include it elsewhere in the book.

To the Reader

BYRD USUALLY BEGAN HIS BOOKS WITH A NOTE TO THE READER. THIS book, like its companions in the *Master Musicians* series, will have readers of many different sorts. Offering a single volume "to serve for all companies" (as Byrd described one of his own songbooks) can be a risky thing. I have not assumed any specialist knowledge of English Renaissance music, although I hope there is something here to interest both amateur and professional audiences. I have not been able to discuss or even mention every individual piece of Byrd's music in the space available. The same is true for the innumerable social and artistic connections that can be drawn between the composer and the world he lived in. Of course it can be disappointing to find one's favorite musical work, or one's favorite Elizabethan character, passed over in silence. Readers interested in more detailed musical criticism will want to consult the magisterial books of Joseph Kerman (on the Latin-texted music) and Oliver Neighbour (on the instrumental music). John Harley's 1997 biography and its 2010 sequel, to which I am greatly indebted, remain the most extensive sources of archival information on Byrd's life and social context. My hope is that this introductory account will encourage at least some people to wade into the more specialized scholarship on Byrd, much of which is musically inspiring and very well written. Appendix E, a brief annotated guide to Byrd literature, has been compiled with such readers in mind.

Another hope is one I share with the composer himself: "Whatsoever pains I have taken herein, I shall think to be well employed, if the same be well accepted, music thereby the better loved and the more exercised." This book is addressed in a special way to those who sing or play Byrd's works and want to know more about the man who composed them. It is intended to encourage more music-making, and more reflection on music-making. He wrote some splendidly accessible (though never simplistic) pieces, and a quick read through the Salisbury pavan or *Ave verum corpus* can be worth a thousand words. My book is also addressed in a special way to students of music: in some ways it is simply the book I would have wanted to read twenty years ago. Byrd more than once signed himself as a "friend to all that love or learn music." He knew that those two things were inextricably linked. If this volume contributes something to either the learning or the love of music, it will have done its job.

Acknowledgments

THIS BOOK COULD NEVER HAVE BEEN WRITTEN WITHOUT THE HELP OF many friends and colleagues. Larry Todd first suggested a new Byrd biography in 2007 and has been a constant source of good advice since then. John Harley gave me several rounds of meticulous commentary on the manuscript. His encyclopedic knowledge of Byrd's life and times has saved me from a few disasters and countless embarrassments. Oliver Neighbour and Andrew Johnstone also went through the text in great detail and offered indispensible advice on matters both large and small. Jeremy Smith helped the book climb free of its rather shaky beginnings, and Richard Turbet kindly shared his bibliographic expertise as it took shape. Benjamin Hebbert led me to the remarkable painting in Chapter 4. Davitt Moroney continues to inspire with his knowledge and love of Byrd's music. David Trendell has been a great encouragement throughout the whole process. Jamie Apgar's skill in producing the musical examples would have been appreciated by Byrd, who knew the value of a good typesetter. My editor Suzanne Ryan and the staff at Oxford University Press have been unfailingly helpful along the way. Bonnie Blackburn was, as always, the best of copyeditors. A special word of thanks is due to Dean Applegate and all the musicians at the annual Byrd Festival in Portland, who continue to bring this music to life year after year. My greatest debt is to Joseph Kerman, whose work first inspired me to start writing about Byrd. This book is dedicated to him with gratitude.

Kerry McCarthy
23 November 2012

Contents

Appendices

BYRD

CHAPTER ONE

Origins

O new, youthful hope of our nation...
—Ferdinando Heybourne, preface to the 1575 *Cantiones*

WILLIAM BYRD WAS ONE OF SEVEN CHILDREN OF A WELL-TO-DO London family. He seems to have come from a musical household. He wrote late in life of his "natural inclination and love to the art of music, wherein I have spent the better part of mine age." His older brothers Simon and John were choristers at St. Paul's Cathedral—Simon went on to leave music books and instruments in his will—and his sister Barbara married an instrument maker and helped run the shop. The details of William's own early life can only be pieced together from genealogical research and informed speculation: we know almost nothing of his activities until he surfaces in his early twenties as the organist of Lincoln Cathedral. He often mentions his friends and colleagues in his writings, but he never mentions his parents or siblings.

There is no surviving record of Byrd's birth or baptism. The best piece of evidence we have is a legal document from October 1598 in which he claims, in his own handwriting, to be "of the age of 58 years or thereabouts." This would place his birth in 1540, or perhaps late in 1539. It looks at first sight like an annoyingly imprecise figure, but "thereabouts" was no more than contemporary legal jargon, a standard disclaimer added to almost all ages given in English court documents: it removed the obligation to add a precise number of months and days. (When Shakespeare made a legal deposition in 1612, his age was recorded as "48 years or thereabouts." It is clear from other sources that he was in fact forty-eight years old at the time.) This sort of language would have come naturally to the middle-aged Byrd, who had already had his share of dealings with the convoluted English legal system, and there is no real reason to doubt his statement here. He does say in his will, dated November 1622, that he is in the "80th year of mine age." That points to a slightly later birthdate, and it certainly deserves consideration, but it is hard to reconcile with the 1598 document. It often took months or years for people to finish drafting their wills. This one appears to have been begun earlier, then revised or recopied without due attention to the passage of time.

Byrd's life began at an unusually volatile moment in English history. 1540 was the year the workshop of Hans Holbein produced the iconic "Rome portrait" of the forty-nine-year-old Henry VIII, glowering at the viewer with fists clenched, the massive canvas barely able to contain his bulk. The "young, lusty, and courageous prince" of his early reign had given way to the capricious tyrant. During this single year, King Henry met, married, and divorced his fourth wife, executed the man who had arranged the marriage, and, on the day of the execution, married for the fifth time. He continued to build up his own musical establishment, often at great expense. In 1540 he brought in the "King's new viols," a full consort of virtuoso southern European string players who would change the character of English instrumental music within a generation. This was also the year he finished dismantling the monasteries and convents—an act that, more than any other, marked the real end of medieval England. The very last to surrender, in March 1540, was Waltham Abbey, a large Augustinian foundation north of London. The royal commission removed the monks and dispersed the lay staff, including a young organist named Thomas Tallis, who left with a pension of £20 and a fifteenth-century manuscript textbook of music theory.

The book still survives in the British Library (now catalogued as Lansdowne 763), with Tallis's name inscribed prominently on the last leaf. It was already a rather old-fashioned book by 1540, but he must have thought it was important enough to acquire, with or without his superiors' permission. (The first page of the manuscript calls down curses on anyone who "maliciously takes away or defaces this book." There was clearly no question of malice here.) The agents who shut down the

English monastic libraries were in the habit of looting them for scrap paper, a practice that the antiquarian John Bale described bluntly in 1549: "some to serve their jakes [toilets], some to scour their candlesticks, and some to rub their boots." This book met a more fortunate fate. It made its way into the musical lineage of the English Renaissance: some of its content resurfaces, in somewhat garbled fashion, in Thomas Morley's 1597 *Plain and Easy Introduction to Practical Music*. Morley could hardly have obtained it from anyone other than Byrd, who was Tallis's most distinguished pupil and Morley's own teacher.

Tallis's music textbook is a collection of twenty short treatises. Some of them are practical materials for working musicians: instructions for sight-reading chant, exercises in musical notation, rules for improvisation set out by the fifteenth-century English composer Leonel Power. There is a satirical poem on the misbehavior of singers and their bad habits in choir:

> Janglers and japers, sleepers, yawners, and drawlers,
> Mumblers, skippers, overrunners...

Other chapters are speculative flights of fancy. One compares the eight Gregorian modes to the movements of the sun and the seven planets; another is an allegorical poem on music featuring a "mystical gamut" allegedly composed by Mary Magdalene. The whole thing is a remarkable portrait of the musical world that Tallis, and the rest of England with him, was leaving behind in 1540. By the time Byrd began his own education, much of that world had already disappeared forever. It is hard to imagine a wider generation gap between a teacher and his student. In fact it is hard to imagine that any other generation before the twentieth century could have had a more chaotic musical upbringing. Before Byrd was out of his teens, he would see three swift and almost total changes (in the late 1540s, 1553, and 1559) in the practice of English sacred music, enforced with strict legislation and in some cases with physical violence. He would also see an unprecedented revolution in the style of secular English poetry and the music to which it was set.

Byrd's later career would be marked by these early experiences, wherever he may have been when they took place. It is entirely possible that he followed his two older brothers into the choir of St. Paul's Cathedral. We may never know for certain: the records for the relevant years are lost.

We do know something about the education received by choristers of that generation, and we can at least speculate about the background of young William, who must have spent time at a similar institution if not the same one. The prime years for training the treble voice were also the prime years for educating a child, and much of a chorister's daily work had (then as now) little to do with singing. A set of sixteenth-century instructions for the teaching of choristers at St. Paul's makes the priorities clear. The children are first of all to learn "the principles and grounds of Christian religion contained in the little Catechism." Only "when they shall be older" are they to advance to "the art and knowledge of music," and, once they are musically literate, to several hours a day of Latin grammar and other scholarly pursuits.

There was also lighter fare for the choristers. They performed on stage, sang ballads, and played viols and other instruments. Some of Byrd's songs allude clearly to the long-standing English Renaissance tradition of choirboy plays, and his brother Simon appears to have owned a manuscript copy of one such play, including stage directions for voices and viols. Young musicians in the Tudor era, even those employed by the church, would doubtless have known and performed all sorts of secular music. Relatively few secular pieces have been preserved from the years around Byrd's birth, but we can reconstruct some of the tradition from what has survived. It seems to have been lively and highly diverse. In the single remaining partbook of a 1530 collection called *Twenty Songs*, courtly chansons and devotional pieces are printed alongside frankly bawdy ballads. The handful of surviving secular manuscripts from the 1530s and 1540s mix settings of English poetry with a sprinkling of foreign music. One of King Henry's most treasured musicians, the Flemish lutenist and composer Philip van Wilder, wrote a large number of chansons in a thoroughly up-to-date French style. The everyday musical landscape of Tudor London was also full of more ephemeral sounds in the form of ballads, folk songs, and the unwritten music of minstrels and city waits. Byrd himself became one of the first composers of the English Renaissance to take popular song seriously and explore its full musical possibilities.

Byrd would have started his formal training as a chorister in the late 1540s, just as the world around him was being irrevocably transformed. After more than a decade of gradual change and accommodation, the

Reformation finally hit the English church with full force. The new Prayer Book of Edward VI was issued in 1549, and all other service books were suppressed. That was also the year clergymen were allowed to marry. (This caused some practical challenges at a place such as Wells Cathedral, where the elegant medieval rowhouses in the Close were suddenly too small. The cathedral authorities responded by knocking out interior walls to accommodate the growing population of wives and children.) Colorful frescoes of angels and saints were whitewashed out, replaced with painted texts from the English Bible, and pulpits were full of revolutionary rhetoric.

The most radical shift of all, from the perspective of a young chorister, must have been the change in everyday musical practice. The daily life of the pre-Reformation church musician had been built around Gregorian chant. Some of this music (such as the psalm tones) was simple, and some of it (such as the great responsories for the night office) was complex and refined. Boys learned Latin by singing the psalms; they memorized an almost unimaginably large repertory of chant; they were taught how to sight-read chant melodies, and how to improvise on them; even their training at the organ was based on plainsong. The endless chanting of the Divine Office, seven times a day and once at night, was the background of their musical life, against which the occasional piece of composed polyphony stood out in sharp relief.

When the Reformers began introducing vernacular services in the 1540s, musicians adapted various pieces of old chant to suit their new needs. The Protestant bishop John Hooper, writing in 1549, grumbled to his European colleague Heinrich Bullinger about this practice: "And that popery may not be lost, the mass-priests, although they are compelled to discontinue the use of the Latin language, yet most carefully observe the same tone and manner of chanting to which they were heretofore accustomed in the papacy." His complaint could hardly have applied to the entire range of pre-Reformation choral chant. Direct adaptation of Latin plainsong into English was only an experiment, and by nature a limited experiment. The new ideal for English services was simple syllabic chanting (Thomas Cranmer's famous injunction: "for every syllable a note"), which automatically ruled out much of the music in the old books. The elaborate scheme of sung day and night offices was cut down to Matins and Evensong, and most of the saints' days were suppressed. The so-called

Proper of the Mass, which called for a vast amount of varied seasonal music, was almost entirely dismantled. By the end of the 1540s, most of the occasions for singing complex chant were already gone.

John Merbecke's 1550 *Book of Common Prayer Noted* ("noted" meaning "set to music") was designed to replace the makeshift adaptations that had sprung up in earlier years. It became, at least for the moment, the official musical setting of the new English rite. This may well have been the first liturgical book Byrd ever handled. Merbecke shows us exactly what was left after the most recent wave of reforms had taken place: "In this book is contained so much of the order of Common Prayer as is to be sung in churches." It is a slim volume, attractively produced and easy to read, with black notes printed on red staves. Much of the music was adapted from the simpler sort of Latin chant: psalm tones, short antiphons, call-and-response formulas. Other pieces were freely composed by Merbecke in a similar style. There is no musical elaboration of any kind that might get in the way of perceiving the text clearly. The whole thing is ingenious but surprisingly austere. Its contents would easily have been mastered by an intelligent ten-year-old chorister within a month or two—quite unlike the luxurious undergrowth of the old service books, which could keep singers occupied, and sometimes perplexed, for decades.

Despite all these changes, some old practices stayed deeply ingrained in the musical life of sixteenth-century England. The first dialogue in Morley's *Plain and Easy Introduction* introduces a pupil looking for basic instruction in music. "Begin at the very beginning," he says, "and teach me as though I were a child." He is promptly initiated into the medieval art of six-syllable solmization, a technique for sight-reading chant (traditionally attributed to Guido of Arezzo) that had remained more or less unchanged for half a millennium. That is how Renaissance choristers learned to sing, and it did not change even when "plainsong" became more a pedagogical fiction than a daily reality. Morley dedicated the *Introduction* to Byrd and offered "what is in it truly spoken, as that which sometime proceeded from yourself." There is no reason to think it did not reflect Byrd's own teaching methods, and, by extension, the basic art of singing as he had learned it in childhood.

When English singers lost the tradition of complex chant, they also began to lose the tradition of improvising polyphony around it. Morley himself, writing at the end of the sixteenth century, said that this kind of improvisation "hath been in times past in England (as every man knoweth), and is at this day in other places, the greatest part of the usual music which in any churches is sung." It was by nature an ephemeral art, and little of it has survived in writing, but it is difficult to exaggerate just how important it was to the musical upbringing of the pre-Reformation chorister. It persisted in more or less stylized form long after Latin chant was banished from services: canons were still composed on the *Miserere*, consort music was still composed on *Gloria tibi Trinitas*, and impromptu counterpoint against a cantus firmus was still a crucial part of every student's work at the keyboard and in the classroom. One of Morley's fictional pupils describes an old teacher who "continually carried a plainsong book in his pocket, [and] caused me do the like, and so walking in the fields, he would sing the plainsong, and cause me sing the descant, and when I sang not to his contentment, he would show me wherein I had erred." (He goes on to describe the old master and a colleague throwing their "plainsong books" at each other's heads during a heated musical argument.) Something of this tradition has persisted to our own day in the practice of teaching species counterpoint, which is always written around a (usually artificial) cantus firmus.

Basic sight-reading and improvisation were central to the young chorister's training, but learning to sing composed polyphony—what we now think of as the great sacred music of the English Renaissance—was equally important. That sort of music also went through some radical changes during Byrd's childhood. By the late 1540s, most of the existing repertory could no longer be used, on grounds of both text (theologically undesirable) and musical style (too elaborate). Singers must have been reluctant to give up polyphonic music altogether, because they scrambled to fill the gaps with various replacements. The most obvious solution, as with chant, was to set new English words to old favorites. This was done widely in the first years of the Reformation, with varying degrees of success. One enterprising musician named Thomas Caustun made a career of adapting secular songs by European composers—Festa, Gombert, van Wilder—to pious English words. French and Italian songs were already popular in England, and their largely syllabic and declamatory style was a good fit for reformist ideals of textual clarity. It was not too far a leap from *Amour me poingt* to *Turn thou us, O Good Lord*, or from

O passi sparsi to *Holy, holy, holy*. A lot of this music was eventually published, and Byrd was very likely acquainted with it, whether or not he knew of its worldly origins. Given the lively cultural cross-fertilization between England and the Continent during these years, he may well have known.

There were also new polyphonic pieces in English, written from scratch to meet the new demands of the Reformation. Many of them are conspicuously lacking treble parts: there is nothing left for the choristers to do. The music of the so-called Lumley and Wanley manuscripts, first-generation English anthems such as Tallis's *If ye love me* or *Hear the voice and prayer*, was written for men's voices only. It is difficult to tell how much polyphony was actually learned by boys during these difficult years of transition. Byrd's earliest surviving works, from the brief revival of the Catholic Latin rite in the mid-1550s, show what was clearly a strong grasp of polyphonic style, although we may never know how and when he first acquired that skill. Many churches simply dismissed their boy singers and continued with a handful of adult professionals. The choir schools at the great cathedrals appear to have gone on more or less without interruption, but the break in continuity is still hard to imagine. To an impressionable young chorister, a difference in age of five or six years can seem like a whole generation. What would it have been like to lose an entire musical tradition in so short a time?

Not all Tudor choristers went on to become professional musicians. If anything, that was the exception rather than the rule. Although Byrd's brothers Simon and John both had a prestigious musical upbringing—a list apparently compiled in the late 1540s features their names together at the head of the ten St. Paul's choristers—they did not take up music as a full-time job once their voices had broken. Singing in a large choral foundation was a valuable way to gain social connections, and families sent their sons to choir schools for what must have been quite diverse reasons. When Simon and John Byrd had finished their musical training, they went on to make their way in the Elizabethan business world. John became a shipowner who engaged in trade and privateering, sending his ships as far afield as West Africa, Brazil, and Cuba. Simon became a successful London merchant. The household inventory drawn up by the executors of his will shows an amateur musician settled comfortably in his music room:

In the study

Item: his books	£5 18s.
Item: a pair of clavichords	20d.
Item: a table and a carpet	12d.
Item: his song books	5s.

A number of Byrd's relatives, including Simon, were involved with the Fletchers' Company, the traditional guild of arrow-makers and, by extension, professional woodworkers. Byrd described the process of revising his own motets as "bringing them back to the lathe and making them more refined." This was the language of his sister Barbara's instrument workshop, dust in the air and wood shavings on the floor. It is clear from almost every note of his music that he had a love of fine craftsmanship—something that was not at all foreign to the rest of his family.

He also shared their business acumen and their rather hard-headed attitude toward the realities of life. Although he was known for his "gravity and piety," he was far from naïve or unworldly. He knew from an early age how to cultivate the interest of the powerful, and he was not shy about seeking connections in high places. He would dedicate his first book of motets to Queen Elizabeth herself, and his first songbook to the Lord Chancellor of England, the successor of Thomas More (to whose great-granddaughter Byrd married off his elder son: we can only regret that there are no surviving descendants of that match.) His brother John, the shipowner and privateer, suffered some assorted contretemps with the English authorities in the 1580s—he was accused of usury and of refusal to do his legal duty—but was eventually pardoned because of his "forwardness in her Majesty's service with his ships against the Spanish Fleet." This must have sounded familiar to William, by then a Catholic dissident who had evaded serious persecution for his faith by, among other things, writing fulsome patriotic music on the defeat of the Spanish Armada. Although he took a different path in life than his siblings did, it is not hard to discern the same underlying character.

CHAPTER TWO

Apprentice Years

It is a knowledge easily taught, and quickly learned, where there is a good master, and an apt scholar.

—*Psalms, Sonnets and Songs,* 1588

WHEN BYRD FIRST APPEARS AS A COMPOSER, HE DOES NOT APPEAR alone: his earliest identifiable work shows him already at the center of the Tudor musical world. It is a four-voice setting of a long Latin psalm, *In exitu Israel,* to be sung during the elaborate ceremonies of the Easter vigil. Unlike the vast majority of sixteenth-century music, it was not written by a single person. The scribe carefully attributes different sections to different composers: the first seven verses to John Sheppard, the last four to William Mundy, and the three in the middle, beginning with the words *Similes illis fiant,* to "Byrd."

The attribution has drawn some understandable skepticism. Who was this "Byrd"? Was the young William Byrd really collaborating on equal terms with two well-established contemporaries? If he worked on this piece, he must have done so during his apprentice years. It was composed between 1553, when Henry VIII's Catholic daughter Mary briefly reinstated the Latin rite, and her death in 1558, after which England became Protestant again. William Mundy (probably born around 1530) was too young to have written his part before the Reformation first began, and the collaboration could not have happened after Sheppard died in December 1558. Even if he had died in the middle of writing the piece, leaving his colleagues to finish it for him, there would have been no practical need for it: with the coronation of Elizabeth I, only a few weeks after Sheppard's death, the reforms were in full swing again, and the Easter festivities in 1559 (and in future years) took place only in English. Whoever composed the three "Byrd" verses wrote them before that happened.

The manuscript source of *Similes illis fiant* gives only the single name "Byrd". There were certainly other musical Byrds in mid-century London, not least William's older brothers, but none of them is known to have composed anything. The musical content of these three verses fits well with what we know of the composer's early creative development. They have a good deal in common with the small handful of other precocious works—some probably from the later 1550s—that have managed to survive in various manuscripts. There is also less reason to be skeptical about William's authorship if we take his recently discovered legal deposition at face value and accept his date of birth as 1540 rather than the traditional 1543. This would have made him eighteen or even nineteen years old when this sort of polyphony was banished for the last time from English church services. It is easy to imagine a composer of that age, or indeed slightly younger, sharing the burden of writing lengthy ritual works with older colleagues.

The psalm composed together by Sheppard, Byrd, and Mundy is a substantial piece of music, taking nearly twenty minutes to perform in full. It is a setting of the fourteen even-numbered verses of Psalm 113 in the Latin Vulgate, each with an alleluia added at the end. (The odd-numbered verses were chanted in unison.) Each verse is built on the same foundation, a pre-existing melody sung throughout by the lowest voice. This bass line is identical in all fourteen verses, give or take some occasional adjustment at cadences and repetition of notes as needed to fit the text. It functions as a cantus firmus, but it is not an actual piece of chant; it is at one remove from chant, a stylized countermelody known as a "faburden," which was traditionally sung below a psalm tone. It is hardly an exciting tune, but it offers more promise than a simple recitation formula would have done. There is a stepwise falling cadence (a welcome sight, then as now, for any student of Renaissance counterpoint) at the end of each of the three phrases, and some inherent harmonic structure, which the composers exploit as best they can.

Ex. 2.1 *Similes illis fiant*, mm. 1–7

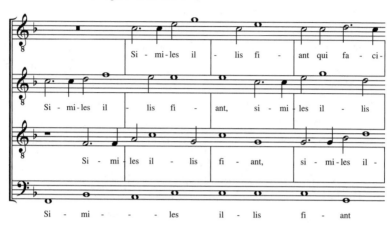

Example 2.1 shows the first notes from Byrd. They do not sound entirely unfamiliar when set beside his later and better-known works. We hear the little melodic gestures reaching upward, *c d f* expanding to *c e g* as the cantus firmus rises and the imitation develops; we hear the recurring 6–5 progressions against the bass; we hear the narrowly avoided false relation between E♭ and E♮ as the top voice cascades down into the cadence. All these things evoke the world of the 1550s in which Byrd received his compositional training. They would work their way into his own distinctive musical language during the years to come.

Similes illis fiant is not a particularly innovative or expressive piece, but it is hard to imagine a more useful first document of Byrd's composing career. It shows his earliest work alongside that of his older colleagues, who respected him enough to collaborate with him in this way. It is akin to the variation sets he loved to write later in life: a number of different approaches to the same musical problem. Byrd's three verses show him responding to a persistent technical challenge—and setting himself an additional challenge in the middle verse, which features a canon between the two upper voices. This sort of two-part canon around a (generally unpromising) plainsong was a mainstay of the English Renaissance compositional workshop. One enthusiastic Elizabethan amateur named George Waterhouse managed to turn out more than a thousand canons on the ubiquitous cantus firmus *Miserere mihi Domine*. Byrd himself joined forces with his Italian-born contemporary Alfonso Ferrabosco (in what Morley called "a virtuous contention") to write a set of eighty canons, now lost, on the same melody. Of course Byrd's youthful setting of *Similes illis fiant* is a practical work, preserved in a collection of real liturgical music, but the idea is a familiar one.

These three little psalm verses also reflect a larger and more interesting musical problem, which mature composers such as Tallis and Sheppard were tackling on a broader scale in the 1550s: how to write real imitative counterpoint around the constraint of an ever-present plainsong melody in long notes. It is worth noting that Byrd fudges the pitch content of the cantus firmus in the middle verse of *Similes illis fiant* so that he can keep the imitation intact between the two canonic voices. (He took the same liberties in his later cantus-firmus motets, where smooth voice-leading often won out over the authority of the chant.) The third part above the plainsong, although it is not officially involved in the canon, takes up all the motives of the two higher parts with remarkable accuracy—including a bold rising seventh at *speravit*, the sort of gesture Byrd would still use with impunity in his mature works. Some of the more unsettling dissonances actually occur in the sections of the piece that are not based on strict canon. At the beginning of the very first *Alleluia*, the alto F smashes unceremoniously into the cantus-firmus E. This could have been avoided easily enough. It is clear that the young composer liked the sound, not least because he built much the same sort of thing into the canonic structure of the next verse.

It is no great surprise to see Sheppard, Byrd, and Mundy working together to complete a large liturgical piece in what may have been some haste. Queen Mary had abruptly restored Catholic worship to England in 1553, and the new demands made on artists during her reign were at least as great as those made during the most active years of the Reformation. This is clearest of all in the records having to do with church buildings and liturgical artifacts: people had to rebuild and repaint and restore what had, in most cases, been physically destroyed just a few years earlier. The situation with music was not much different. A whole repertory of complex sacred music had been (at best) left to lie fallow and (at worst) systematically eradicated. Now composers, scribes, and singers were required to build it up again from scratch. A lot of artistic collaboration went on during these years, some of it from sheer necessity. Various London churches (including Mundy's own parish of St. Mary at Hill) borrowed boy trebles from the Chapel Royal, the private musical establishment of the English monarchs, whose choir school seems to have continued unbroken through the Reformation. Sheppard and Tallis, who were both employed by the Chapel in the 1550s, worked together on an impressive series of polyphonic hymns and reponsories for the restored Latin liturgy. Byrd's own work in *Similes illis fiant* was very much a part of that tradition.

The mid-1550s also brought a new influx of European art and culture to England. Queen Mary was the daughter of Catherine of Aragon, and she was married soon after her coronation to King Philip of Spain, who joined her in England with most of his court in tow. The royal wedding was celebrated with an extended visit by Philip's Capilla Flamenca, a large group of professional musicians (mostly Flemish: hence the name) who provided sacred music for the Spanish monarchs. They even sang a joint mass with the Chapel Royal during Advent 1554. All of this international exchange must have made an impression on the young Byrd. The cultural message was clear: England was going to reverse its years of proud isolation and become part of a reunited Catholic Europe. The intellectual atmosphere of the moment was a peculiar mixture of Counter-Reformation zeal and cosmopolitan Renaissance humanism. A visitor to Oxford could attend an open scholarly debate and see dissenters burned at the stake, sometimes on the same day. It must have been an exciting and unsettling time to be a young student of music.

Most of the musical sources from these years have vanished without a trace. We are lucky to have a set of four handwritten partbooks that preserve a more or less unique snapshot of English church music during the 1550s. This collection, now known as the Gyffard partbooks, is the only surviving source for Byrd's *Similes illis fiant*. In fact it is the only surviving source for most of the music it contains. Judging from the evidence of the manuscript itself, it may even have been compiled as an exercise in nostalgia or wishful thinking after its contents had already been banned from public worship. Of the ninety-four pieces in it, eighty-eight are unique—including, by good fortune, virtually all the extant four-voice Latin works of Taverner, Tallis, Sheppard, Tye, and Mundy. Unlike some of the more eclectic manuscript collections that have come down to us from sixteenth-century England, the four Gyffard books show us what professional singers—most likely a group of church musicians in and around London—were really using from day to day. There is a wide selection of music for the daily Lady Mass, for the evening services of Vespers and Compline, and for the various other needs of a mid-century urban church choir. The Gyffard set also preserves the three "Western Wind" masses, the only English mass settings of their generation to be based (as so many European ones were) on a secular tune.

None of the music in Gyffard is written in more than four parts, and much of it has a relatively restricted vocal range. We have to look elsewhere for the elaborate scorings and soaring treble lines so often associated with Tudor church music of this generation. Quite a few works on a larger scale have managed to survive, mostly in retrospective manuscripts put together by various Elizabethan collectors. The most notable of these enthusiasts was probably John Baldwin, a singer and scribe of Windsor and eventually one of Byrd's colleagues at the Chapel Royal, who undertook a one-man antiquarian effort to preserve the repertory that had been sung by English choirs during the last years of the Latin rite. He seems to have had free access to the music in the royal archives, and he made the most of it. Iconoclastic zeal was apparently not as strong there as it was at many cathedrals and parish churches, because there was still plenty of old music left for him to copy.

Baldwin's greatest surviving collection of Latin-texted polyphony is a set of five partbooks (the sixth is missing) now in the library of Christ Church, Oxford. Mundy and Sheppard are both featured prominently in them. Sheppard is such a familiar figure that some of his works are simply labeled "S." His contribution to the Baldwin partbooks is mostly practical music for the liturgy—if the word "practical" can be applied to a splendid piece such as *Verbum caro*, a virtuosic setting of a Christmas responsory that blazes out into an eight-part chord at its final cadence. Almost all of this music is built, like *Similes illis fiant*, around an ever-present cantus firmus in long notes. It sounds like a thankless task, but Sheppard clearly enjoyed it. He was the sort of composer who could take strict liturgical forms and turn them into something truly distinctive. Perhaps the most memorable of these pieces is his vast Lenten antiphon *Media vita*—"in the midst of life we are in death"—whose cantus firmus moves at a glacial tempo, in breves (double whole notes) rather than the usual semibreves. This produces more than twenty minutes' worth of music, unfolding on a monumental scale, with a complex system of internal repetitions and refrains. The final variation features an unexpected change in vocal scoring, with a single bass voice below an ethereal quartet of divided sopranos and altos. This was the sort of piece Byrd himself would have known and sung as a young colleague of Sheppard's. It will show later in his talent for gradual musical development, his ability to give shape to even the largest-scale works.

Mundy was also composing twenty-minute pieces during these years. One particularly striking example is *Vox patris caelestis*, a setting of a florid Marian prayer adapted (by the poet and music collector William Forrest, one of Mundy's associates) from the biblical Song of Songs. Of the nearly two hundred works in Baldwin's manuscript collection, this is the one he could not resist inscribing with *laus Deo*, "praise be to God." It is a glorification of vocal sonority in all its forms, a perfect fit for its lush, rambling, frankly erotic text. The last section uses much the same multiple divisi as *Media vita*—four high voices played off against a pair of low basses—before launching into a full-choir invocation to the Virgin and a final Amen on the grandest possible scale. We can only imagine the impression this ecstatic music would have made on a fifteen-year-old raised on a diet of Merbecke and metrical psalms.

Byrd's own contribution to the musical culture of the 1550s, or what little has survived of his contribution, is on a more modest scale. *Similes illis fiant* is the most obvious and best-documented example. Another Latin-texted work, a pair of short three-voice Alleluias with their verses

(*Confitemini Domino* and *Laudate pueri*), almost certainly dates from the same years. There would have been no practical need for these pieces in later decades, and their style closely reflects what we hear in *Similes illis fiant*, including various forays into canonic writing and some harsh moments of dissonance.

His earliest instrumental pieces are harder to pin down. They do not have any specific liturgical function, and people went on writing instrumental music on Latin plainsong long after the original melodies had been banished from church. Byrd's two-part organ settings of *Miserere* and *Gloria tibi Trinitas* may well have been written at the same time as his earliest vocal music: they show some signs of being student exercises, and they closely reflect the keyboard style of older composers such as Tallis, Redford, and Blitheman. The same can be said of a few early three-part consort pieces by Byrd. It is difficult to know how many of his early instrumental works were written before he arrived at Lincoln in 1562. In any case he was probably much busier there, having taken on the full-time post of organist and choirmaster, and had less time to compose music not immediately needed for the Anglican liturgy.

Some other pieces by Byrd are also worth at least reconsidering as early works from the last years of the Latin rite. His six-voice setting of *O salutaris hostia* is one of the strangest things he ever wrote. Unlike almost all his other surviving six-part motets, it was passed over in discreet silence when he published his six-part anthology in the 1591 *Cantiones sacrae*. The omission is not too surprising. *O salutaris hostia* is a three-voice canon at various pitch levels, interwoven with three freely-composed parts, all undertaken with the breeziest possible attitude toward dissonance treatment. The result (Example 2.2) is layer upon layer of grating discord and tonal instability. It may well be the most appallingly dissonant piece of sacred music written in the sixteenth century. The music still has an unmistakable confidence—even authority—although it is hardly the kind of thing Byrd would have composed (much less circulated) later in life. Could this have been another student work of his, perhaps written at the age of seventeen or eighteen, while the Latin motet was still universal currency among English musicians? The taste for acrid false relations and irregular suspensions was doubtless something Byrd picked up from his London colleagues in the 1550s, though it must be said that even Sheppard never wrote anything quite like this. Similar

Ex. 2.2 *O salutaris hostia*, mm. 30–34

questions linger around some mid-century manuscript works dubiously attributed to Byrd, rather rough cantus-firmus compositions such as *Reges Tharsis* and *Sacris solemniis*, which use chant melodies also set by Sheppard and may conceivably be early attempts by the younger composer to write in the same style. In any case John Baldwin, who was close to Byrd and to his musical world, was ready to say they were by him.

The extraordinary musical flowering of the 1550s was the product of a particular cultural moment. This moment ended quickly when Queen Mary died, and Byrd and his associates went their own ways. William Mundy took the Oath of Supremacy, left the perfumed garden of *Vox patris caelestis*, and became a well-respected Protestant church musician. John Sheppard, who had written such an impressive meditation on mortality in *Media vita*, died only a few weeks before he would have had to do the same. He left his two children in the care of a Chapel Royal colleague. He asked to be buried in Westminster Abbey, as princes and statesmen (and, in later centuries, great artists) were, with an inscription showing the date of his death—or, "if I cannot be suffered to lie there," in his nearby parish church. He ended up in the parish church. Byrd was no older than nineteen at the time, an accomplished young musician whose practical training had once again been declared obsolete. He could hardly have known where the next six decades would take him.

CHAPTER THREE

Lincoln Cathedral

When the old store of the musicians be worn out which were bred when the
music of the church was maintained (which is like to be in short time), you
shall have few or none remaining.

—Thomas Whythorne, ca. 1570

ON 25 MARCH 1563, BYRD BEGAN HIS DUTIES AS ORGANIST AND MASTER
of the choristers at Lincoln Cathedral. He was twenty-three years
old. If this was his first real job—and there is no surviving evidence of an
earlier appointment—he was doing very well. He had been invited to
lead one of the rare musical establishments that had survived the English
Reformation without serious damage. The choir was thriving, with
twelve adult professionals and nine choristers, and the cathedral itself was
(and still is) among the most splendid in England. Life at Lincoln would
bring some political troubles for Byrd, and he must have suffered from a
sense of isolation in the provinces, nearly a week's journey from his native
London. It still turned out to be, at least in retrospect, an ideal place for
him to spend his twenties. He came of age as a composer during his years
in Lincoln. He arrived as a gifted but inexperienced church musician and
left with an impressive fluency in a wide variety of musical styles.

We do not know how Byrd was chosen for the job, or what he was
doing before he came to the cathedral. We know that he was a pupil of
Tallis, and he may well have undertaken his musical studies with him in
the late 1550s and early 1560s, after his duties as a chorister were finished

and he was free to pursue composition as a full-time vocation. It is easy to imagine Tallis putting a word in for his most talented student when he heard of a vacancy at Lincoln. However Byrd spent his apprentice years, they left him qualified to run a large musical establishment and compose new works for it. He also emerges in later documents as a well-educated man, fluent in the humanistic Latin of the Renaissance, a reader and collector of books. It is possible that he spent some time in his late teens and early twenties (as his son Thomas, Tallis's godson, would later do) studying the humanities, studying law, or even traveling abroad. Richard Fleming, an early-fifteenth-century bishop of Lincoln, had founded an Oxford college (Lincoln College) which maintained close ties with the cathedral and might conceivably have been the scene of some of Byrd's education during these formative years.

Whether or not Byrd knew it at the time, he was unusually fortunate in his situation at Lincoln. As his fellow-musician Thomas Whythorne noted in his autobiography a few years later, the profession was in a precarious state. We tend to think of the Elizabethan era as a golden age of church music, but the daily reality was less glamorous. Although Elizabeth's injunctions on sacred music provided for the maintenance of cathedral and collegiate choirs, this was often overlooked (or blatantly disobeyed, as when the choir of St. John's, Oxford was disbanded in 1575) in favor of more pragmatic or puritanical views. The supply of qualified professional musicians was dangerously short at times. Many singers had to live on fixed stipends that had not been raised, despite rampant inflation, since the time of Henry VIII. One anonymous observer (whose notes on music are preserved in the manuscript now known as BL Royal 18.B.xix) lamented that "whereas in former times of popery divers benefactions have been given to singing-men . . . the same is swallowed up by the deans and canons"; a contemporary singer's salary, he said, "doth not answer the wages and entertainment that any of them giveth to his horse-keeper." Byrd was one of the lucky few with a living wage, but he still had to augment it with private teaching.

When he arrived at Lincoln, Byrd was given a formal contract outlining the duties and benefits of his post. A copy of this document has survived. It shows what was expected from the director of music at a busy Elizabethan cathedral. Byrd was actually taking on two separate jobs, with separate requirements and salaries. The first post was that of "song master or master of the choirboys," whose task was to "diligently instruct and teach the choristers...in knowledge of the art of music." The contract itself does not go into detail about what this involved, but it is clear from other sixteenth-century records at Lincoln that the choir-master did not just lead the choir: he also gave instruction in music theory, composition, and organ playing. Byrd's predecessor James Crawe was told to choose two or three especially promising boys and give them additional tuition on the "clavicordes." The records during Byrd's time at the cathedral show expenditures on parchment, paper, and ink for the use of his choristers, and, in 1568, the appointment of an extra teacher to instruct them, presumably in non-musical subjects. Byrd also shared the responsibility for recruiting young singers when their numbers ran low. He made several journeys around the East Midlands, funded by the cathedral, in search of new talent.

Byrd's second post, which provided the other half of his salary, was that of organist: *joculator organorum*, the same office Tallis had occupied as a young man at Dover Priory in the early 1530s. Unlike some other English cathedrals, Lincoln did not destroy its organ at the Reformation or let it fall into long-term disuse. A substantial amount of money was spent on organ repairs just a few months after Byrd arrived. He attended the daily offices of Matins and Evensong, giving the choir their starting pitches, overseeing their singing of the psalms, and accompanying them as needed. He also seems to have done a good deal of improvising or playing more elaborate music, at least judging from the severe restrictions imposed on him in the end by an increasingly straitlaced cathedral chapter.

Byrd was not appointed to Lincoln Cathedral as a composer, at least not in explicit terms. Although we can place quite a few of his works more or less confidently in the Anglican cathedral milieu of the 1560s, there is no surviving musical source that can be traced directly to his years at Lincoln. His colleagues there copied out polyphony and pur-chased books of music, but we can only guess at the contents of those books and manuscripts. His original contract says nothing about writing new music. He was only described as a composer much later, during the mid-1570s, in an effort to retain at least some of his loyalty after he had left to join the Chapel Royal: he was offered a lifetime annuity of one-fourth his former salary on the sole condition that he provide—or, one assumes, *continue* to provide—"well-composed songs and divine services" for the cathedral.

For some Elizabethan church musicians, such a good first job would have been the end of the road. The composer Osbert Parsley came to Norwich Cathedral as a singing-man at the age of twenty-four and stayed until his death ("as falleth mellowed apples from the tree," his epitaph tells us) half a century later. Byrd's contract certainly seems to have been drawn up with a long tenure in mind. It invited him to continue at Lincoln "to the end and for the term of his natural life if the said William Byrd is willing so long to occupy and exercise the said post." The contract included provision for "sickness, feebleness of mind or old age," and allowed him the use of a deputy as necessary, as long as he continued to provide for the education of the choristers and the organ music needed at services. He was also given a bonus in the form of a lease on a nearby rectory, granted for forty-one years, due to expire in 1604. His employers at Lincoln had every reason to hope that he would stay until retirement.

Byrd's most lasting tie with Lincolnshire would turn out to be his marriage in 1568 to a local woman named Julian Burley. The cathedral provided a rent-free house at what is now 6 Minster Yard for them and their growing family. Their son Christopher was born in 1569, and their daughter Elizabeth in 1572. Three more children would follow after the family moved to London. Julian proved to be, among other things, an unusually stubborn Catholic. She was the first member of the Byrd family to be prosecuted for recusancy—refusal to attend Church of England services—and she remained a regular presence in legal records for many decades. At one point it was claimed that she gave her household staff extra work on Sundays, effectively preventing them from going to church. She herself "refused conference" with the authorities when they came knocking. Her husband was, she said, away from home. Nothing is known about her own background, but she may well have contributed to Byrd's increasingly Catholic convictions during the first years of his career.

There are some hints that he may in fact have conformed to the state religion for a while as a younger man. When he took his post at Lincoln, he would certainly have had to submit to the Elizabethan Acts of Supremacy and Uniformity, as his colleagues at other cathedrals did. We also have an astonishing musical manuscript with a piece attributed to "Birde," an English version of a well-known Lutheran prayer: "from Turk and Pope defend us, Lord."Whether or not this was actually by our composer, one early Elizabethan scribe was ready to think it was. It is hard to believe in any case that the dean and chapter of Lincoln Cathedral would have hired an outspoken religious nonconformist as their organist and choirmaster. That side of Byrd's character developed later.

After some quiet years at Lincoln, Byrd began to run into trouble with the authorities. His nemesis appears to have been the puritanical John Aylmer, who was appointed archdeacon there in 1562, shortly before Byrd arrived. Aylmer was a strict reformer with little sympathy for elaborate ritual. The Protestant chronicler John Strype described him pointedly as having "purged the Cathedral Church of Lincoln, being at that time a nest of unclean birds." The archdeacon and the composer would cross paths again. In 1577, Aylmer (by then Bishop of London) was the first to cite the Byrd family for recusancy. In 1583, he led the commission to crack down on irregularities in the London book trade, an effort aimed in part at monopolies such as those held at the time by Byrd and Tallis. Aylmer's signature often appears near Byrd's in the Lincoln cathedral archives. The conflict of personalities can almost be seen on the page: the austere, polished *Ælmer* alongside the flamboyant *Byrde* with its multiple loops and flourishes. There is no other signature like the young Byrd's in the contemporary account books at Lincoln. It is not hard to read a certain youthful arrogance into it.

There may also have been some conflict with Francis Mallett, who was Dean of Lincoln from 1554 until his death in 1570. Mallett had been a musical child. A letter of recommendation written on his behalf as a young man reports that he had been "apt to many worldly pleasures, for when he was but ten years of age, he could sing discant, play the organ, recorders, lute, and other instruments; for this reason Lord Latimer had such pleasure in him that he lay with him nightly." (This was John Neville, the third Baron Latimer, who was briefly married to Henry VIII's last wife, Katherine Parr.) Mallett seems to have soured on the experience as he grew older: "and yet it pleased our sweet saviour Jesus to kindle his heart so fervently with the fire of his love that he despised all vain pleasures, and then worldly men set nothing by him." It is easy to imagine that he was suspicious of Byrd's elaborate musical and pedagogical program at Lincoln, or at least that he was reluctant to support it fully.

The greatest problem seems to have been Byrd's organ playing. The conflict was serious enough for Mallett and the cathedral chapter to suspend his salary for eight months in 1569–70. Given the ascendancy of puritanism at Lincoln during these years, it is no surprise that Byrd's colleagues were dismayed by lavish displays of instrumental music. He was eventually told to play the organ "only for the guidance of the choir," before the four main canticles of the Anglican liturgy: Te Deum and Benedictus at Matins, Magnificat and Nunc Dimittis at Evensong. It is hard to know just what the authorities had in mind here. They may have expected brief preludes along the lines of Italian Renaissance *intonazioni*, keyboard flourishes designed to set up the appropriate tonality for the singers. John Case wrote about this practice in England in his 1586 *Praise of Music*: "When the organs do play without the addition of the voices, it is to give the singers a fit tune to lead them into the song, lest otherwise the same would be set too high or too low for the voices." Byrd's own short keyboard preludes would have filled that role very well.

The orders may have been yet more severe, telling him to do nothing but give opening pitches to the choir. The other instruction he was issued at the same time—to leave the organ bench and sing along with the choir during the anthem—certainly implies a desire to limit his organ playing to an absolute minimum. If he was only allowed to give pitches, he was playing just a few notes a day, a task any of his young choristers could have taken on with a little training. It is no great surprise that he became restless and sought employment elsewhere.

These restrictions seem even worse when we look at the music Byrd was actually composing for the keyboard during the 1560s. We can see his musical personality unfolding in his earliest keyboard works, from student experimentation—influenced by mid-century composers, the generation of John Redford and Thomas Preston—to a voice of real authority and creativity. By the time he became well established at Lincoln, he was fit for much more than giving singers their notes.

Byrd's three keyboard settings of the plainsong melody *Clarifica me*, one each in two, three, and four parts, show the early evolution of his technique. Judging from the various musical influences they display, they were probably written during his first years at Lincoln. The two-part *Clarifica me* may well have been the first composed. It begins as a straightforward little exercise in counterpoint over a paraphrased cantus firmus and takes on more rhythmic complexity as it goes along: stately quarter notes, then running eighth notes, then accelerating variations in triple time, rounded out by a slightly queasy 9-against-4 passage. This gradual process of rhythmic intensification was something Tallis worked through in his later keyboard pieces—most notably in his two *Felix namque* settings, preserved in manuscript with dates of 1562 and 1564. Byrd must have been attracted to that process during the same years, because he returned to it in the three-part *Clarifica*, now played out in a busier texture with an extra layer of syncopation added near the end.

The surprise comes in Byrd's four-part setting, where such elaborate devices are put away in favor of a different, more balanced approach. Instead of creating interest by cramming more ornamentation into each successive phrase of the cantus firmus, he gradually builds up the web of counterpoint and broadens the sweep of his melodic lines. There are no triple-time fireworks or unusual rhythmic proportions. When the running eighth notes appear, they present themselves as a distinct imitative idea, a rising-and-falling figure that produces a playful onslaught of false relations. The original chant melody runs out ten bars before the end of the piece. The increased gravity of this last setting is balanced by a coda around the long-held final note D, during which the imitative points are at last given a chance to unwind. Byrd is taking a new approach to musical development here. His first two settings of the *Clarifica* melody owe much to the late medieval practices absorbed by Tallis, in which the numerical ratios between voices become more and more complex until they emerge together (if all goes well) in a triumphant final cadence. In his four-part setting, Byrd takes the same material and fashions it into a much more modern artifact. These three pieces, played one after the other, bridge the gap between one generation of keyboard style and the next. They also bridge the gap between apprentice and professional.

The four-part *Clarifica* holds to tradition in one important way. Like most of the mid-century English keyboard music that survives in written form, it is still composed around a plainsong. The cantus firmus provided a sound tonal scheme (*Clarifica me*, like its more popular cousin *Gloria tibi Trinitas*, is an elegant little first-mode melody with cadences in all the right places) and a convenient framework around which to build up the counterpoint. A piece of chant such as this was the ideal raw material for a two-minute or three-minute keyboard piece. Any composer who wanted to write a ten-minute keyboard piece faced different problems. What worked so well on a small scale was not always conducive to larger projects. The *Felix namque* settings by Tallis may be the most convincing exceptions to this rule. They are both based on a very long chant melody, almost two hundred notes long, with each measure of the finished work (except for the introduction and coda) composed around a single note. Tallis approaches them as large-scale exercises in rhythmic and melodic variation, starting with straightforward counterpoint and moving on to impressive displays of virtuosity.

When Byrd started writing large-scale keyboard music of his own, he took Tallis as a model and inspiration. The clearest example of this influence is Byrd's A-minor fantasia, the first of his really memorable keyboard works. It has a number of parallels with the 1564 *Felix namque*, from the gradual process of rhythmic elaboration to some brief passages that Byrd simply repeats note for note from Tallis. There is of course one major difference between the two works. Byrd's fantasia is freely composed, without any systematic use of pre-existing material (although the new tune introduced at measure 82, near the halfway point, appears to have been borrowed from an Elizabethan popular song.) The Renaissance fantasia was a product—as its name makes clear—of the composer's own imagination. Morley called it "the most principal and chiefest kind" of instrumental music, precisely because of the musical freedom it offered. In the fantasia, as he defined it,

> a musician taketh a point at his pleasure and wresteth and turneth it as he list, making either much or little of it according as shall seem best in his own conceit. In this may more art be shown than in any other music because the composer is tied to nothing, but that he may add, diminish, and alter at his pleasure.

Byrd enjoyed this liberty to the fullest. His A minor fantasia takes in a broad variety of styles, from stately imitative counterpoint to lively dance-like rhythms. The opening bars are an exposition on the standard 5–4–5–1 theme known and loved by countless European Renaissance composers as the intonation (A–G–A–D) of the chanted *Salve Regina*. What follows is a succession of more than a dozen varied textures and thematic ideas. Byrd "makes much of" some, and leaves others behind after a little exploration. The energy never flags throughout the whole process. When the inevitable syncopations and metrical shifts do appear, they feel like natural developments rather than a series of technical feats.

As in so many of Byrd's other large works, there are also a few surprises. Perhaps the strangest moment comes near the end, just before a triple-time passage lifted from Tallis's second *Felix namque*. The harmony and the right-hand figuration seem to be heading inexorably toward some sort of tidy ending. What we get instead is the most deceptive of cadences (Example 3.1). The bass resolves to an F rather than the expected A, and the prominent upper voice overshoots the expected resolution by a semitone and lands on a grating dissonance against the tenor. This gesture would make very little sense if it were not for the equivalent passage a bit later on (Example 3.2), which sets up the same situation, resolves triumphantly onto the expected chord, and goes on into a magnificent plagal coda—once again reminiscent of Tallis, whose *Felix namque* shifts in its final bars from the rather dry atmosphere of the pre-Reformation organ loft to the blaze of a Gabrieli toccata.

Listening to the cadence (or non-cadence) in Example 3.1, we catch a glimpse of Byrd thinking through the problems of large-scale musical structure. In the most basic terms, it is no more than a crude prolongation device, delaying the final resolution long enough to fit in some new musical material (including the most obvious quotes from Tallis)

Ex. 3.1 Fantasia in a (BK 13), mm. 155–59

Ex. 3.2 Fantasia in a (BK 13), mm. 184–88

and enjoy a bit more rhythmic play. The end result is slightly more subtle than that. Byrd is willing to do something bold—even something ugly—trusting that his listener will accept the gambit and follow him deeper into the structure of the work. When the real cadence does come, it is all the more convincing for the risk taken earlier. This fantasia shows Byrd discovering for himself how to plan an extended piece of music. The result is nearly two hundred measures long, on a scale similar to his most elaborate Latin motets or the longer canticles of the Great Service. The young Byrd would have known very few (if any) big works which were not either composed on a text or based on some kind of pre-existing musical material. When he took up the challenge in his early keyboard fantasias, English instrumental music came into its own for the first time.

If Byrd was indulging in this sort of thing during services at Lincoln, it is no wonder that the cathedral authorities wanted him to cut down on his organ playing. They seem to have appreciated him more in his other capacity, that of choirmaster and composer of vocal music. When he first arrived there in 1563, the musical repertory of English cathedral choirs was just beginning to settle down into a distinctive style after a period of uneasy experimentation. Byrd helped forge a new standard that would persist, with various developments and refinements, well into the seventeenth century. He was influenced by the slightly older group of musicians (Sheppard, Farrant, Tye) who had worked so hard to build up the first generation of vernacular church music in the 1540s and early 1550s. Not surprisingly, he also took Tallis as a model for many of his English church works.

Merbecke's *Book of Common Prayer Noted* had offered simple chant settings, one note per syllable, of the new English liturgy. The earliest choral service music to come out of the English Reformation was more or less a harmonized version of the same idea. The iconic work of this first generation was Tallis's Short Service, better known in later centuries as his "Dorian" Service, an austere and almost entirely syllabic four-voice setting of the choral parts of Matins, Holy Communion, and Evensong. Its severe beauty appealed to musicians long after the rules had loosened to permit more elaborate music. It has been sung in cathedrals, more or less without interruption, ever since it was first written. One earnest Victorian connoisseur praised it for its "gloomy grandeur and ponderous solemnity." It reflects the moment when the English liturgy had been stripped down to nothing and was being, rather cautiously, built back up again. This new musical language was quintessentially Protestant, but it also borrowed much of its effect from the European chansons and other secular songs so popular in mid-sixteenth-century England: straightforward and memorable harmonies, with a clear focus on the text. The curt declamation of Tallis's *Holy, holy, holy*, over in no more than thirty seconds, is a shock after the luxurious Sanctus settings of his early Latin masses, but it is entirely convincing music on its own terms.

Byrd took surprisingly well to this way of composing. His own Short Service, the simplest of his four surviving English services, was written in the same tradition as Tallis's and was nearly as popular in its day. It begins in four voices, as little more than a carefully calculated succession of chords. There is some unbending toward a more relaxed style in the course of the seven movements. The later sections, especially the Magnificat and Nunc Dimittis, indulge in a freer interplay among voices and some touches of ornamentation at cadences. Byrd also becomes more generous with his vocal scoring. The alto and tenor lines split and rejoin freely, creating five-part and, briefly, even six-part textures. The same flexibility is found in many of his other English sacred works. It is not unlike the approach he took in his polyphonic keyboard writing, where the number of voices is rarely consistent for long. The justification for this was entirely practical: each Elizabethan cathedral choir in fact performed as two separate choirs, one on each side of the chancel. The two groups sang almost everything back and forth in alternating verses (a practice derided by the more severe reformers as "tennis play") and could be called on to cover multiple parts as needed. Byrd would go on to exploit the antiphonal layout of the English choir most fully in his Great Service, which uses ten different vocal parts in almost all imaginable combinations.

His so-called Verse Service, a setting of the two evening canticles, is an entirely different sort of piece. Contemporary sources described it as a "service with verses to the organs" or "for a man alone." It is built around a series of solo passages with organ accompaniment. These alternate with sections sung by the whole choir. The "verse" style of church music seems to have originated in the practice—especially common among Elizabethan choristers—of singing solo songs to the accompaniment of viols or keyboard. This developed into a new way of writing service music, a change from the well-established "short" style cultivated by many composers. It offered an appealing variety of musical textures, encouraged soloists to show their talents, and gave organists a creative opportunity to fill in what were usually no more than bald two-part written accompaniments. By the end of Byrd's life, it had become the favored medium of English church composers.

If Byrd's Verse Service was not the very first of its kind, it was among the earliest, and it set the precedent for a whole group of similar works. It shows some signs of having been an experiment, especially in its solo sections, which incorporate a rather odd mixture of styles. The Magnificat and the Nunc Dimittis begin with almost identical solos, linking the two movements together. Another solo passage ("As he promised to our forefathers") is a harmonized chant melody, the same *tonus peregrinus* Bach featured in his own Magnificat a century and a half later. Yet another ("To be a light") is, somewhat unexpectedly, a solo quartet of high voices. The choral sections are written in five parts throughout, with touches of more elaborate counterpoint and the occasional glimpse of real imitative writing.

In some ways this music is less self-assured and more formulaic than its counterpart in the Short Service. The difficulties are already clear in the opening pages of the Magnificat, where the chorus grinds out half a dozen "English cadences" (near misses between the leading tone and the flat seventh, creating a characteristic little dissonance) in its first minute of singing. The gesture is striking at first, but it wears thin with repetition. Morley complained a generation later that the English cadence formula, by then a hoary cliché of Anglican church music, was "robbed out of the capcase of some old organist." It is not too hard to imagine that he had this passage in mind as he wrote.

The English liturgy offered a handful of other direct opportunities for musical elaboration. Byrd wrote some five-voice settings of special psalms to be sung on festive occasions. Most of them are organized, like his Short Service, as a simple dialogue between the two sides of the choir. *Teach me O Lord* is a more experimental piece, including solo verses. The words of these psalms are often colorful and expressive: "fear and trembling are come upon me, and an horrible dread hath overwhelmed me"; "God is gone up with a merry noise, and the Lord with the sound of the trump"; "the mountains skipped like rams, and the little hills like young sheep." Byrd resists every temptation to showy text-setting and keeps the music on an even keel throughout. The underlying aesthetic of his liturgical psalm settings, and the related Preces and Responses, is not unlike that of his earliest secular songs: clarity, decorum, and moments of quiet but distinctive beauty.

Byrd's employers at Lincoln asked him for a continuing supply of "divine services"; they also requested "songs" for use in church. By "songs" they meant what we now call English anthems. Queen Elizabeth's ministers gave a definition of the church anthem in 1559 in the forty-ninth article of their Royal Injunctions on religious practice. After issuing the order that service music must be "modest and distinct," they added an escape clause of sorts:

> And yet nevertheless, for the comforting of such as delight in music, it may be permitted that in the beginning or in the end of common prayers, either at morning or evening, there may be sung a hymn or suchlike song to the praise of God, in the best sort of melody and music that may be conveniently devised, having respect that the sentence of the hymn may be understood and perceived.

This was a rare moment of musical freedom in what was otherwise a strictly defined regime of daily services, and musicians took advantage of it. Some of the earliest Anglican "anthems," as we have seen, were no more than thinly veiled versions of fashionable French or Italian songs. Others were almost indistinguishable from the pious English domestic songs cultivated in Tudor households. There was inevitably a lot of crossover between ecclesiastical music sung in public and devotional music sung in private, but the English church anthem soon took on a life of its own. The story of its developing style can be read in the uneasy dialectic between the last two phrases of Elizabeth's 1559 injunction. Composers were to devise the "best sort of melody and music" possible, but without obscuring the all-important "sentence," the verbal text.

One memorable essay in the new anthem style was Byrd's setting of *O Lord, make thy servant Elizabeth,* a prayer for the health and well-being of the queen. This was one of his most popular ecclesiastical works, preserved in a wide variety of manuscripts. If it was written during the 1560s, as seems likely from its adventurous and rather archaic treatment of dissonance, it remained topical for almost half a century. It shows a composer who is conscious of both Elizabethan ideals: musical sophistication and textual clarity. Much of the piece is a tug-of-war between the two. It begins in five-voice harmony with the simplest of chordal invocations, taking in the all-important name of the monarch herself. It then wanders into a thicket of intricate six-voice counterpoint (some well-meaning scribes took it upon themselves to simplify this passage) with, at one point, six different words being sung at once. Much the same thing happens in the second half of the anthem, where another straightforward invocation—"but prevent [go before] her with thine everlasting blessing"—soon dissolves into another round of elaborate and closely-spaced imitative writing. No one would have had trouble recognizing the text of a final Amen, and Byrd takes the opportunity to write the most luxurious passage of all (Example 3.3), with five-part filigree under a long-held note in the soprano. "The best sort of melody and music" has obviously triumphed here over reformist ideals of clarity and declamation.

Byrd's English anthems and services, along with some keyboard pieces most likely written for the organ, occupy a unique place in his musical output. They are his only works that cannot be classified as chamber music. They provide a rare opportunity to observe him composing in a truly public voice, one he seems largely to have abandoned in later years

Ex. 3.3 *O Lord make thy servant Elizabeth*, **mm. 45–end**

for both musical and political reasons. Some of this repertory was doubt-less lost, since Byrd himself made no effort to preserve it in print. We owe our knowledge of what is left to the enthusiasm and industry of English church scribes, some of them working several generations after Byrd's death. His services and anthems were his best-known works for a long time. Most of his seventeenth-century or eighteenth-century admirers could hardly have known that these pieces made up just a small percentage of his surviving music, or that the vast majority of English Renaissance churchgoers, despite persistent and appealing myths of an Elizabethan golden age, never heard this kind of music at all.

Byrd's garrulous colleague Thomas Whythorne was very much a man of the Reformation—he had little sympathy for "papists" and wrote bawdy verses on the misadventures of a lecherous friar—but he was quick to rec-ognize the damage done to the English musical tradition in the course of the sixteenth century. "In times past," he said, "music was chiefly main-tained by cathedral churches, abbeys, colleges, parish churches, chantries, guilds, fraternities, etc., but when the abbeys, and colleges without the uni-versities, with guilds, and fraternities, etc. were suppressed, then went music to decay." In most Elizabethan churches, right up to wealthy urban parish churches, singing during services was limited to metrical psalmody and the simplest kind of chanting. Elaborate polyphony of the sort composed by Byrd was sung only in the royal household, a relatively small group of cathedrals, and a handful of colleges. Even the best-established choirs were subject to the whims of Calvinist clergy (some of them stricter than Aylmer) and what seems to have been a chronic shortage of music deemed appropriate for common prayer. The situation, as it turned out, only got worse in the years after Byrd left Lincoln. He would never hold another full-time cathedral post.

CHAPTER FOUR

Musical Explorations

When nothing could my fancy please,
at last I fell into a dream:
methought I saw upon the seas
a ship that sailed against the stream....
—*Content is rich*, consort song by Byrd

ALTHOUGH BYRD SPENT MOST OF THE 1560S AS A CATHEDRAL ORGANIST, his interests during those years went far beyond the realm of church music. He was equally involved in other aspects of Elizabethan musical life: the cultivation of English solo song, the general enthusiasm for viol playing, and the revival of the Latin motet (now banished from church use) as sophisticated chamber music. Much of the music he wrote during his years at Lincoln had little or nothing to do with the practical needs of the cathedral. At this early stage in his career, he was already exploring a variety of styles and genres. His versatility would ease his eventual transition into court life, where sacred and secular music of all sorts was in demand.

Byrd composed a large number of Latin motets in his twenties. That may seem surprising, given the change in official policy about what could and could not be sung in church. There was no real public role left for motets after the Elizabethan religious settlement of 1559. A Latin translation of the Book of Common Prayer was duly produced for the universities in the following year, but there is no sign that it was widely used (even well-established Cambridge choral foundations such as King's and Trinity seem never to have acquired copies) or that anyone was setting it to music. Latin polyphony, however harmless the text, appears not to have been sung in public worship at cathedrals, colleges, or even the Chapel Royal. Latin-texted pieces are in any case completely absent from Elizabethan ecclesiastical manuscripts.

None of this could drive composers away from what had already become one of the most important musical genres of mid-sixteenth-century England. They simply went on cultivating the motet in a different context. It was now private music to be enjoyed among small groups of connoisseurs. Byrd himself described these circles in the dedication to one of his motet books: he expressed his gratitude to "some people joined to me by true bonds of friendship, and of good reputation" who had acquired manuscript copies of his motets and noticed that errors were starting to creep in. In terms of social function, the Elizabethan motet was much closer to the secular instrumental music of its age than it was to the sacred music being sung in cathedrals. Latin-texted polyphony was no longer welcome in the choir stalls, so it resurfaced in academic lodgings, the private rooms of the well-to-do, and the sometimes heroic efforts of amateur scribes and collectors.

Byrd's early motets followed the precedents set by colleagues such as Parsons, White, and Mundy. Some of these pieces were written on a quite ambitious scale. Now that settings of the Catholic mass (the traditional grand genre of Renaissance music) were out of the question, the motet offered English composers their chief opportunity for writing large vocal works in complex counterpoint. They generally kept clear of old-fashioned devotional texts and glorifications of the Virgin Mary, although Parsons managed to produce a justly famous *Ave Maria* before his premature death.

One popular approach was to set an entire Latin psalm to music. The so-called "psalm-motet" was ideologically acceptable among a wide variety of singers, even the stricter sort of Protestant. It also provided a link with the international musical traditions of the Renaissance. This is illustrated well by an anonymous English family portrait from the 1560s (Figure 4.1), now in a private collection, which shows a solemn black-clad group of four children making music. The older boys are holding open partbooks, one of which is so realistically depicted that it can be

FIGURE 4.1   Master of the Countess of Warwick (fl. later 1560s), unidentified English
children with a Josquin motet

transcribed from the painting. It contains the bass part of the Josquin
motet *Domine ne in furore*, a polyphonic psalm setting of the exact sort
cultivated by so many Elizabethan composers. The source, copied down
to the tiniest detail, is a German motet book printed by Johannes Petreius
in the late 1530s and imported to England at some point before this portrait was made. Whether or not the thirteen-year-old boy (his age carefully inscribed above his head) could actually manage the bass line on his
own, the ideal celebrated in the painting is clear: cultivation of musical
skill and decorum within the well-educated Elizabethan family. The
Latin psalm-motet, whether native or imported, was a perfect fit for the
situation.

Many early Elizabethan psalm-motets were more or less direct stylistic
descendants of mid-century English works such as Mundy's *Vox patris*.
These were large pieces with kaleidoscopic variations in texture, often
concluding with an unusually impressive Amen. White's *Exaudiat te
Dominus* is a good example of the type, as is Parsons's *Retribue servo tuo*.
Byrd took a different approach to writing his first big motets. He was not
interested in chopping his text into numerous little phrases and assigning
each one to a different combination of singers. His two earliest psalm-
motets, both almost certainly dating from the 1560s, are scored on a
grand scale—one in nine voices, the other in eight—and all the parts are

heard almost all the time. This produces a complex tangle of polyphony, much of it consistently dissonant, especially in the nine-part *Domine quis habitabit*. The effect is monumental, gritty, and a bit precarious in places. There is nothing else quite like it in the surviving repertory of English Renaissance music. Byrd clearly enjoyed the emotional intensity he could build up in such long stretches of uninterrupted imitative writing. He also seems to have enjoyed the sheer noise he could produce with such a large group of voices.

Domine quis habitabit was a favorite psalm among English composers despite its rather dry and moralizing text, less a prayer than a checklist of good behavior. (Given his brother John's irregular financial activities, Byrd may have raised an eyebrow at the denunciations of usury and greed.) There were already numerous contemporary settings of this psalm by the time Byrd made his own. He began with a fresh and unusual idea, a leap of a minor sixth, which creates an unexpected harmonic jolt the first time it is heard. This melodic figure passes through all nine voices, one by one, and the waves of counterpoint close in over the singers, who do not resurface again until the final cadence. The only relief in the unrelenting nine-part texture is a brief passage during which two of the three bass voices are silent. Byrd still manages to give the work a more or less convincing musical shape, with the highest notes of all cutting through the clamor of the last pages. He does much the same thing in the eight-part *Ad Dominum cum tribularer*, a more overtly expressive piece, where the voices (especially the sopranos) fall into pairs and trade increasingly urgent exhortations with one another:

> With those who hate peace I was a peacemaker.
> I spoke peace, and they shouted together for war.

The constant harangue of imitation at the unison (Example 4.1) is a rather blunt instrument, but it creates as convincing an effect as we find in any of his other early motets.

Byrd never published these two big psalms, most likely for practical reasons of scale. They were experiments he did not repeat. When he came back to sustained eight-part writing in his musical exchange with Philippe de Monte during the 1580s, it was at the invitation of a European colleague for whom eight-voice polyphony meant something rather different. What comes through most clearly in Byrd's large-scale psalm

Ex. 4.1A *Ad Dominum cum tribularer*, mm. 144–52

settings is the desire to try out extremes of musical texture. There must have been a similar impulse behind his serious cultivation of three-part music a few decades later, with all its particular challenges and limitations. He was never satisfied for long with a conventional layout of voices.

Another popular source for the Elizabethan motet was the biblical book of Lamentations. These laments, which mourn the destruction of Jerusalem and the exile of the Jewish people, are among the most expres-

Ex. 4.1B

sive and tragic passages in all of Scripture. They were incorporated into
medieval Holy Week services and eventually became favorites among
composers of polyphony. A number of Byrd's older English contemporaries set them to music. Judging from the excerpts they chose, they seem
to have known each other's work well and made an effort not to duplicate
it: the same text is never set twice. One feature shared by all these
polyphonic Lamentations is the creative setting of the initial letters. The
poem is an alphabetical acrostic in the original Hebrew, and each verse

Ex. 4.1C

in the Latin Vulgate begins with the relevant Hebrew letter. This offered composers a chance to break up the text with long passages of abstract music, in much the same way that medieval scribes punctuated their manuscripts with illuminated initial letters. Byrd took full advantage of the opportunity in his own Lamentations, writing elaborate settings of the letters *heth*, *teth*, and *jod*. He also added the traditional liturgical prologue ("From the lamentation of Jeremiah the Prophet") and epilogue ("Jerusalem, Jerusalem, return to the Lord your God").

This complex form gave Byrd some much-needed guidance. He could not follow the method of his big psalm-motets and produce a steady onslaught of imitative counterpoint until the piece was over. The music had to be divided into many small sections, each with its own expressive trajectory and its own place in the larger whole. He was happy to elide or avoid cadences in these early years—a piece such as *Da mihi auxilium* or the canonic *O salutaris hostia* could go on for a very long time without a definitive full close—but the structure of his Lamentations required at least eight of them. The result is an eccentric, somewhat uneven, and in the end quite arresting work. In many ways it is a response to Tallis's two sets of Lamentations. The unusual final cadence with its plunging bass line is taken directly from Tallis, quoted as plainly as Byrd quoted from his keyboard works in these early years. We also catch a first glimpse here of the expressive semitone that will color so many of Byrd's later imitative points. Tallis uses it for *aleph*, the first of his five Hebrew letters; Byrd adapts it to the crucial word *lamentatione*. Tallis's first set of Lamentations shows an astonishing chromatic flexibility, with opening and closing sections based on E and a central section based a tritone away on B-flat. We can see Byrd's own reply to this in the lurching modulations of his last pages, where he covers as much ground in an even less predictable manner. Even the rich and distinctive vocal scoring of Byrd's Lamentations—five low voices, the bass regularly descending below the staff—is borrowed from the older composer.

There are also a few notable differences. Unlike Tallis, and like many of his Continental contemporaries, Byrd brings in some pre-existing musical material. Near the end he cites the Gregorian chant melody of the Lamentations with its repeated exhortations of "Jerusalem, Jerusalem." (He will allude later to this idea at the beginning of his lament *Ne irascaris*, with its slow rising figures and glacial major chords.) The Tallis Lamentations gain much of their dramatic effect from groups of voices that declaim the text simultaneously, often set in sharp relief against an isolated solo voice. Byrd has no interest in copying this technique. He never brings in more than two parts at once. His English liturgical music from the 1560s shows that he knew perfectly well how to write in a declamatory style, but his fascination with sustained counterpoint prevails here over his desire for immediate rhetorical effects. Byrd even edits the biblical text (thus dropping all pretense of liturgical decorum) to suit the needs of his musical style: his Lamentations discard the second half of each verse. If he had not made those cuts, the music, unlike Tallis's more concise Lamentations, would quickly have grown to an unmanageable size.

Some of Byrd's most complex polyphony did not have a text at all. It was during his Lincoln years that he began to write substantial pieces for groups of viols, which were popular instruments among English Renaissance choristers and formed part of the official musical curriculum at many cathedrals. Boys played the viol in theatrical productions, pageants, and other entertainments, a trend that reached its peak during the 1560s. The master of the choristers at St. Paul's, Sebastian Westcote, who trained Byrd's two older brothers and perhaps Byrd himself, owned a "chest of violins and viols," which he left to his successor "to exercise and learn the children and choristers." Lincoln Cathedral maintained its own viol consort by the late sixteenth century, and there is no reason to believe that viols were not already being played when Byrd was there. A number of his early string works have a distinctly pedagogical air, although others are elaborate musical experiments that probably had little to do with the everyday curriculum he offered his choristers.

The line between music for voices and music for strings was not always strictly drawn. Some of the best-known pieces in sixteenth-century England began in one genre and migrated to another. A brief section of a polyphonic mass by John Taverner was copied out as a textless work which eventually spawned well over a hundred imitations. One of Byrd's earliest large-scale pieces for viol consort reappeared in his first motet book, shoehorned under his own supervision into a Latin psalm text. Various pieces by Tallis and other Tudor composers underwent a similar transformation. Morley was still complaining at the end of the century about the widespread habit of performing vocal music without its text. The surviving evidence shows that voices and viols were sometimes considered interchangeable in the early Elizabethan years—a situation that Byrd and his colleagues exploited to the fullest.

Byrd's six-part string fantasia in F, the one he later adapted for voices, is quite unlike his more free-wheeling keyboard fantasias. It is hard to believe these pieces were written by the same composer at more or less the same time. The viol fantasia falls into four sections, each one based on a jaunty little melodic idea that is imitated relentlessly at the unison and the fifth. Three of the four sections are repeated note for note to drive the point home. There is not much change in texture or atmosphere, although the long final section unwinds a little with its more leisurely melodies and its brief nod toward the minor mode. The whole piece is yet another experiment in pervasive imitation, now in a very different style. This was the style used by slightly older contemporaries such as Mundy and White in their more fiercely constructivist moods: symmetry, strict repetition, regular cadences, and rather little that could be called musical development in any meaningful sense. Byrd must have been satisfied with the experiment, because he eventually revised and published it in 1575—one of only a handful of consort pieces he ever printed—as the Latin motet *Laudate pueri Dominum*. (He must have been in urgent need of material for his new motet book, because the adaptation for voices is not entirely convincing.)

Other early consort works by Byrd are in a more relaxed and imaginative style. The most important of these works are his group of In Nomines. Despite their Latin name, these are not sacred pieces. They are textless compositions based on the chant melody used by Taverner in his early sixteenth-century mass *Gloria tibi Trinitas*. (The unusual title comes from the sung text of the mass: the original In Nomine was simply a straight instrumental transcription of a four-voice passage from the Benedictus, at the words *in nomine Domini*.) The form survived for a very long time—it was still being cultivated by Henry Purcell in the late seventeenth century—and it produced some of the most famous music in the English consort repertory. The practice of writing and playing In Nomines was closely associated with the choir schools and the musical education of boys. String playing and creative improvisation around a fixed melody were, as we have seen, two important parts of a chorister's training, and the two met in the musical form of the In Nomine, which was taken up (at least in passing) by nearly all English Renaissance composers. By the middle of the sixteenth century, some of them were accepting the tradition as a sort of challenge, producing more and more audacious settings. Christopher Tye and Osbert Parsley wrote In Nomines in 5/4 time. An obscure Elizabethan musician named Picforth managed to write one in which each of the five parts uses its own distinct time value throughout. Many of these pieces were given eccentric or obscure names. Tye's output of In Nomines includes *Seldom seen*, *Blameless*, *My death bed*, and *Farewell my good l. forever*. His 5/4 In Nomine is aptly titled *Trust*.

Byrd wrote a number of In Nomines during his years at Lincoln. Most of them are in five parts, with one part providing the set melody in long notes while the others weave an increasingly complex web of counterpoint around it. Byrd does not indulge in the sort of overt showmanship we see in Tye's settings. His settings are adventurous but ultimately quite serious. He took the more conservative side of the Elizabethan In Nomine tradition, which kept to the precedents established by Taverner two generations earlier: minimal tampering with the cantus firmus, and an emphasis on melodic beauty over virtuosity or cleverness. Byrd's group of In Nomines for five voices traces the broad outlines of his early development as a consort composer. The first (and probably earliest) begins with a slightly wooden theme, reminiscent of his consort fantasia in F, and ends with an enthusiastic but ultimately unconvincing triple-time section. The second is more lyrical, with a higher concentration of dissonance, and develops its musical material in a more compelling way. By his fifth and last In Nomine (whose opening measures are shown in Example 4.2), Byrd emerges as a self-confident composer who is shaping the form rather than being guided by it. As in the four-part *Clarifica me* setting for organ, the cantus firmus—when we notice it, which is not too often—has become an unobtrusive piece of deep structure. The last pages are full of rhythmic complexities, but they seem to arise naturally from what has come before. This final setting was by far the most famous in Byrd's own day. It survives in more than a dozen manuscripts.

In most of Byrd's early works, whatever their background or style, we see a young composer who was interested above all in experimentation. He wanted to try out new ideas and tackle a variety of problems. Some groups of pieces were clearly conceived as multiple responses to the same challenge. By the time he left Lincoln, he was already well versed in many of the musical genres he would cultivate in later years. There were only two important exceptions to this rule: keyboard pavans and galliards, which he did not begin writing until the 1570s, and Catholic liturgical

Ex. 4.2 In Nomine, 5v, no. 5, mm. 1–8

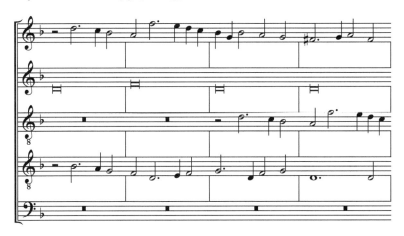

music, which he had dabbled in as a young apprentice but seems not to have revisited until the early 1590s.

Some other types of music seem to have fallen by the wayside as his career went on, but even the genres he eventually lost interest in (the English verse service, the In Nomine, the massive psalm-motet) still exercised an influence on his later works. There are numerous echoes of his accompanied English church music in his more serious secular songs. His fascination with cantus-firmus composition and its less strict derivatives lasted into the early seventeenth century. Most important of all, his delight in imitative counterpoint—played out in audacious, colorful, and sometimes crude ways in so many of his early works—remained central to his musical thought until the end of his life.

The art of counterpoint was doubtless the most crucial skill Byrd acquired as a young composer. It seems also to have provided him with an intellectual and aesthetic refuge of sorts in an increasingly contentious age. As a purely musical technique, it was not subject (except in the relatively narrow confines of the cathedral choir stalls) to any kind of ideological constraint. Morley hinted at something similar when he praised "those famous English men ... Fayrfax, Taverner, Sheppard, Mundy, White, Parsons, Master Byrd, and divers others, who never thought it greater sacrilege to spurn against the image of a saint than to take two perfect chords of one kind together [i.e. write parallel fifths or octaves]." Morley is saying here—rightly or wrongly—that the art of good composition was ultimately every bit as strong a cultural force as the religious convictions of the era. Byrd would doubtless have bristled at the suggestion that he would sooner desecrate the image of a saint than write parallel fifths, but his student, with his characteristic wry humor, had touched on something important. The musical craft Byrd perfected during his early years did not guarantee him immunity from political or religious controversies, but it certainly eased his path through them.

CHAPTER FIVE

Royal Patronage

How precious a thing is Music
—Richard Mulcaster, preface to the 1575 *Cantiones*

IN THE LAST DAYS OF JANUARY 1572, ROBERT PARSONS, GENTLEMAN OF the Chapel Royal, drowned in the River Trent. The usually laconic record-keeper of the Chapel found the cause of death unusual enough to note in his chronicle. Byrd was almost immediately invited to fill the vacant place, and he wasted no time in accepting it. On 22 February, less than a month after Parsons's death, Byrd was sworn in as his replacement. He was following several older generations of distinguished composers into the royal service. The best church musicians in England had already begun to converge on the Chapel when Henry VIII dissolved the abbeys, monasteries, and chantries in the late 1530s, effectively concentrating much of English musical life in his own court. Byrd's new post gave him access to unequaled musical resources and close contact with many of the country's leading musicians. It also gave him a chance to pursue his considerable social and economic ambitions.

The Elizabethan Chapel Royal was the largest choir of its kind in England. The Queen maintained a Chapel staff of thirty-two gentlemen (most of them musical laymen like Tallis and Byrd, along with a smaller number of clerics) and twelve children. Even with the usual rotation of duties among adult singers and the difficulties caused by illness or absence, Elizabeth's choir was still an impressive force. She could muster more than forty singers for major feast days and state occasions. Byrd and his colleagues were rewarded with a generous salary, and their appointments were for life. Very few of their counterparts elsewhere in England were as fortunate.

Byrd's swearing-in as a Gentleman of the Chapel involved a solemn declaration that the Queen "is and ought to be, by the word of God, the only supreme governor of this realm…as well in all spiritual or ecclesiastical things or causes, as temporal." It also called for a renunciation of "all foreign jurisdictions, powers, superiorities and authorities." The oath was a slightly more elaborate version of the standard Oath of Supremacy required of any aspirant to church or court office. Almost two years to the day before Byrd entered the Chapel, Pope Pius V, who had grown frustrated by the political situation in England, issued the notorious injunction known (by the first words of the papal document) as *Regnans in excelsis*. This decree excommunicated the Queen, released her Catholic subjects from allegiance to her, and—most relevant to Byrd's case—anathematized any subject who continued to "obey her orders, advice or laws." By the time Byrd took the oath in 1572, the Catholic hierarchy would have considered it grounds for his own immediate excommunication. Whatever Byrd's religious convictions were at this point, he was still willing to make the compromise. He appears never to have renounced the oath, at least not in any formal way.

Queen Elizabeth herself had a pronounced taste for good music, sacred as well as secular, and she made room for it at her court. Her private musical establishment enjoyed some immunity from the puritanical tendencies imposed by many parish and cathedral clergy. She seems to have had little patience with ideologues who saw all complex church music as inherently suspect. Whatever her own theological leanings may have been, cultivating a certain kind of high churchmanship was also in her best diplomatic interest. Catholic visitors from the Continent, who had doubtless been regaled with stories of dour northern Calvinism, were often surprised at what they saw and heard in her private chapel. For the visit of the Italian duke Virginio Orsini in January 1601, she reportedly gave orders "that the communion table should be adorned with basin and ewer of gold and evening tapers and other ornaments (some say also with a crucifix), and that all the ministry should be in rich copes." A visitor to the Chapel Royal at Whitehall in September 1565—a guest at the christening of the child of Lady Cecile, marchioness of Bawden—left a vivid description of the place where the Queen's choir sang:

> The back part of the stalls wherein the Gentlemen of the Chapel do sing was hanged with rich tapestry representing the twelve months [the signs of the zodiac], and the front of the said stalls was also covered with rich arras. The upper part of the chapel, from the table of administration to the stalls, was hanged with cloth of gold, and on the south side was a rich traverse [private box] for the Queen. The communion table was richly furnished with plate and jewels. On the north side of the choir between the organs and the upper window stood seventeen candlesticks double gilt, with seventeen lights; and on the tops of the stalls were fastened certain candlesticks with twelve lights.

We do not know much about Byrd's regular routine as a Chapel musician. Given the extensive travels and "removes" of the Elizabethan court, it is hard to say what an average day looked like, although the quiet round of services at Whitehall was probably more the exception than the rule. Tallis was probably close to seventy when Byrd joined him at the Chapel—he was described by the late 1570s as "very aged"—and he may well have taken the opportunity to pass along the burden of his duties to his student. Most of the singers spent alternating months on and off active duty for much of the liturgical year. This normally meant that their attendance was required only seven or eight months out of twelve. Parsons was clearly on post-Christmas leave from court (or on an external assignment: perhaps the recruiting of choristers?) when he drowned in Nottinghamshire. The Chapel organists, who may also have been in charge of rehearsals, were bound to a more regular schedule. In 1577, Byrd complained in a petition to the Queen that "his daily attendance in your Majesty's said service" prevented him "from reaping such commodity by teaching as heretofore he did, and still might have done, to the great relief of himself and his poor family." Four years later, in 1581, he wrote to Robert Petre that "my attendance here at the Court is so requisite that I cannot have as yet any spare time to come to London." Whenever he had his own music printed, he described himself on the title page either as Organist of, or Gentleman of, the Chapel. In his Latin books, he preferred the internationally understood "organist," the term also used by émigrés such as Peter Philips and Richard Dering who went to serve at the great courts and chapels of Europe. In his English books, he used the distinctively English title of Gentleman. When he dedicated a volume to the Queen in 1575, he took advantage of both titles.

Byrd's new position at the Chapel brought him from the provinces to the center of English cultural and economic life. He seems to have had the ear of powerful people at court almost as soon as he arrived there. Within a few years, he and Tallis had negotiated a royal patent for the printing and distribution of music in England. The patent, granted by Elizabeth in January 1575, gave "full privilege and license unto our well-beloved servants Thomas Tallis and William Byrd" to edit and publish music in England for the next twenty-one years. The decree also barred all other English entrepreneurs from selling "songs made and printed in any foreign country." The official penalty for dealing in such musical contraband was the Queen's "high displeasure," a fine of 40 shillings, and forfeit of the offending pieces to the two composers, whose libraries would doubtless have been enriched by any enforcement of this rule. Their monopoly extended even to the specially printed staff paper on which many musicians made their manuscript copies. Byrd himself claimed personal expenses for "partition paper" in the 1570s.

Privileges and monopolies of this sort were nothing unusual in Tudor and Stuart England. They were often granted as royal favors to preferred clients, including some of Byrd's own associates. Edward Somerset, the earl of Worcester, to whom the composer dedicated his first solo publication of Latin motets, was given a commission from King James in 1607 "for the making of saltpeter and gunpowder." This may have raised a few eyebrows, coming as it did just after the Gunpowder Plot of 1605, a narrowly foiled attempt by a group of Catholic extremists to assassinate King James and most of his government by detonating kegs of gunpowder during the ceremonial opening of Parliament. Henry Howard, the patron of Byrd's first book of *Gradualia*, had the monopoly on the production and importation of starch. This was not a trivial matter, given the elaborate starched ruffs and collars in fashion at the time. Although printed polyphony was certainly more of a niche market than laundry or explosives, the 1575 music patent had a lasting influence on the generations that followed. The privilege was inherited in full by Byrd and his younger son after Tallis's death, was eventually secured by Thomas Morley, and persisted well into the seventeenth century. Music publishing in England seems to have been at its most vigorous and diverse during the brief interludes (such as the years 1596–98) when the monopoly was *not* in force.

Tallis and Byrd were quick to show their gratitude to Elizabeth for the music patent. By the end of 1575, they had dedicated a joint collection of Latin motets to her and seen it through the press. It contains seventeen pieces by each composer, mostly in alternating groups of three. Tallis takes the place of honor at the beginning of the book and ends it with a dazzling display of canonic skill. Byrd's contribution is in many ways the more novel and varied of the two, and arguably the more uneven. The volume is a retrospective for the older composer, a showcase for the younger, and a collaboration between two musicians whose training lay on either side of the major cultural watershed of their day.

The composers gave their book a strange and somewhat evasive title: *Cantiones quae ab argumento sacrae vocantur,* "songs which on account of their subject matter are called sacred." The shared contents of the *Cantiones* reveal two rather different approaches to writing sacred songs. Tallis had worked for a number of English musical foundations, including the Chapel Royal itself, before the Latin liturgy was finally dismantled. Some of his contributions to the 1575 book are older works, mid-century pieces of liturgical polyphony (of the same vintage as the teenaged Byrd's *Similes illis fiant*) which recall a period of relative stability. Byrd was never publicly active as a Catholic composer in the way Tallis had been. Producing a substantial set of motets was a different undertaking for him. He did not already have a portfolio of Latin-texted ritual music at his disposal, and his own motet style was in a state of considerable flux at the time. Tallis himself had gone on experimenting with new compositional devices in his old age, perhaps under the influence of his adventurous student. The result of all this was an unusually diverse book: a broad sample of English polyphonic music, along with some distinctive rereadings of the sixteenth-century Continental tradition. The composers seem to have reveled in the sheer variety of their collection. They made no attempts to disguise that variety—in fact they emphasized it through the unusual ordering of the contents.

This was almost certainly *not* practical music to be sung in services at court. Even among the rich tapestries, gilt candlesticks, and general grandeur of Elizabeth's Chapel Royal, there is no evidence that Latin-texted polyphony was cultivated or even tolerated. Reports by foreign dignitaries show, if anything, that even the Queen's most solemn services were sung in the English vernacular. When a Habsburg ambassador visited Whitehall in 1565, "the Earl of Sussex interpreted the hymns and anthems" for him. A Russian diplomat who came to England in 1601 had to be told during the royal communion service that "they are singing the psalms of David." Diplomats of this sort would doubtless have been able to understand Latin without difficulty, so their testimony hints that the singing must have taken place in English—although Elizabeth certainly seems to have encouraged complex music in English well beyond the austere declamatory ideals of the reformers. Despite the public dedication to her, this was music she would only have heard in private.

The 1575 book of *Cantiones* was the first Renaissance musical anthology shared with complete equality between two musicians. Gathering more than one person's music in a single book was something generally done by printers and editors, not by composers themselves, and the anthologist's work was as often eclectic as systematic. Byrd himself, at a more advanced age, would be given the place of honor in the early seventeenth-century keyboard anthology *Parthenia*: he supplied the first eight of the twenty-one pieces, with the rest allotted to John Bull (seven) and Orlando Gibbons (six). The 1575 book of *Cantiones* is organized in a more even-handed way. Its unusual layout of two times seventeen motets, made to come out even by some creative renumbering of multi-part pieces, may itself be a tribute to Queen Elizabeth, to whom the composers offered the book in the seventeenth year of her reign. The anniversary of her accession day was celebrated on the seventeenth of November, quite possibly the occasion on which it was presented.

Tallis and Byrd speak at some length in the preface to the 1575 *Cantiones*, addressing the Queen directly in the first person. There is no shortage of the usual courtly flattery ("when you are compared with the greatest artists you easily surpass them, whether by the elegance of your voice or the agility of your fingers"), but the preface reveals something of the sincere musical optimism and creativity that prevailed at court in the mid-1570s. The composers could easily (as they say) have summoned learned arguments for the value of music, but, given the Queen's own musical talent and taste, they prefer to let their work speak for itself. They finish with a short and rather poignant valedictory poem in Latin:

We commend these first-fruits to you, gentle reader, as a woman still weak from childbirth entrusts her infant to the care of the nurse, for your favor will be their milk. Thus nourished, they dare to promise an abundant harvest; if fruitless, they will fall by an honorable sickle.

The introduction to the book also includes a group of Latin poems by other authors extolling the skill of the composers. These poems take a less modest tone. The central idea, expressed at times in frankly milita-ristic terms, is that English music ("already contemplating battle") was now ready to appear in print and take on its famous Continental rivals: Lassus, Gombert, Clemens, the familiar litany of mid-century masters. The Latin motet, the most learned and cosmopolitan of Renaissance musical genres, was a perfect vehicle for such ambitions. Ferdinando Richardson's prefatory poem is worth quoting at some length for what it says about the composers' motives, or about contemporary perceptions of them:

When bountiful Music perceived that her heralds sprang from foreign soil...Orlando singing harmoniously with his divine voice and composing his works for boundless posterity, sweet Gombert pouring out his delightful melodies, Clemens harmonizing his tranquil measures, Alfonso the Phoenix of our time, producing songs that Apollo might pass off as his own...but without a solitary English name printed in any book, she nearly began to lose her temper and to charge our British composers with being unworthy of her gifts. Eager to put an end to such a stern complaint, Tallis, an aged man worthy of great respect, and Byrd, born to honor such a great teacher, promise that henceforth what was before will be no longer. And they direct the printing of their songs, both allowing them to be read by others.

Of course Tallis and Byrd were not working in splendid isolation. There were many connections between the music in the 1575 *Cantiones* and the work of the foreign "heralds" named by Richardson. Byrd was very much interested in European musical styles and compositional processes during these years. One foreign musician who seems to have made a distinct impression on him was "Alfonso the Phoenix of our time," the Italian composer Alfonso Ferrabosco, who spent the years from 1562 to 1577 in the employment of Queen Elizabeth. Ferrabosco seems to have used his frequent international travels as an opportunity for intrigue and espionage of various sorts. He was embroiled in a scandal surrounding the murder of an Italian colleague; he attracted the surveillance, at different times, of both the Inquisition and the English Protestant authorities; and he gained a reputation in some circles, notwithstanding his skill and his documented friendship with other musicians, as "a most evil-spirited and evil-minded man." His services were clearly still valued at the English court. By his mid-twenties he was already being paid £100 per year, more than three times Byrd's salary as a Gentleman of the Chapel.

Ferrabosco's music remained almost unknown in his native Italy, but a good number of his motets and madrigals were preserved in English manuscripts. English musicians spoke highly of him, and, as we have seen, he earned a place among the illustrious foreigners in the preface to the *Cantiones*. At a time when rather little up-to-date Continental music was readily available in England, he was a perfect match for his Elizabethan contemporaries, given their insatiable thirst (mixed with a dash of suspicion) for foreign luxury goods. Byrd knew him personally and engaged in friendly musical rivalries with him. The most notable of these was a set of eighty canons, now lost, on the plainsong *Miserere*. Henry Peacham, in his 1622 *Compleat Gentleman*, refers to their "friendly emulation," and Morley describes their "virtuous contention in love." A number of Byrd's 1575 motets, especially those near the beginning of the book, have affinities of various sorts with Ferrabosco's own Latin works.

Byrd's opening salvo in the *Cantiones*, the motet *Emendemus in melius*, comes as something of a shock after the intricate web of polyphony woven by Tallis in his first three pieces. For most of this brief work, there is no counterpoint, no imitation, only flickers of melodic independence in the inner voices. The result has very little to do with preconceived notions of how a late Renaissance motet should sound. Byrd's chosen text does not begin with a prayer or a reflection, but with a call to arms, a gauntlet thrown down to the listener: "Let us make amends where we have sinned through ignorance." We are exhorted to leave the old and begin something new. Byrd follows suit in his musical setting. He declaims the words urgently, with driving bursts of syncopation, frequent short pauses, and, especially in the second half, some arresting harmonic turns. Not a single chord is out of place. Only in the final measures of the piece does the taut homophony unwind fully into radiant imitative counterpoint.

The only other piece of Elizabethan music that looks anything like *Emendemus* is a setting by Ferrabosco of some verses (*Qui fundasti terram*) from Psalm 104. Their opening measures can be compared in Examples 5.1 and 5.2. This unusual pair of works can be read either as Byrd's direct response to a promising musical influence or as a well-timed act of

Ex. 5.1 *Emendemus in melius*, mm. 1–9

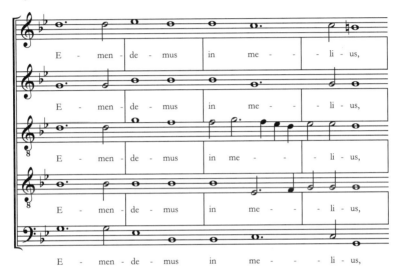

Ex. 5.2 *Qui fundasti terram* (Alfonso Ferrabosco), mm. 1–8

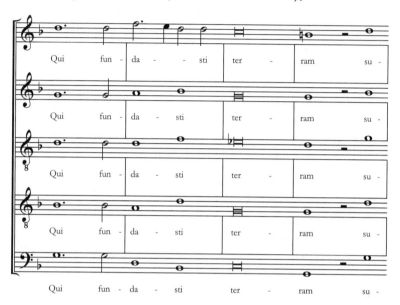

homage (or plagiarism?) on the part of his Italian friend. However Byrd arrived at the distinctive stylistic idea, he took it and made it his own.

There is also an obvious kinship between *Emendemus* and the lucid, transparent declamation of English vernacular church music, where clarity of text was—at least ideally—valued above all else. The language Byrd had learned as a young cathedral choirmaster is present almost everywhere in the little piece he chose to launch his publishing career. It was not a gesture he would repeat often. He avoids such long stretches of simultaneous text-setting in his later motets, with a few exceptions such as the famous *Ave verum corpus*. He tends to use this sort of declamation as a pungent seasoning rather than a main ingredient. In *Emendemus* we taste it briefly at full strength.

Byrd explores a number of different musical techniques in the rest of the *Cantiones*. The most important of these, not too surprisingly, is pervasive imitation among voices. It is used only briefly in *Emendemus*, as a special gesture at the end, but it is the stylistic foundation of most of the other motets. *Peccantem me quotidie*, his third piece in the book, is a good example of this basic imitative type. Its first pages are everything *Emendemus* is not: polyphonic, discursive, a gradual exploration of a single musical idea. The idea is the one already featured in Byrd's Lamentations a decade earlier, the dissonant, claustrophobic semitone that, in extreme cases, could and did set the musical program for a whole piece. The half-step may sound at first like a confining melodic figure, but for Byrd it was a liberating gesture which often carried the music into unexpected tonal areas. It appears here at several different pitch levels: first D/E♭, then A/B♭, and finally E♮/F—the last something of a surprise, because the musical scale used by Byrd contains a naturally occurring semitone in only two places. As often as not, he introduces a third or even a fourth semitone as he develops the material further. In *Peccantem*, as in so many other serious imitative works, he combines this sort of harmonic flexibility with a robust (and quite un-Palestrinian) approach to dissonance treatment.

Ferrabosco also wrote a setting of *Peccantem me quotidie*. The two pieces keep to the same basic proportions until the last sentence, a final plea for mercy and salvation. Byrd's response to the concluding words "Miserere mei Deus et salva me" is twice as long as Ferrabosco's and much more complicated. He brings two complementary musical ideas into play, one belonging to the phrase *Miserere mei Deus* and the other to *et salva me*. He then works out this double point with unusual tenacity, chasing it around the circle of fifths and testing out all its contrapuntal possibilities. There is a brief respite, with a thinning of texture and a bittersweet turn to the major mode, before the voices rise to a climax and converge on the final cadence. At this stage in his life, Byrd liked to develop his final imitative points almost to excess: he does much the same thing with the ending of *Da mihi auxilium*, later on in the 1575 book, where his rich, complex, anguished setting of the four words "ut plangam iuventutem meam" ("that I might lament my youth") is itself the length of some of his more direct and declamatory motets. There are few people more earnest than a still quite young artist who has taken it upon himself to lament the sins of his youth, and Byrd made the most of the opportunity (Example 5.3).

Byrd's opening group of three pieces, including *Emendemus* and *Peccantem*, keeps to a penitential mood throughout. This atmosphere is intensified by the persistent minor mode based on G with two flats in the key signature, quite far into the flat side of the tonal system by sixteenth-century standards. The imagery in all three motets is of death and its terrors, the inexorable passage of time, the struggle between light and shadow. It was an uncompromising way for a composer to break into print in his mid-thirties. The words of *Peccantem me quotidie* speak for themselves:

> While I sin every day, and do not repent,
> the fear of death troubles me:
> for in hell there is no redemption.
> Have mercy on me, O God, and save me.

The mood will become even darker in his next series of published motets—most of all in the first half of the 1589 *Cantiones*, a musical cycle with few rivals for sustained gloominess until the nineteenth century. Of course Elizabethan England was full of ostentatious displays of melancholy, both secular and religious, and it is risky to draw conclusions about a composer's personality from the prevailing mood of a small group of pieces. Among Ferrabosco's forty-three surviving motets, more than half are overtly penitential, of a kind much less often found in the works of Palestrina or even of Lassus. It would be surprising if an Elizabethan

Ex. 5.3A *Da mihi auxilium,* mm. 101–17

Ex. 5.3B

Ex. 5.3C

composer were to turn out more happy pieces than sad. These dark, sometimes anguished texts were also an ideal vehicle for Byrd's favorite expressive techniques. Whether he chose them himself, was handed them by a serious-minded older patron (as seems to have been the case from time to time), or was merely reacting to the spirit of the age, they were a remarkably good fit for him.

Despite his lifelong taste for what Peacham called "gravity and piety," Byrd could and did also write motets in a cheerful vein. The 1575 book contains a number of lighter pieces, although lightness in the Elizabethan motet is always a matter of degree. His six-voice *Attollite portas* is a perfect example of the type. The text is "Lift up your heads, O ye gates," and he sets it to a bounding subject that quickly rises through an octave, the light-hearted opposite of the grave semitone that haunts other Byrd motets. This piece seems to have become a favorite in cathedral choirs, where a version adapted to English words was sung widely during the seventeenth century.

Some of Byrd's more upbeat motets are printed in the fashionable *note nere* ("black notes") characteristic of Italian madrigals: the note values are reduced by a factor of two, which in practice turns out a much darker printed page and a livelier sense of declamation. All of Byrd's *note nere* motets are based on Latin metrical poetry, and they owe much to Italianate and humanistic ideals of clear, accurate text-setting. *Siderum rector* sets an obscure text, an adaptation of a hymn in honor of female saints who fall into the somewhat ungrateful category of "neither virgin nor martyr." Byrd seems to have picked it as neutral material on which to practice his new-found enthusiasm for setting poetry in classical meters; once again there is a link with Ferrabosco, who set a hymn in a more or less identical way. Byrd's *O lux beata Trinitas* is another *note nere* piece in the Italian style. The strict three-in-one canon in the final verse, where a single part unfolds in three voices at different pitch levels, is clearly a musical reflection of the Trinity to whom the hymn is addressed. The result is an uneasy coupling: a breezy, modern piece that suddenly lapses into thick, rather old-fashioned counterpoint in the last pages.

Some of Byrd's 1575 motets are old-fashioned all the way through. His share of the *Cantiones* moves, in broad terms, from the progressive to the conservative. The newest material appears first. He begins with expressive declamation and tightly organized imitation, and he ends with canons, cantus-firmus settings, and leisurely, expansive music that recalls the older English polyphonic tradition. If the first part of the book had somehow been lost, we would be left with a quite different image of what Byrd was doing in the early 1570s. (Tallis seems to have taken an opposite tack. He reserved some of his most forward-looking pieces, such as the astonishing chromatic essay *In ieiunio et fletu*, for the end.)

One of Byrd's most traditionally-minded contributions to the *Cantiones* is the tripartite motet *Tribue Domine*. Here he faced a problem that was already familiar to him: how to keep up interest through an unusually large-scale work. His solution in *Tribue Domine* was to use the old technique of breaking up a long text and setting it to different combinations of voices, while bringing in a more modern taste for systematic imitation and large-scale tonal planning. He took the text from a well-known book of *Meditations* attributed to St. Augustine, which circulated widely on both sides of the sectarian divide in Renaissance England and even appeared in a manuscript linked to Queen Elizabeth herself. There are many moments worth relishing in this piece. One is the splendid old-fashioned dissonance (Example 5.4) on the word *imperium* as the first soprano sails up a seventh to a high F and the second soprano responds with a simultaneous F-sharp at the lower octave. This is the pungent sound ubiquitous in English Catholic ritual works of the previous generation, especially those of Sheppard, who could hardly follow through an imitative point without it occurring somewhere (and who almost invariably resolved it with the accented 6–5 progression also found here.) It is hard not to hear a touch of grateful triumphalism as Byrd reflects on the "kingdom" described in the text. This was, for him, the sound of the old order.

Another self-consciously archaic aspect of the *Cantiones* is the emphasis on canons, which are listed in their own special index at the end of each partbook. They seem to have earned Tallis and Byrd some prestige among admirers who were easily impressed by technical feats. Byrd's *Diliges Dominum* is an eight-voice retrograde canon that makes up in ingenuity and rich sonority what it lacks in genuine contrapuntal interest. If the writings of English theorists and antiquarians (Morley, Charles Burney, John Hawkins) are anything to go by, *Diliges Dominum* was the most admired of the *Cantiones* for the following two centuries. Tallis's own contribution to the list of canons, the seven-voice *Miserere nostri*, is a

Ex. 5.4 *Tribue Domine*, mm. 231–33

beautiful and rather intimidating piece that proceeds by fourfold augmentation and inversion. It is just within the realm of possibility that the
two composers worked together on it: Byrd's name appears on one of the
seven printed parts, the longest and most complete voice of the
four-in-one canon, though this may well have arisen from a printer's
error rather than from any musical involvement by Byrd.

Both Tallis and Byrd contributed a number of cantus-firmus settings
to the *Cantiones*. Tallis included half a dozen chant-based hymns and
responsories for the old liturgy, drawn from the impressive portfolio he
had built up over four decades. He seems to have dug deep into his own
musical past for the best pieces he could find—although he scrupulously
avoided printing anything with an overt reference to the Virgin Mary,
the saints, or the mass. For a musician of Byrd's generation, composing
on a cantus firmus was a different sort of task, more speculative than

practical. The classic example in the *Cantiones* is his setting of *Miserere mihi Domine*. There was already a well-established tradition of treating the *Miserere* as an abstract, non-liturgical cantus firmus by the time Byrd set it to polyphony. Its narrow range, stepwise motion, and simple contour made it a favorite assignment for several generations of counterpoint students, and more experienced composers took it as a challenge to produce interesting music under severe constraints. Byrd had already made several instrumental settings of the *Miserere* by the time he tackled this vocal setting, which pays tribute to the tradition with a rich and elaborate four-part canon—conveniently begun just where the cantus firmus leaves off.

Libera me Domine de morte aeterna, the last piece by Byrd in the book, is another old-style cantus-firmus work. The equal-note plainsong is more prominent here than in *Miserere mihi*, and Byrd features it in the top voice instead of burying it in the bass. This motet also forms part of a larger and more distinct group in the 1575 collection: responsories and readings for the old Roman funeral liturgy, the Office of the Dead. Byrd seems to have taken on these texts in a fairly systematic way. He found a precedent in the funeral responsories set by Parsons and Ferrabosco during the 1560s and early 1570s. Unlike Parsons and Ferrabosco, he also showed interest in setting the matching readings to music. The result was a systematic group of pieces drawn from the great Matins of the Catholic funeral office. This group of works can be summarized in a table. (*L* stands for lesson and *R* for responsory, of which there are nine each in the actual service.)

Ferrabosco:
R1 Credo quod Redemptor
R5 Heu mihi Domine
R7 Peccantem me quotidie

Parsons:
R1 Credo quod Redemptor
R7 Peccantem me quotidie
R9 Libera me Domine de morte aeterna

Byrd:
L6 Cunctis diebus (first part)

R6 Domine secundum actum meum
L7 Libera me Domine et pone me
R7 Peccantem me quotidie
L9 Cunctis diebus (second part)
R9 Libera me Domine de morte aeterna

There was no real chance of this music being used in any public ritual context by 1575—even less than for the numerous sets of Lamentations (nominally for the Holy Week liturgy) turned out by early Elizabethan composers. The new Prayer Book burial service used in England took an entirely different set of texts and, more importantly, followed a different ethos. This became a major point of cultural contention during the second half of the sixteenth century. The ongoing conflict between the reformed English church and the remaining Catholic loyalists was nowhere sharper than at the time of death, burial, and the immediate remembrance of the deceased. Many Elizabethans with Catholic convictions were willing to conform in public to preserve social ties or avoid financial ruin, but when the hour of death came, they wanted to be accompanied by the old-fashioned last rites, buried as Catholics, and, perhaps most crucially, commemorated as Catholics by those willing to pray for their souls. The entire structure and background of the pre-Reformation funeral service was rooted in the idea of intercession and prayer for the dead. The reformers saw this as rank superstition and forbade it. By 1575, when Byrd started publishing, the old funeral observances were considered archaic at best and deeply threatening at worst.

When Byrd turned to these traditional funeral texts as a young Elizabethan, he was linking himself to England's religious past—not too surprising an approach for a book he shared with an older colleague. The pre-Reformation funeral ceremony was still within living memory for much of the adult population in 1575, and it persisted much longer in folk memory. Here, as often happens, etymology has preserved in the English language what theology has discarded: the common term for solemn funeral music is still "dirge," from the Latin *dirige*, the first word of the service of Matins for the dead. Byrd's grandfather, who died the year his grandson was born, provided in his will for the singing of "diriges" after his death. Byrd himself did no such thing. All he could do eight decades later was to affirm that he died a "true perfect member of the Holy Catholic Church" and ask to be "honestly buried." Not that all was forgotten; hints of the old funeral tradition persisted everywhere in Elizabethan and Jacobean culture, from the courtly laments of Sidney:

> Let dirge be sung, and trentals rightly read,
> For Love is dead. . . .

to the half-remembered choristers' chatter in one of the rounds collected by Thomas Ravenscroft for his 1609 *Pammelia*:

> Ut re mi fa mi re ut,
> Hey derry derry, sing and be merry,
> *Quando veni quando coeli,*
> Whip little David's boom, boom, boom, boom. . . .

Amid all this cheerful nonsense is an echo of the haunting responsory *Libera me*, the final piece of the long funeral Matins, evoking that awful day *quando coeli movendi sunt*, when the heavens will be shaken, when God will come to judge the world by fire. Byrd, like other young musicians of his generation, would have sung that responsory many times during the brief Catholic restoration of the 1550s. As we have seen, he also wrote a polyphonic setting of it and chose it to conclude his first book of motets. There is no mistaking what it meant to him and his contemporaries.

Despite Byrd's musical curiosity and progressive tendencies, he was haunted by the past as few other sixteenth-century composers were. He could be nostalgic in a way that Tallis (who had survived much greater changes) seems never to have been. His nostalgia was that of a young man for something he had never really known. Modern readers can obtain a facsimile of the 1575 *Cantiones* reproduced from the unusually well-preserved partbooks in the Royal College of Music. The partbooks are so well preserved because their Elizabethan owner had them bound in sheets of vellum from a brutally dismembered pre-Reformation chant manuscript. As dubious as this sort of recycling may seem to twenty-first-century minds, it is not too different from what Byrd himself was doing in many of his 1575 pieces: salvaging old material deprived of its context, rescuing what he could of threatened or obsolete traditions.

The *Cantiones* did not turn out to be the triumph Tallis and Byrd had hoped for. They were not unlike the first few musical prints made by Ottaviano Petrucci in early sixteenth-century Venice: unprecedented, elegantly produced, and released (perhaps too soon for their own good) into a culture where most music was still being copied by hand. Despite the lavish promises in the introductory poems that these motets would be "published throughout the world" and "borne through foreign lands to be appraised by the judgment of artists," most of the copies not only remained in England but went unsold. 717 sets of partbooks (out of a presumed print run of no more than a thousand) were still gathering dust on the shelves several years later. By 1577, the composers were keenly aware of their failure and felt the need to ask Queen Elizabeth for additional income. She responded by granting them leases on property in eight locations across central and southern England, some of which had been confiscated a generation earlier when her father dissolved the monasteries. Tallis and Byrd collected the rent on these lands, and were exempt from the usual taxes and fees "in consideration of service." They were required only to supply "drink and lodging for the Queen's Majesty's steward and surveyor and their servants, and sufficient hay and provender for their horses" on their yearly visit.

This new arrangement, like the printing monopoly, was valid for twenty-one years. It seems at least temporarily to have solved Byrd's financial problems. He did not try to publish another collection of music for more than a decade.

The failure of the *Cantiones* may well have been inevitable: there was, in the end, not much of a market for printed polyphony in early Elizabethan England. That sort of music was still something that circulated primarily in manuscript among small groups of cognoscenti. Printed music, to most people, meant no more than broadside ballads or simple psalm settings. Thomas Vautrollier, the enterprising Huguenot exile who printed the 1575 motet book, had recently suffered a similar financial failure when he produced an elaborate book of French songs (the Lassus *Recueil du Mellange*) for English consumption. When Thomas Whythorne published a collection of his own music in 1571, he soon found his printer complaining that "it was not bought of him so fast as he looked for." Whythorne blamed the printer, saying the man's earlier publications had been "very false printed" and a "discredit" to anything that might come later. It is clear from Whythorne's other writings that he was well aware of the real problems: musical illiteracy, philistinism, and simple lack of interest. Commercial music printing would eventually grow under Byrd's influence into an important part of the Elizabethan cultural landscape. In the 1570s, its time had not yet come.

CHAPTER SIX

Byrd the Reader

*In the words themselves, as I have learned from experience, there is such
obscure and hidden power ...*

—*Gradualia* I, 1605

SOMETIME AROUND 1580, BYRD WROTE HIS NAME ON THE TITLE PAGE OF
a book: *Wm* on the left side, *Byrde* on the right. The book was an
unusual choice for a musician's library. It was a slim volume called *The
New Arrival of the Three Graces into Anglia, Lamenting the Abuses of the Present
Age*, by an illustrator and antiquarian named Stephen Bateman. The contents are as eccentric and learned as their author. The book features
elaborate speeches by the allegorical figures of the three Graces, who
denounce the prevailing vices of Elizabethan England with a wide variety
of classical and biblical allusions. Bateman was a staunchly Protestant
cleric—a close associate of Archbishop Matthew Parker, for whom he
acquired thousands of books—and his writing reflects the anti-papist
sentiment that prevailed in England at the time. He was also a skilled
artist who put considerable effort into the design and layout of his own
works. Bateman's comments on the pope are illustrated by a grotesque
woodcut (Figure 6.1), his version of an image which can be traced back
to the propaganda of the early sixteenth-century German Reformation.
It is a fitting accompaniment to the tirade in *The New Arrival of the Three
Graces* against "the wicked government of papal dignity." Even more surprising than the image itself is the fact that Byrd, now settling into his

¶ In Anno 1041.this picture was found in the temple of the *Iacobines* in *Geneua*, againſt the wicked gouernement of papall digniue.

FIGURE 6.1   Stephen Bateman, illustration from *The New Arrival of the Three Graces into Anglia*

identity as a prominent English Catholic, owned this volume and inscribed his name in it. The book itself was produced by none other than the London printer Thomas East, who began a close partnership with Byrd in 1588 and went on to print nearly all of his published works through the early seventeenth century.

This book was not unique. We have a dozen others signed by Byrd, with dates of publication ranging from 1580—*The New Arrival* is the oldest of the group—to 1602. The signature and its spelling changed slightly over the years, but the style and the format (*Wm* to the left of the title-page ornament, *Birde*, *Byrd*, or *Byrde* to the right) remained the same. There were many people named William Byrd in Elizabethan England, and some of them certainly owned books, but this group of signatures clearly belongs to the composer. It is easy to compare one of the title pages signed in 1602 with a 1598 legal document in which Byrd wrote his own name several times. The handwriting (Figure 6.2) is all but identical. (By this time, Byrd's signature had changed considerably from the flamboyant hand seen in the Lincoln Cathedral records of the 1560s.) The 1602 title page had already been noticed in passing during the Victorian era, but the corresponding legal document did not surface until the later twentieth century, which would rule out forgery by an imaginative connoisseur of old books. It is unlikely that any forger would also have gone to the trouble of creating incremental changes in the detail of Byrd's signature over more than two decades. It is even more unlikely that a forger would have decided to associate such a library with a well-known recusant composer. Almost all of Byrd's surviving books are works of political or religious controversy, and they all take the Protestant side.

The signature shown in Figure 6.2 appears in a book called the *Unmasking of the Politic Atheist*, a Puritan diatribe by the Cambridge don and controversialist John Hull. The charge of "atheism" here was essentially the charge made against Socrates two thousand years earlier: it meant not worshipping the right gods, or the gods approved by the state. The "atheist" of Hull's title is anyone who does not share his particular type of devout Protestantism. He pours a considerable amount of scorn

FIGURE 6.2 Byrd's signature in 1602 book (left) and 1598 legal deposition (center and right)

on the musical and liturgical practices of English Catholics. He condemns "organs, and instruments in the church," as well as "musical measures," "*Antiphonae* and nine times *Kyrieleison*," and the singing of "*Ave maris stella*...that blasphemous hymn." He rejects a list of "superstitious" holidays, including Candlemas, All Saints, Corpus Christi, St. Peter ad Vincula, and many others for which Byrd provided elaborate musical settings. "Musicians" appear next to prostitutes as papal courtiers and hangers-on. We are also informed that Pope Sixtus IV gave the whole entourage of the Cardinal of Santa Lucia "a dispensation to use sodomy in June, July, and August." (The story is pure legend, but it captures the tone of much of the book.) Even the institution of the Latin mass is traced to the inauspicious year 666.

Hull denounces the "railing, slandering, lying & blaspheming" of "the Rhemish testament," the official English Catholic version of the New Testament, which was well known in Byrd's musical and social circles. He also devotes a substantial part of his book to the papal excommunication of the Queen in 1570, or, as he calls it, "the thundering Bull of Pius Quintus, roaring and breathing out his beastly threats against our gracious Sovereign Queen Elizabeth." The decree brought up some urgent questions of policy and practice, including one mentioned by Hull: "whether the Catholics may take an oath that Elizabeth is the true Queen of England." It may well have been a sore point for Byrd, who took an oath of exactly that kind when he entered the Chapel Royal.

A number of Byrd's books deal with international politics rather than events at home in England. There is a proliferation of titles such as *A Caveat for France* and *The Restorer of the French Estate.* Some of these books are direct translations of French Protestant originals. There was a lively trade in foreign controversial literature at the time: during the single year 1589, at least twenty-five imported French political books and pamphlets were produced for the English market. Other books in Byrd's library catered to the Elizabethan taste for gossip about the Spanish and their colonial ambitions. The 1588 *Copy of a Letter Sent out of England* retells the recent defeat of the Spanish Armada, with ample commentary on the cruelty and dishonesty of Spaniards. *A Brief Discourse of the Spanish State,* published two years later, is a lurid account of Spanish vices, from military atrocities in the New World to "the daily use of garlic."

Byrd's collection also included a sixteenth-century travel guide to Europe, an English version of a German original. It is an extensive check-list of what the well-informed tourist should observe—weather, geography, food, architecture, local traditions and customs—"so that the traveler (although in that course a novice) after his rangings and peregrinations shall retire himself a man of skill, and bring more to his home from overseas." The English translator, Philip Jones, dedicated his edition to the consummate world traveler Sir Francis Drake: "if either I regard yourself, or your present business, I cannot sort and single out a man more fit to whom the same may be offered." It is no great surprise to find a travel guide in Byrd's library given the activities of his brother John, a merchant who sent his ships into a wide variety of foreign lands. William himself was anything but a consummate world traveler. Unlike many other Elizabethan Catholic musicians, he seems never to have set foot outside England, which makes his rather international collection of books even more noteworthy.

One book in Byrd's collection was quite closely tied to his daily life and his interests. It was a 1594 handbook of English law, a digest of important cases and precedents compiled by Richard Crompton, one of the great legal specialists of Elizabethan England. It is not too unexpected to see Byrd reading a legal handbook—certainly less so than seeing a devout Catholic reading anti-papist screeds, or a settled landowner who never left England reading a travel guide. He was constantly mired in lawsuits and other legal intrigues; he also seems to have been in the habit of writing at least some of his own legal materials. Among the few autograph sources we have from Byrd's own hand are law documents of various kinds. We hear from a third party that one of his lawsuits in 1591 had to be thrown out and restarted from scratch because two crucial words were omitted, which may well point to some sort of amateur legal activity.

Whatever Byrd was doing with Crompton's legal textbook, the simple fact that he owned it reveals him as someone who was naturally curious, and probably ambitious, well beyond the requirements of his job as a professional musician. Like the travel book, it shows that his non-musical interests were broader than mere polemic or controversy. It also offers an unusual glimpse into his education and intellectual background. The book is entitled *L'authoritie et iurisdiction des courts de la maiestie de la*

Roygne. Most of it is in a specialized language known as Law French, a version of medieval Norman French that remained the official parlance of the English law courts well into the seventeenth century. By Byrd's time, Law French was characterized by a total disregard for the finer points of French grammar and a habit of dropping in untranslated English words whenever the writer's or speaker's vocabulary came up short. The following passage, from Crompton's discussion of cases tried in the English court of Star Chamber, is typical:

> Diverse de Countie de Middlesex aver pris money destre favore al L. Grevel prisoner in le Tower pur suspition destre accessorie all murder, sils serront returne sur son deliverance, et sur cel fueront convicts per bone proofe, et fueront fined in ceo Court al graunde fines, et trois de eux did were papers, de Fleete usque la sale de Westminster, et la auxi, et back again.

> (Some people of the county of Middlesex took money to buy the favor of Lord Greville, who was imprisoned in the Tower on suspicion of being an accessory to murder, on the understanding that it would be returned after he was set free; they were convicted of this by good proof, and they were fined in this court with great fines, and three of them wore papers [were paraded in public with placards showing their crimes] from Fleet Street to Westminster Hall, and there, and back again.)

This sort of archaic, macaronic language was used out of centuries of habit. By Byrd's time it had become a marker of status and collective identity among legal professionals who might otherwise have found it more convenient to use plain English or Latin. It finally died out after the English Civil War, although numerous vestiges remain in modern legal jargon. Legal documents are still full of old French terms—*force majeure, voir dire, cy pres*—and some English-speaking courts are still convened with a shout of "Oyez, oyez," Law French for "Hear ye, hear ye." One of Byrd's own songs, the humorous *My mistress had a little dog*, features a mock trial called to order with "Oyez, oyez."

Assuming Byrd did not just own this legal book for show, its place in his library implies that he could read complex documents in Law French and make practical use of them. Of course any Tudor composer would have been familiar with French chansons and other simple poetic texts, but this sort of technical knowledge was something more specialized and more unusual. It is worth asking whether Byrd might even have been intended at some point for a legal career but rejected it in favor of music. His son Thomas spent some time in his late teens studying English law, as we know from the records of the English College at Valladolid in Spain: when he entered the College at the age of twenty, apparently with plans for ordination to the priesthood, he had been instructed in "the humanities and the municipal laws of England" for a year. He arrived with another English student of law, a like-minded companion who had decided to emigrate to a place where his Catholic beliefs were better tolerated. Thomas Byrd, as it turned out, was not a good match for Spanish seminary life. He was expelled from Valladolid after three years, "because" (in the laconic words of the record-keeper) "he was not considered suitable for this institution." He appears to have inherited something of his father's litigious temperament along with his musical talent. When the elderly composer made his will two decades later, he included a pointed note: "if my son Thomas Byrd do seek by law or other ways to disturb or trouble my executors," he was to be deprived of his inheritance.

Byrd's library, as it stands at present, is the largest identifiable and physically intact library we have from any single Renaissance composer. There is certainly evidence that other musicians collected books. Guillaume Dufay's late fifteenth-century will includes a long list of books, including some law books, though no signed copies have ever been found. His English contemporary John Dunstable signed a collection of mathematical and astronomical treatises. John Bull, a younger colleague of Byrd's, owned a number of music books, including Arbeau's dance collection *Orchésographie* and the medieval treatises of Boethius and Guido. Thomas Tomkins acquired a copy of Morley's *Plain and Easy Introduction*, wrote his own name on the title page, and added a number of colleagues (including Mundy, Gibbons, Bull, and Morley himself) to the author's list of distinguished English composers. Tallis signed the fifteenth-century compendium of music theory he rescued from Waltham Abbey and appears to have taken good care of it for the rest of his life. It reveals a certain antiquarian bent on Tallis's part, or at least a desire to preserve the traditions of the past. Byrd's collection of books, with its political and legal intricacies, is a quite different sort of artifact. Waltham Abbey was dissolved the year he was born, and he might well have made a serious effort to collect old musical sources if they had still been available to him.

He started assembling his own library a full generation later. What it shows most clearly is a keen interest in the controversies and troubles of the present.

We may never know exactly why Byrd, by now a convinced Catholic, was filling his library with Protestant books. There were warrants for the search of Byrd's house in the aftermath of some of the more notorious political plots of the 1580s, and the Victorian collector Edward Rimbault, who briefly owned the signed copy of the *Unmasking of the Politic Atheist*, assumed that it was a decoy to mislead anti-Catholic spies and government officials. Did Byrd just want to stay informed about current political issues in England and abroad? Was he, like so many politically engaged readers, most inspired by listening to the opposition? Did he simply enjoy works of controversy? He was a loyal subject of the Queen and apparently patriotic in matters that did not conflict with his religion. How much of this material (the anti-Spanish gloating, the Elizabethan cultural triumphalism) might he have found inoffensive or even congenial?

Perhaps the most surprising thing about Byrd's library, or what we can reconstruct of it, is what is still missing. There is no music and very little poetry, although music or poetry is sometimes mentioned in passing, usually in the service of some ideological argument. What survives of the library shows signs of having been a particular group of books concerned with political and legal controversy, a small piece of a larger puzzle. The rest of his collection may well come to light some day. Until then, we can certainly make some informed speculations about what else he read. There is no other English musician of his generation whose literary background can be traced with such confidence. He was acquainted with a wide variety of texts—poetry and prose, secular and sacred, courtly and rustic. His songbooks feature a number of distinguished Elizabethan poets (along with many less distinguished ones), and, as we will see in the next chapter, he was arguably the first composer to treat their poetry with the art and seriousness it deserved.

CHAPTER SEVEN

Sundry Songs

Since singing is so good a thing,
I wish all men would learn to sing.
—*Psalms, Sonnets and Songs, 1588*

B YRD BEGAN HIS FIRST ENGLISH SONGBOOK WITH AN INVITATION:

Benign Reader, here is offered unto thy courteous acceptation Music of various sorts, and to content divers humors. If thou be disposed to pray, here are Psalms. If to be merry, here are Sonnets. If to lament for thy sins, here are songs of sadness and piety...Whatsoever pains I have taken herein, I shall think to be well employed, if the same be well accepted, music thereby the better loved and the more exercised.

The production of *Psalms, Sonnets and Songs* in 1588 was a leap of faith for Byrd. He had been so badly stung by the financial failure of his 1575 motet book that he waited thirteen years to go back into print. The 1580s had also been a difficult time in his private life. He spent most of the decade under constant suspicion of illegal Catholic activities. Letters were intercepted, his property was searched, fines were exacted, and he may even have been kept for a short time under a relatively mild form of house arrest. As the English authorities uncovered a long string of papist plots and intrigues—some real, others imaginary—Byrd became one of the usual suspects. He was already named in 1580 in a list of people who gave support to Catholic emigrants ("great friends and aiders of those beyond the seas"). He was a close associate of Thomas Paget, a Catholic and a keen amateur musician who fled to France in 1583 after becoming implicated in an unsuccessful attempt to depose Queen Elizabeth. Byrd was in regular contact with the Paget family, sending money abroad and forwarding letters, one of which was seized and used as incriminating evidence. By the mid-1580s, his name was appearing with alarming regularity in official memoranda. One suspect in a Catholic plot admitted under interrogation in 1586 that he had been in the habit of singing "songs of Mr. Byrd and Mr. Tallis, and no other unlawful song."

Byrd's position at court may even have been temporarily suspended at the height of his troubles. In May 1585, a warrant for the search of his house called him "Byrd of the chapel"; in November of that year, he was described in a list of recusants as "sometime [formerly] of her Majesty's chapel." If "sometime" is to be taken at face value, it marks a particularly sad moment in Byrd's life. His friend and Chapel Royal colleague Tallis died that same month, November 1585, leaving the generous sum of £3 6s. 8d. "to my company the gentlemen of her Majesty's chapel toward their feast." Byrd witnessed Tallis's will with his own hand, and went on to compose *Ye sacred Muses*, a finely crafted musical elegy for him.

By the late 1580s, Byrd was eager to reassert himself as a respectable and valued courtier. Everything about the *Psalms, Sonnets and Songs*, from the star-studded roster of poets (Raleigh, Sidney, Oxford, Ariosto, Ovid) to the elegant layout and typesetting, was designed to make an impression. This new venture was undertaken in partnership with a new printer, Thomas East, who was equipped to produce complex musical prints and seems in the end to have tolerated (or perhaps even sympathized with) Byrd's religious leanings.

The 1588 songbook was dedicated to the Lord Chancellor of England, Sir Christopher Hatton, a royal favorite and a well-known patron of the arts. Byrd mentioned Hatton's musical gifts in the dedicatory preface ("your judgment and love of that art") and suggested that he might enjoy the songs in his own moments of leisure. Much of the title page (Figure 7.1) is taken up by a large woodcut illustration: Hatton's own coat of arms, which featured a golden hind, a female deer. The *Golden Hind* was of course the name of Sir Francis Drake's galleon, the first English ship ever to circumnavigate the world. Drake had expressed his gratitude to Hatton, who paid for the voyage, by rechristening the ship in his honor

BASSVS.

Pſalmes,Sonets,& ſongs of ſadnes and pietie, made into Muſicke of fiue parts : whereof, ſome of them going abroad among diuers,in vntrue coppies, are heere truely corrected , and th'other being Songs very rare & newly compoſed,are heere publiſhed,for the recreation of all ſuch as delight in Muſick: By _William Byrd_, one of the Gent.of the Queenes Maieſties honorable Chappell.

Printed by Thomas Eaſt, the aſſigne of W.Byrd, and are to be ſold at the dwelling houſe of the ſaid T.Eaſt,by Paules wharfe. 1588. _Cum priuilegio Regiæ Maieſtatis._

FIGURE 7.1 _Psalms, Sonnets and Songs_ (1588), title page

in 1578. The patriotic associations would have been clear to any Elizabethan reader who saw Byrd's title page. Those associations were even stronger by the end of 1588, after the triumphant naval defeat of the Spanish Armada under Drake's command—which Byrd duly celebrated with the song *Look and bow down*, a setting of Queen Elizabeth's own verses of thanksgiving. He had chosen an auspicious year to relaunch the English music-publishing industry.

The preface to Byrd's *Psalms, Sonnets and Songs* includes an unusual and charming list of "Reasons briefly set down by the author to persuade everyone to learn to sing":

> First, it is a knowledge easily taught, and quickly learned, where there is a good master and an apt scholar.
>
> 2 The exercise of singing is delightful to nature, and good to preserve the health of man.
>
> 3 It doth strengthen all parts of the breast, and doth open the pipes.
>
> 4 It is a singular good remedy for a stuttering and stammering in the speech.
>
> 5 It is the best means to procure a perfect pronunciation, and to make a good orator.
>
> 6 It is the only way to know where nature hath bestowed the benefit of a good voice: which gift is so rare as there is not one among a thousand that hath it: and in many, that excellent gift is lost, because they want art to express nature.
>
> 7 There is not any music of instruments whatsoever comparable to that which is made of the voices of men, where the voices are good, and the same well sorted and ordered.
>
> 8 The better the voice is, the meeter it is to honor and serve God therewith: and the voice of man is chiefly to be employed to that end.

Many of Byrd's "reasons" are non-musical: the study of singing encourages good health, strengthens the body, cures difficulties in speech, cultivates correct pronunciation, and leads to success in public speaking. All those points would have appealed to ambitious Elizabethans who wanted the best for themselves and their families. Byrd taught his trade to a whole generation of professional musicians; he also served as music tutor to young amateurs such as the twelve-year-old daughter of Henry Percy, Earl of Northumberland. He had discovered early in life that a good musical upbringing, like that enjoyed by his two older brothers in the choir of St. Paul's, could be the gateway to social success and a lucrative career in any number of fields. There is little doubt that he was angling for the good will of middle-class audiences, and, in short, trying to sell more books. (A scrupulous reader might have paused at the suggestion that not even one person in a thousand had a good voice, but it seems not to have hurt Byrd's sales.)

Psalms, Sonnets and Songs was the ancestor of the endless collections of madrigals and light canzonets that would overwhelm the English musical press within a generation, but its actual contents had little in common with them. Byrd's 1588 pieces had almost all begun life as songs for solo voice accompanied by viols. He was quite clear about that in the preface. When he published these songs, he revised and retexted them for five-part vocal ensemble, "framed in all parts for voices to sing." It is hard to know exactly why he took this radical step, although he must have been aware of the new vogue for amateur group singing and wanted to make his book appeal to the widest possible audience.

The book includes psalm settings, devotional and moralizing songs, a smattering of funeral elegies, and a group of more light-hearted "sonets and pastorals." Even the light-hearted pieces are deceptively complex. "If there happen to be any jar or dissonance," Byrd remarked drily in his preface, "blame not the printer." Some of the songs were "very rare and newly composed," while others had been circulating in manuscript and were now "here truly corrected." Even after they appeared in print, Byrd still worked hard at improving them. He brought out three editions of his *Psalms, Sonnets and Songs* within the year—something almost unheard-of in English Renaissance music publishing—and each new edition was full of tiny corrections and lists of errata. It is clear that this music was being performed, and that Byrd was keeping a close eye on its progress and its integrity. His note to the reader includes a plea: "If in the composition of these songs there be any fault by me committed, I desire the skillful either with courtesy to let the same be concealed, or in friendly sort to be thereof admonished, and at the next impression he shall find the error reformed." He seems to have kept his promise.

When Byrd started to compose songs in English, he was wading into an unusually rich and complex literary tradition. English poetry had been transformed earlier in the century by a group of authors, most notably Thomas Wyatt and Henry Howard, Earl of Surrey, who began to emulate the poets of the Italian Renaissance. They borrowed subject matter, rhyme schemes, and other conventions from various Italian models. This was the generation of the first English sonnets, which were more or less direct imitations of Petrarch. As the sixteenth century went on, a native style of Renaissance poetry began to develop and flourish in England. By Byrd's day, the current poetic language was almost as deeply indebted to the older English tradition of courtly literature as it was to more recent Continental models. The work of Edmund Spenser, the Elizabethan courtly poet par excellence, owes nearly as much to Chaucer as it does to Tasso or Ariosto. Elizabethans were fascinated by the medieval and the pseudo-medieval, by jousting and heraldry and pageantry, and much of their poetry has a surprisingly archaic cast to it. (The fashion for Chaucerian diction was eventually picked up by lesser poets: we need look no further than the anonymous late sixteenth-century epitaph on Tallis and his "loyal wife whose name yclept was Joan"). The peculiar mixture of old and new was well suited to Byrd's own musical aesthetic, which was itself balanced—uneasily at times—between tradition and innovation.

For Elizabethan authors, the art of poetry was very much a rhetorical art, an art of persuasion. As perhaps the most rhetorical and argumentative of sixteenth-century English composers, Byrd took naturally to their ideals. Some of his songs even deal explicitly in the language of legal debate. *My mistress had a little dog*, with its shouts of "Oyez, oyez," is only one among several examples. *O you that hear this voice*, a poem from Sidney's *Astrophel and Stella*, is an argument over the relative merits of Music and Beauty, with multiple "lawyers" and "witnesses" called to the "bar." *Where Fancy fond* is an even more elaborate courtroom allegory, with a huge cast of characters including Fancy, Pleasure, Reason, Sweet Delight, Beauty, Grief, Hope, and Despair. All of these poems are long and complex, with witty arguments developed at leisure over a number of stanzas. Their dimensions are entirely typical of Byrd's song texts. More than two-thirds of the pieces in his first songbook, the 1588 *Psalms, Sonnets and Songs*, include extra verses—sometimes as many as seven or eight—printed alongside the music.

A long strophic song makes special demands on its composer. There is no room here for the illustrative gimmicks cultivated by the English madrigalists, who usually set their texts through from A to Z with no musical repetition. A clever piece of word-painting in one verse may well sound ridiculous when the music recurs in the next verse. Even the basic issue of poetic meter can be a minefield when a single tune has to serve for many stanzas. The composer risks problems as soon as the poet begins to use variable rhythm or reversal of accent, as Sidney does with the all-important words "music" and "beauty" set by Byrd in O *you that hear this voice*. Rather paradoxically, the tune of a strophic song must not be too well suited to any individual verse. What is required is a well-wrought piece of music that can stand up to multiple performances and accommodate subtle (or not so subtle) changes in diction and mood.

The style Byrd chose for so many of his songs was uniquely suited to these needs. He described it himself as "made for instruments to express the harmony and one voice to pronounce the ditty": a solo singer declaims the text, one measured phrase at a time, accompanied by a group of viols. Pieces of this sort eventually came to be known as consort songs. Their combination of subdued vocal melody and rich polyphonic accompaniment fit well with the serious large-scale poems favored by Byrd. Almost all of his secular vocal music was influenced on some level by the fundamental aesthetic of the consort song: restraint, melodic beauty, harmonic richness, and respect for the formal integrity of the text. It was a very English way of setting poetry. At its most formulaic, as in some of Byrd's metrical psalms, this technique produces a dignified but not particularly memorable piece of music. In more inspired moments, such as some of his funeral elegies, the result can be stunning.

Byrd probably became acquainted with consort songs early in life. The genre seems to have originated in the mid-sixteenth-century English theatrical world, where boy choristers were often featured in leading roles. The traditional layout of the consort song, with a high-pitched solo voice (or occasionally a pair of high voices), reflects the preference for young actors. This device allowed individual characters to sing elaborate harmonized songs, and some stage directions even provided discreetly for the entrance of the necessary viol players. The poetic quality of these early consort songs was somewhat mixed. They tended to occur at points of high drama or tragedy, and many of them are laments of the overwrought type so deftly skewered by Shakespeare in the Pyramus and Thisbe scene of *A Midsummer Night's Dream*. Byrd himself must have indulged in some of this as a young chorister. He satirizes the genre in songs such as *Who made thee Hob forsake the plough?*, where a pair of decidedly rustic characters trail off into repeated protests of "I die, I die, I die."

Some of Byrd's consort songs are based on unusual texts. A handful of them are not even in English. *Quis me statim* is a little set-piece written to adorn an Oxford performance of a Latin play by Seneca; *Adoramus te* is a Latin devotional song accompanied by viols; *La verginella* is a setting of an untranslated stanza from Ariosto's epic poem *Orlando Furioso*, the only Italian-texted solo song that has survived in the whole Elizabethan repertory. Even Byrd's famous elegy on the death of Tallis, *Ye sacred Muses*, is an English version of a Continental original. The anonymous text reads:

> Ye sacred Muses, race of Jove,
> whom Music's lore delighteth,
> come down from crystal heavens above
> to earth, where sorrow dwelleth,
> in mourning weeds, with tears in eyes:
> Tallis is dead, and Music dies.

This is simply a translation of a venerable lament on the death of Josquin des Prez, set to music by (among others) Josquin's student Nicolas Gombert:

> Musae, Jovis ter maximi
> proles canora, plangite,
> comas cypressus comprimat:
> Josquinus ille occidit.
>
> (Muses, melodious offspring of thrice-great Jove, weep,
> let the cypress weigh down your locks: Josquin is dead.)

These more exotic texts are the exception rather than the rule. Byrd set more than a hundred and fifty English poems to music, and most of them fall squarely within Elizabethan and Jacobean literary norms. There are a great many metrical psalms and almost as many secular moralizing poems. *My mind to me a kingdom is*, one of the secular pieces in Byrd's

1588 songbook, is typical of contemporary taste. It was attributed variously to the Earl of Oxford and Sir Edward Dyer, and eventually became one of the most popular poems of the English Renaissance. The singer adopts a Stoic persona, revelling in his perfect detachment from envy, greed, ambition, and the other evils of Elizabethan public life. He concludes triumphantly: "Thus do I live, thus will I die: would all did so as well as I." This kind of self-satisfied smugness did not sit well with some readers. By 1599 it was already being mocked by the playwright Ben Jonson, who made one of his characters denounce "these patient fools" who "sing 'My mind to me a kingdom is' when the lank hungry belly barks for food." Other songs by Byrd take up a related commonplace of Renaissance literature, the glorification of the quiet life far from the noise and corruption of the court. *What pleasure have great princes* is perhaps the most characteristic, with its naïve (or pseudo-naïve) melody and its praise of "herdsmen wild" whose bucolic life is innocent of riches, hypocrisy, and "lawyers and their pleading." Byrd eventually took the advice of his own songs by moving from court to country in the mid-1590s—although his troubles, not too surprisingly, followed him there.

His songbooks, like other poetic anthologies of their age, are notable for their easy mingling of sacred and secular. A piece such as *Susanna fair*, retelling the biblical story of the virtuous Susanna and the lecherous elders, could appear only a few pages from the mischievous *In fields abroad*, where various feats of military prowess are finally scorned as inferior to the joys of seeing a beautiful woman naked. Both songs were unusually well received in their day. *Susanna fair* enjoyed a great deal of popularity, not least among Catholic musicians who seem to have admired the song's stalwart heroine as an allegory of Mary, Queen of Scots. *In fields abroad* even made its way in the 1580s into the staid and scholarly Dow partbooks. Some modern editors have been less tolerant. The twentieth-century clergyman and musicologist Edmund Fellowes, assembling the first complete edition of Byrd's songs, declared that the words of *Susanna fair* were "not entirely suited to the requirements of modern taste" and published the piece with some anodyne verses of his own making. The nineteenth-century compiler of *Musa Madrigalesca*, the first great anthology of Elizabethan song verse, simply censored the last stanza of *In fields abroad*, which restored decorum but made nonsense of the poem.

Byrd seems to have acquired some of his poetry through his Chapel Royal contacts. One of the most ubiquitous Elizabethan verse anthologies, the *Paradise of Dainty Devices*, was compiled by Richard Edwards, a Gentleman of the Chapel who served for some time as master of the Queen's choristers. He advertised the poems as "aptly made to be set to any song in five parts, or sung to instruments." Edwards's successor William Hunnis published several collections of metrical psalms and other devotional poems which remained popular fodder for musicians throughout the Elizabethan era. Byrd obtained song texts from both of these colleagues. He even borrowed a melody from one of them. His devotional song *Alack, when I look back* is an arrangement of a tune by Hunnis—a tribute Byrd never paid to any other song composer, with the single exception of John Dowland, whose famous *Lachrimae* (*Flow my tears*) he reworked for the keyboard.

Other songs by Byrd were drawn from the most refined circles of the English literary world, from poets whose social status kept them (unlike Edwards and Hunnis) from publishing their works for mass consumption. Byrd himself had no such scruples by the late 1580s. His musical settings of Sidney and Raleigh were, rather astonishingly, the first poems by those authors ever to appear in print. Some of his consort songs set experimental texts in the manner of the Elizabethan "new poetry." *Constant Penelope* is an anonymous humanist translation of the first lines of Ovid's *Heroides*: an English poem fitted to the traditional form of Latin hexameters, with stress determined by syllable length rather than natural accent. Byrd must have been aware of these metrical principles, because he observed them scrupulously in his music. Sidney was a strong advocate of such experimentation, and Byrd's two elegies on his death use very modern poetic styles. One of them (*Come to me grief for ever*) imitates classical Greek meter in a manner cultivated by Sidney himself. The other (*O that most rare breast*) is in the ostentatiously avant-garde form of the blank-verse sonnet.

Byrd went on writing consort songs well into the seventeenth century. Some younger composers followed his lead—the handful of surviving Jacobean examples include the famous *Cries of London* by Weelkes and Dering—but the genre's days were numbered. English musicians fell under the spell of Italian fashion, just as their poetic counterparts had done a generation or two earlier. By the 1590s, most composers of

English secular music were writing various imitations of the late Renaissance Italian madrigal, with a heavy emphasis on elegant (and very particular) musical illustration of the text. They were also taking up lighter musical textures inspired by dance-songs. Byrd's song style continued to evolve, but he did not follow in the footsteps of his younger contemporaries. This was the point at which his secular music acquired its lasting reputation for "gravity and piety." There were no *balletti* or fa-la-las in his songbooks. He also avoided the increasingly popular lute-song form, although quite a few of his works were arranged by other musicians for lute and solo voice. At one point he was persuaded by friends to write two Italianate madrigals (four-part and six-part settings of *This sweet and merry month of May*) in honor of Queen Elizabeth. He seems to have reconciled himself to their style in the end—he even included one of them in his last printed collection of songs in 1611—but he never wrote another madrigal. As we can already see in his first song-book, his loyalties lay elsewhere, with older ideals of text-setting and musical expression.

The generally serious atmosphere of the 1588 songbook was in tune with the spirit of the age. In the first decades of the Elizabethan era, domestic singing had largely meant the singing of metrical psalms and other poetic paraphrases of the Scriptures. John Day's 1562 *Whole Book of Psalms Collected into English Meter* went through multiple reprintings and became the best-selling musical book of its time in England. On the title page, readers were invited to use Day's collection of psalms "in private houses for their godly solace and comfort, laying apart all ungodly songs and ballads, which tend only to the nourishing of vice and corrupting of youth." The same interest in domestic performance is clear in Tye's *Acts of the Apostles* ("to sing and also to play upon the lute, very necessary for students after their studies to fill their wits") and Tallis's settings of Archbishop Parker's psalter ("to such as will sing or play them privately"). Some books of devotional music even included brief instructions in sight-reading or solfege for the less experienced singer. A few elite groups of musicians were already starting to import Italian secular music for domestic use—the madrigals of Marenzio had certainly made their way into some English circles by the 1580s—but most middle-class enthusiasts of this generation still chose metrical psalms to sing around the table and elsewhere in the home.

Despite the taste for severe Calvinist repertory, domestic singing in Elizabethan England could be a lively affair. An English–French phrase-book (*The French Schoolmaster*) from the early 1570s, compiled by a Huguenot refugee living in London, offers an after-dinner vignette:

— Roland, shall we have a song?

— Yea sir. Where be your books of music? For they be the best corrected.

— They be in my chest. Catherine, take the key of my closet, you shall find them in a little till at the left hand. Behold, there be fair songs at four parts.

— Who shall sing with me?

— You shall have company enough. David shall make the bass, John the tenor, and James the treble. Begin, James, take your tune. Go to. For what do you tarry?

— I have but a rest.

— Roland, drink before you begin, you will sing with a better courage....

— Oh see, what a funnel, for he hath poured a quart of wine without any taking of his breath.

— I should not be a singing-man except I could drink well.

The conversation continues in this vein for some time. When the singers eventually get around to performing something, it is an unnamed "good song" by "Master Edwards," a Chapel Royal musician who contributed to Day's *Whole Book of Psalms* and was also one of the pioneers of mid-century English secular song. Of course this is an artificial and didactic scene, but it gives us a glimpse into the social context in which Elizabethan domestic music was sung. The "books of music," a set of four partbooks, are valued for their accuracy ("the best corrected") and are considered precious enough possessions to be kept in a locked chest. The performance itself is one to a part, as could be expected in a small family group. The lady of the house has access to the books, but she seems not to be a singer herself; the treble part is taken by a young boy, James, who appears to be more musically astute than his father. (His initial protest that "I have but a rest" can also be taken as a hint that this was genuine polyphonic music. In metrical psalms and similar pieces, all the voices start together.) The music itself may have been sacred or secular, but there is no sign that it was being sung as any sort of overt devotional activity: this is how a well-educated and convivial family spent the hours after dinner.

Byrd's 1588 book appears to have been a great success among English audiences of this sort. By early 1589 he was already confident enough to publish a substantial sequel, which he called *Songs of Sundry Natures*. He began once again with a note to the reader:

> Finding that my last impression of music (most gentle reader) through thy courtesy and favor hath had good passage and utterance: and that since the publishing thereof the exercise and love of that art have exceedingly increased: I have been encouraged thereby to take further pains therein, and to make thee partaker thereof, because I would show myself grateful to thee for thy love, and desirous to delight thee with variety, whereof (in my opinion) no science is more plentifully adorned than music.

"Variety" is the watchword in Byrd's new book. He uses it again in his dedicatory preface: "the variety and choice of songs is both a praise of the art and a pleasure to those delighted therein." As the title suggests, it is a sundry collection, much more so than its predecessor. It includes music for three, four, five, and six voices, composed in highly diverse styles. There are severe penitential psalms, songs about nightingales and Cupids and young lovers, "carols for Christmas day" with instrumental accompaniments and delightfully frothy refrains, and some carefully-wrought introspective songs of the sort familiar from his 1588 book. The texts in Byrd's second songbook are less obviously connected to the rarefied circles of the Elizabethan courtier-poets, although he includes one memorable Sidney setting (*O dear life*) and a fair number of classical allusions.

Byrd dedicated his 1589 *Songs of Sundry Natures* to another well-placed patron: Henry Carey, Lord Hunsdon, a first cousin of the Queen who served as her Lord Chamberlain and was a highly influential figure at court. (He also funded, among other things, the voyage of the explorer and privateer Thomas Cavendish, who followed Francis Drake as the second Englishman to sail around the world.) Unlike most of Byrd's patrons, Carey seems not to have been a musician himself. His primary artistic interest was in the theater. He supervised court entertainments, supported several groups of actors, and was the founder and patron of the Chamberlain's Men, Shakespeare's own theatrical company. As the chief administrator of the royal household, he was at least indirectly responsible for the welfare of Byrd and his musical colleagues. In his dedication to Carey, Byrd acknowledges his debt to him "for many favors to me shown, being most deeply bound unto your Honor, having not in me any other power of serviceable thankfulness than in notes and tunes of music."

Some of Byrd's songs enjoyed success at court as well as in more modest domestic circumstances. The Earl of Worcester wrote in September 1602 that "we are frolic [joyful] here in court … Irish tunes are at the time more pleasing, but in winter Lullaby, an old song of Mr. Byrd's, will be more in request, as I think." This sort of wintertime recreation was nothing unusual: one of Thomas Paget's friends, writing in October 1581, had offered him "a song which must by your good help be set in parts to sing about the fire in a winter's night." *Lullaby*, a subtle and witty Christmas carol, seems to have become an iconic piece over the years. It was copied into numerous manuscripts and arranged for lute, for keyboard, and for lyra viol. When the rights to Byrd's first songbook were transferred in the early seventeenth century, the register of the Stationers' Company did not list the book as *Psalms, Sonnets and Songs*: the whole thing was simply called "Byrd's Lullaby of 5 parts." (The London bookseller Thomas Playford did the same a generation later, advertising it as "Byrd's 5 parts wherein is Lullaby.") With its substantial chorus and four verses, the song was ideal for the long, gloomy winter evenings so evocatively described by Byrd's younger musical contemporary Thomas Campion:

> Let now the chimneys blaze
> And cups o'erflow with wine,
> Let well-tuned words amaze
> With harmony divine.
> Now yellow waxen lights
> Shall wait on honey love
> While youthful revels, masques, and courtly sights
> Sleep's leaden spells remove.

Other songs were better suited to springtime revelry. *Though Amaryllis dance in green* is a light-hearted pastoral whose spirited and refined cross-rhythms, 3/2 alternating with 6/4, are borrowed from the Elizabethan galliard. The dance-like quality of the music (Example 7.1) is an apt illustration of the text. Byrd clearly enjoyed the rhythmic freedom offered by triple time, because he used it in half a dozen of his 1588 "Sonnets and Pastorals"—including more serious-minded pieces such as *My mind to me a kingdom is* (with the resulting air of

Ex. 7.1 *Though Amaryllis dance in green, mm. 1–4*

smug nonchalance that so infuriated Ben Jonson) or *O ye that hear this voice* (where the galliard-like second half introduces the courtly debate between Beauty and Music). The choruses of some carols, *From virgin's womb* and *An earthly tree*, are yet livelier experiments in this sort of rhythmic flexibility, with two nesting levels of triplets: the traditional medieval carol was, after all, a dance.

The most unusual piece in Byrd's early songbooks is probably *La verginella*, his single surviving Italian work. It reveals a composer who was eager to write in Italian but not entirely comfortable with the language. Example 7.2 shows the last phrase alongside two other representative settings of the same text by Andrea Gabrieli and Giaches de Wert. Byrd's line is musically the most graceful of the three, but he is completely ignorant of the Italian system of elision—an oversight that produces far too many syllables in the line of poetry, sixteen rather than eleven. He is also confused about how words are divided (he gives "tempie" three syllables instead of two) and where the accents fall (he writes a-*ma*-no instead of *a*-ma-no, which at least produces an attractive descending sequence in the melody.) Henry Peacham wrote in 1622 that "his Virginella …cannot be mended [improved] by the best Italian of them all." It could easily have been mended by the best Italian of them all; it could have been mended by any eight-year-old Italian schoolboy. Byrd appears to have

Ex. 7.2 Text-setting in *La verginella* (Ariosto, *Orlando Furioso* I. 42, line 8); B = Byrd (Oxford, Christ Church, MS Mus. 984); G = Andrea Gabrieli (*Libro primo de madrigali a tre voci*, 1575); W = Giaches de Wert (*Madrigali a cinque voci, libro primo*, 1558)

made it well into his forties without hearing and absorbing a single piece of Italian poetry read out loud, which would have solved most of his scansion problems. Barely a year after this song appeared in print, Thomas East published it in English in his anthology *Musica Transalpina*, a pioneering collection of anglicized Italian madrigals. It included a new second verse from Ariosto, which had clearly been translated first and only then presented to Byrd for musical setting. It appears he either was uninterested in composing another Italian piece or could not be trusted to get it right.

Byrd's "songs of sadness and piety" are not all as spectacular or stylish as his more experimental works, but they are equally self-assured. By the time he published his two songbooks in the late 1580s, he was the acknowledged master of grave English song. Even his metrical psalms were often a cut above the usual Calvinist fare, offering complex counterpoint and an interesting selection of texts. The seven penitential psalms set to music in the 1589 *Songs of Sundry Natures* seem in fact to have been paraphrases made by the poet and courtier Emilia Lanier (née Bassano), Henry Carey's mistress at the time, who belonged to two distinguished musical families and was closely linked to musical circles at court. Byrd's settings of her texts use only three voices, suitable for the smallest household groups. Other devotional songs, such as the six-part *Christ rising again*, are composed on a large scale with elaborate accompaniment; a few such pieces even made their way into the musical repertory of cathedrals and other great churches.

Many Elizabethan songbooks ended on a somber note with elegies or laments for the recently deceased. Byrd himself seems to have set the fashion in his 1588 book: it concludes with two songs in memory of Sidney, who had died of wounds received in battle while defending the Netherlands against the incursions of the Spanish. He was hailed as a national hero, given a grand public funeral in February 1587, and honored with a vast profusion of elegies, many of them in an overwrought and sentimental vein. Byrd's own contributions, *Come to me grief forever* and *O that most rare breast*, were of a more tasteful variety. The former was an austere metrical piece in a neoclassical style, an imitation of Sidney's own poem *When to my deadly pleasure*. The latter was especially notable for being a full setting of a sonnet. (Despite his use of the fashionable word "sonnet" in the title of two of his songbooks, Byrd set the classic fourteen-line form only a handful of other times in his life.)

O that most rare breast was already circulating before 1588 as an accompanied solo song, which means that Byrd must have received its text and composed it very quickly indeed after the news of Sidney's death reached England. In this elegy, he takes the gloomy conventions of the old consort-song lament and recasts them in his own distinctive voice. The song begins with sobbing declamation—the singer can barely begin the first line of the poem—above rich harmonies and sweeping melodies in the lower parts. The four-part accompaniment is itself as intricate as many of Byrd's string fantasias. The sonnet unfolds line by line in a leisurely manner, producing the longest through-composed piece of music to appear in any of Byrd's English songbooks. By the final outcry of "dieth"—Example 7.3 shows the passage in its original form for solo voice and viols—it is clear that the English consort elegy has finally moved out of Pyramus and Thisbe territory and become something genuinely heart-breaking.

The Sidney elegies are not the only music of their kind in the 1588 book. They are immediately preceded by a grave and elaborate song called *Why do I use my paper, ink, and pen?*, which appears at first glance to be a tribute to the Christian martyrs of ancient times. It is in fact the beginning of a notorious twenty-stanza lament on the execution of the Jesuit missionary Edmund Campion in 1581. The printer of the original poem was apprehended and suffered the gruesome punishment of having his ears cut off. John Bolt, one of Byrd's musical associates, was interrogated about the piece as late as 1594. The two harmless-sounding extra stanzas printed in Byrd's songbook are, as it turns out, no more than pious decoys. His Catholic readers, and anyone else well versed in current affairs, would have known what really followed. It was a risky gesture that prefigured his even greater boldness in publishing three Latin masses a few years later.

Byrd chose to end his first songbook with elegies for a pair of distinguished Elizabethans who died too young, victims of the political strife of their era. One was widely venerated as a Protestant martyr, the other as a Catholic martyr. Both were professional wordsmiths, masters of rhetoric and persuasion. Sidney used his art in defense of poetry; Campion used his in defense of his faith. Although they worked in very different spheres, there was one point in their lives when they met and talked at some length. This happened in 1577, when they crossed paths in Prague: Campion teaching at the university, Sidney on a diplomatic mission. Campion recalled that Sidney "had much conversation with me—I hope

Ex. 7.3 *O that most rare breast*, **mm. 148–end**

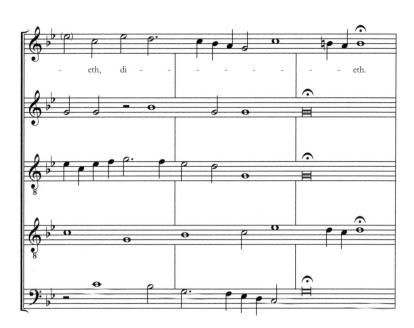

not in vain, for to all appearance he was most eager." Campion's Jesuit colleague Robert Persons claimed that "after much argument [Sidney] professed himself convinced, but said that it was necessary for him to hold on the course which he had hitherto followed; yet he promised never to hurt or injure any Catholic, which for the most part he performed." Although Persons's talk of conversion may well have been wishful thinking, it is poignant to imagine two such gifted and intelligent men as Campion and Sidney meeting face to face and perhaps even coming to some sort of understanding. Their joint place of honor in the last pages of Byrd's songbook reflects the composer's own situation in the late 1580s, walking the fine line between establishment and subversion.

CHAPTER EIGHT

Sacred Songs

Naught so sweet as melancholy
—Robert Burton, 1621

WHEN BYRD WROTE THE PREFACE TO HIS FIRST ENGLISH SONGBOOK in 1588, he was already hinting at a new and different project: "some other things of more depth and skill to follow these, which being not yet finished, are of divers expected and desired." He wasted no time in finishing them. In October 1589, just a few months after he published his *Songs of Sundry Natures*, he brought out a collection of sixteen Latin motets. He was confident enough to call it *Liber primus sacrarum cantionum*, "the first book of sacred songs." A second book duly followed in 1591. Byrd's two new volumes of *Cantiones* fell into the same pattern as his pair of English songbooks: first a polished and rather severe five-voice collection, then a more diverse, experimental set. These two motet books are among Byrd's greatest achievements. They contain some of the most profound and emotionally compelling music he ever wrote.

By the late sixteenth century, Latin-texted music was considered rather exotic in England. The fashionable Elizabethan production of psalm-motets, so characteristic of the 1560s and early 1570s, had slowed down to a trickle. Byrd's mature Latin motets were almost unique in their day. His European contemporaries—and he must have known this well—were writing a steady supply of motets and publishing them in mass-market editions. The motet books of Lassus, only one prolific composer among many, are enough to fill an entire library shelf on their own. Priorities were different in Byrd's musical circles. Thomas Morley offers, as usual, some contemporary perspective on the issue: although the Elizabethan motet was admirable "both for art and utility," it was "notwithstanding little esteemed, and in small request with the greatest number of those who highly seem to favor art, which is the cause that the composers of music who otherwise would follow the depth of their skill, are compelled for lack of maecenates [patrons] to put on another humor."

Byrd managed to find two patrons who were unusually well suited to his project. He dedicated his first book of Latin motets to Edward Somerset, earl of Worcester, with whom he had many cultural and musical interests in common. They spent Christmas 1589 together at the country house of their mutual friend John Petre, who shared their Catholic sympathies. The revellers must have enjoyed performances of Byrd's newly published five-part motets, along with what seems to have been a variety of instrumental music: when the festive season was over, Petre made a generous payment "to five musicians of London…for playing upon the violins by composition in the Christmas time." One of Worcester's daughters went on to marry Petre's son in 1596, in the lavish wedding immortalized by Spenser's *Prothalamion*. Worcester was the correspondent who said in 1602 that he hoped to hear Byrd's *Lullaby* at court after the fashionable country dances and Irish tunes of autumn had run their course. He seems to have been a keen musician in his own right: he wrote in 1581 that "I remain in music still; I have a daughter that will almost serve for a treble at the first sight, and my boy cometh well towards the same." He even noted in a letter to a friend that Byrd had helped him with his own efforts at composition. An inventory taken at his house in London included a Palestrina motet book from the 1570s, a set of feast-day motets by Luca Marenzio, and Latin "sacred songs" by Orazio Vecchi, Peter Philips, and others. There was also an ample selection of Italian secular music. Byrd had a private lodging there—he mentioned it in his will—and it is hard to imagine he did not take advantage of the musical riches at hand.

For his second set of *Cantiones*, Byrd chose an equally apt patron. John Lumley was a scholar and bibliophile who owned an impressive hoard of music, including a large number of imported motet books. This was the Continental music Byrd was emulating most closely in his own motets: Clemens, Lassus, Gombert, Willaert, and a whole series of distinguished mid-century European anthologies. Byrd praised Lumley in his 1591 dedicatory preface for his love of the arts, "the daughters of the Muses," as well as his "sweetness" and "unusual beneficence." Lumley kept a large collection of instruments in his home and supported a number of singers. Like Worcester and Petre, he also had a religious affinity with Byrd. Despite his cordial relationship with Elizabeth during the later years of her reign, he never accepted the Elizabethan ecclesiastical settlement and had spent most of the early 1570s in custody (at one point in the Tower of London) for his presumed role in a series of unsuccessful Catholic plots. Byrd must have felt a bond of empathy with him in his own political troubles.

Although Byrd's motets were dedicated to important public figures, they had almost nothing to do with the ostentation and ceremony of the English Renaissance court. They were a very private sort of art, as private as the richly tapestried Elizabethan rooms where they were copied and sung. The composer Martin Peerson, a generation younger than Byrd, captured their essence in the title of one of his own books: *Motets or Grave Chamber Music*. Byrd's motets can aptly be described as "grave chamber music." They circulated among skilled musicians of all sorts: Catholic and Protestant, male and female, courtly and bourgeois. These were the same people who relished Byrd's instrumental music and his more serious English songs. His motets may have raised a few eyebrows among opinionated Calvinists who considered long prayers in Latin to be politically suspect, but the language was still common currency among educated Elizabethans (as we can see from the incessant use of Latin tags in public sermons), and Latin-texted polyphony seems to have been widely accepted and loved across sectarian lines.

These two books of *Cantiones* were the result of more than a decade of hard work. Composing motets was a gradual and painstaking process for Byrd. He may have stopped publishing them temporarily after the chilly reception of his 1575 book, but he never stopped writing them. He did not claim, as he did for his English songs, that any of this music was "rare and newly composed." Much of it had been passed around in various manuscript versions for years (he described the situation as a "farrago") and was in urgent need of sorting out. It was in his 1589 Latin preface that he used the vivid metaphor of bringing his music back to the lathe and gradually smoothing out its imperfections. By the end of the 1580s, he had found sympathetic patronage, enough time to edit his own work thoroughly, and a skilled and trustworthy printer in the person of Thomas East, whose shop had done such an expert job with his English songbooks. He finally had all he needed to complete his new project.

The motets Byrd wrote in middle age have little in common with the serene piety of many Counter-Reformation motet books. Most of his *Cantiones* are anguished confessions of sin, pleas for rescue from tribulation, or laments over the fall of an allegorical "Jerusalem" or "holy city." It is hard to avoid the conclusion that many of them were inspired by Byrd's distress at the increasingly dire predicament of the English Catholic community. This is clearest of all in the 1589 collection, where the prevailing mood ranges from gray to black, with the occasional flash of red—most notably in his extraordinary *Deus venerunt gentes*, with a text taken from the brutal Psalm 79 (78 in the Latin Vulgate), what appears to be a thinly veiled protest in the manner of *Why do I use my paper, ink, and pen?* at the executions of Elizabethan religious dissidents.

Defecit in dolore, the opening number of the 1589 *Cantiones*, seems to have been written specially as an introduction to the book. Unlike the fifteen motets that follow it, it never circulated in pre-publication manuscripts. It may not be the most striking or memorable piece in the whole collection, but it is a very effective one, and it illustrates many of the distinctive musical techniques Byrd used in his motets. The text is cobbled together from several different psalms:

> My life has wasted away in pain, and my years in groaning.
> My strength has failed in poverty, and my pain is renewed.
> But you, O Lord, have become my refuge, and in your mercy I am consoled.

Byrd sets these words in a low vocal range, with an almost obsessive prevalence of minor chords. In fact the first two-thirds of the 1589 motet book is an unrelieved series of minor-mode pieces. *Defecit in dolore* begins with Byrd's most familiar expressive figure, the rising and falling semitone, which is inverted for additional effect in the outer voices. It will return with even greater intensity when the word "dolor" reappears later in the piece. The music begins with this single gesture and gradually unfolds (Example 8.1) into grave, close-knit counterpoint, flowing on unbroken from one phrase to the next. "To return to our Motets," says

Ex. 8.1A *Defecit in dolore,* mm. 1–17

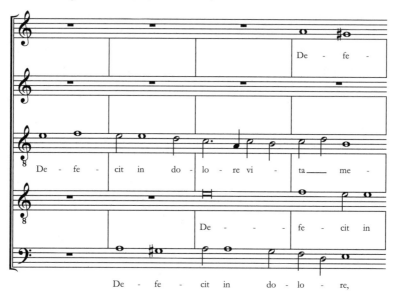

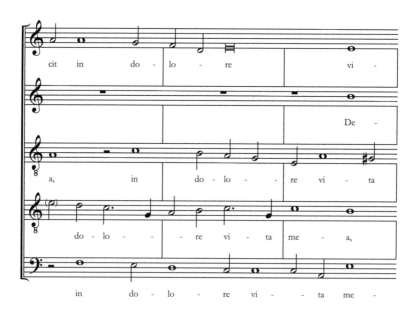

Ex. 8.1B

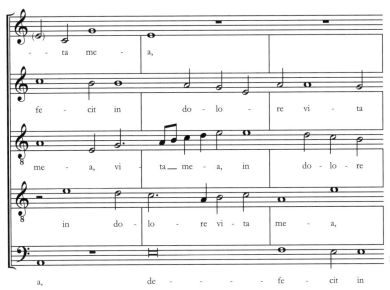

Ex. 8.1C

Morley, "if you compose in this kind, you must cause your harmony to carry a majesty, taking discords and bindings [suspensions] so often as you can." Morley's description could have been written with these rich, somber, slightly claustrophobic first pages in mind.

The gloomy atmosphere does not persist to the end of the piece. It is already clear from the text that *Defecit in dolore* has a two-part structure, with goodness and mercy finally prevailing in the second part. Byrd responds to the shift with a sudden change to C-major sonorities, a splendid cascade of falling scales to depict consolation from heaven, and, in the end, a more or less convincing expression of hope. Here, as in other 1589 motets such as *Tristitia et anxietas* or *Vide Domine afflictionem nostram*, the second part begins with a quite literal antithesis introduced by the word "but" (*sed*). This is the same device used in so many Petrarchan sonnets, the *volta* or abrupt emotional shift that takes place about three-fifths of the way through. In Italianate love poetry, the *volta* is usually a sudden descent into despair; Byrd's sacred songs tend to do the opposite. It was an effect he may well have picked up, consciously or unconsciously, from secular models.

All of these devices reappear in many of Byrd's other motets, some-times in more subtle forms. *Tristitia et anxietas* is a particularly beautiful example. It is a long and elaborate work, reminiscent of the numerous mid-century Franco-Flemish motets collected by Lumley. Byrd bor-rowed the somber text and the general plan of *Tristitia* from the opening number of Clemens's 1553 *Cantiones ecclesiasticae*. His own setting echoes the most effective musical techniques in the older piece: obsessive semi-tonal figures, evaded cadences, insistent suspensions, and a general air of unrest. It is in the very last pages, after a tentative return to hope and consolation, that Byrd departs definitively from Clemens's model. He edits the rambling coda down to a terse *miserere mei*, "have mercy on me," and gives those simple words the most expressive music of all. The central idea is no more than a rising and falling four-note scale, but Byrd takes this most basic of materials and builds it up through multiple layers of counterpoint (Example 8.2) until it is transformed into something pro-foundly moving.

Ne irascaris, another serious piece from the 1589 book, was probably the most popular of Byrd's large motets. One laconic Elizabethan copied it out with the comment "good song." Byrd treats the mournful text from Isaiah with solemnity and insistence. From the very first bars, he shows that major chords can also create a grave effect. Josquin already knew this a century earlier when he built his renowned lament *Planxit autem David* around similar sounds, which he borrowed—as Byrd also seems to have done—from the traditional major-mode Gregorian chant used for the Lamentations of Jeremiah. (The only musician who missed the point was the enthusiastic early seventeenth-century English church scribe who adapted Byrd's motet to the text *Behold I bring you glad tid-ings*.) The long, brooding conclusion of *Ne irascaris* shifts the center of gravity to the final cry that "Jerusalem is desolate." This is reiterated again and again for several minutes, beyond what any contemporary singer or listener would have been likely to expect. It finally ebbs out with some flat sevenths in the alto, an audible image of weariness and desolation.

Some of Byrd's motets are virtuosic exercises in text-setting, as close to the world of the Elizabethan madrigal as anything he ever wrote in English. *Laudibus in sanctis*, the opening number of the 1591 *Cantiones*, is a good example of this type. Like its counterpart at the beginning of the 1589 collection, it seems (given its complete absence from manuscript

Ex. 8.2A *Tristitia et anxietas,* mm. 156–end

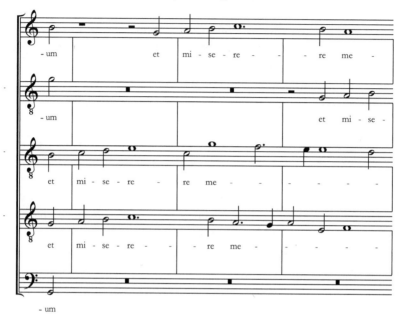

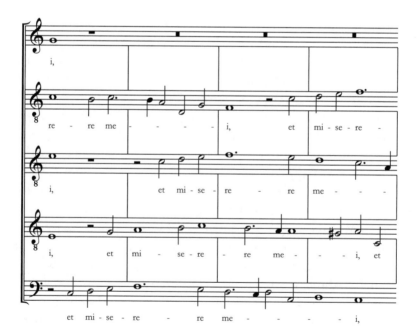

Ex. 8.2B

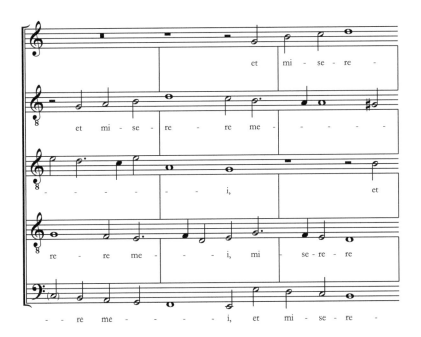

Ex. 8.2C

sources) to have been written as a special introduction to the new book. The text of *Laudibus in sanctis* is a well-crafted fourteen-line poetic paraphrase of Psalm 150, the quintessential musician's psalm, in a neoclassical Latin meter. We do not know who wrote the text, but it recalls a number of the poetic experiments in Byrd's English songbooks, and there is a good chance that it was made expressly for him to set to music. He handles the endless parade of illustrations—trumpets, drums, organ music, cymbals, dancing—with wit and technical facility. Even the dramatic slow-down in the final measures is a pun on *tempus*, meaning both "time" or "season" and the time signature in musical notation. The prevailing note values are suddenly doubled, producing an unexpected but magical effect. *Vigilate* is a similar treatment of a New Testament parable (Mark 13:35–37: "be watchful") with some striking musical depictions of the text. The ebullient Easter motet *Haec dies* is every bit as madrigalian as Byrd's two stylish little settings of *This sweet and merry month of May*, which were roughly contemporary with it.

The 1591 book, unlike its predecessor, includes a group of six-voice motets. Byrd appears to have saved the additional trouble and expense of producing a sixth partbook by holding this music back for his second collection. Some of the six-part pieces are among his finest. *Domine salva nos* is a musical epigram, with a text only nine words long:

> *Domine, salva nos, perimus: impera et fac, Deus, tranquillitatem.*
> Lord, save us, we are perishing: give the command, O God, and create peace.

Byrd sets these words with remarkable tonal flexibility and a keen sense of drama. C major yields unexpectedly to A major, G to E major, as small groups of voices gradually merge (Example 8.3) into a rich six-part scoring. The musical texture is dense and paradoxical. It has rather little in common with either of Byrd's favorite techniques at the time, pervasive imitation and declamatory homophony. He seems to be trying here for something new, something more closely akin to the well-wrought expressiveness of sixteenth-century Italian secular music, the language of Marenzio, Cipriano de Rore, Philippe de Monte, and all the other madrigalists treasured by Elizabethan connoisseurs. *Domine non sum dignus*, another six-voice work in the 1591 book, is a closely related piece with a similar appeal. In some ways these motets—probably quite late additions

Ex. 8.3 *Domine salva nos, mm. 1–8*

to the project—are even more refined than the leisurely penitential exercises that fill Byrd's motet books. They show a different approach to writing sacred songs, one that will come fully into its own in the following two decades.

Infelix ego, yet another six-part motet, is anything but an epigram. It is the most monumental of all Byrd's *Cantiones*. It sets a deathbed meditation by the fierce Italian Renaissance reformer Girolamo Savonarola, written shortly before his execution for heresy. John Lumley, to whom Byrd dedicated his 1591 collection, seems to have treasured this motet: his personal library included a small devotional book in his own handwriting, featuring the full text of *Infelix ego*. Most of the lengthy text is not a prayer at all. It is (as the title suggests) a first-person monologue, an arresting and intimate portrait of a man arguing with himself, fighting off despair, and eventually arriving at a heartfelt plea for mercy. A number of Renaissance composers recognized the dramatic appeal of this monologue, and it had already been set to music half a dozen times by the late sixteenth century. When Byrd himself turned to it, he followed the example set by his English Catholic predecessors in dealing with long devotional texts. He divided Savonarola's meditation into several sections, began each section with a quiet imitative trio, and let the successive musical paragraphs develop on a large scale. (The similarities were not lost on Byrd's historically astute colleague John Baldwin, who copied *Infelix ego* next to two equally substantial works from the 1550s, Mundy's *Maria virgo sanctissima* and *Vox patris caelestis*.)

The whole piece is full of dramatic momentum, following the complex, agitated rhetoric of the text. The most striking passage comes at the end: a caesura in all voices, followed by a sudden, unexpected progression to a major chord on the remote pitch of A♭ (barely hinted at in the rest of the piece) and the most solemn and expansive of final cadences. This happens at the crucial last appearance of the word *misericordiam*, "mercy," something the speaker (like the speaker in *Tristitia*) has hardly even dared to hope for until these final pages. It recalls the point of emotional crisis reached in a simpler piece such as *Defecit in dolore*, but what happens here is not just a turn to the relative major mode and some optimistic musical gestures: it is a moment of real transformation. When that moment arrives, we realize that Byrd has been setting it up all along, preparing for it through almost a quarter-hour of varied and increasingly expressive polyphony. Here he can be seen writing on a truly symphonic scale.

In many of his motets, Byrd seems to be striving for a general mood, an emotional effect, more than a literal setting of the text. The mood is very often a dark one—most of all in the first half of the 1589 *Cantiones*, a display of sustained earnestness that is probably unequalled in any other Renaissance motet book. The closest contender may be the uncommonly gloomy first section of Clemens's 1553 *Cantiones*, a volume that seems to have served as an inspiration for Byrd as he composed and collected his own motets in the 1580s. Byrd spent these years under ongoing surveillance for his Catholic activities, and some of his fellow recusants suffered much more than suspicion and inconvenience. It is tempting but risky to deduce much about his own personal mindset from the prevailing atmosphere of his motet books. Although he shared the English Renaissance taste for melancholy and introspection—there was something of Hamlet about him as he approached middle age—this was the same composer who delighted in popular song, brought echoes of Elizabethan dance into unexpected places, and wrote (when the music called for them) some of the most exuberant alleluias of his day. His more serious *Cantiones* were certainly products of their difficult times, but they cannot be explained as a simple reaction to them. A composer steeped in personal bitterness, or obsessed with political wrongs, would surely have produced music of less lasting value.

The impression left by Byrd's mature motets is one of unfailing musical creativity and exploration. Morley described the motet as the type of vocal music which "requireth most art," equivalent in status and complexity to the instrumental fantasia. As in the fantasia, the composer "taketh a point at his pleasure and wresteth and turneth it as he list." In many of Byrd's motets, the "wresting and turning" takes on a life of its own, quite separate from the verbal phrases on which it hangs. His two motet books can be read as studies in imitative counterpoint and all its possibilities, from the grave opening of *Defecit in dolore* to the grand and triumphant six-voice alleluia that ends *Haec dies*, the last piece in the 1591 collection. Byrd is certainly willing to break the flow of imitation from time to time and bring the voices together in simultaneous declamation, but this occurs as a deliberate gesture, a rhetorical figure, rather than (as in *Emendemus* or so much of his English church music) a consistent way of speaking. As every Renaissance author knew, rhetorical figures lose their power if they are overused. Byrd's strategic use of homophony gains much of its effect—unforgettably so in a piece like *Infelix ego*—through contrast with what surrounds it.

Morley observed that a well-composed motet "moveth and causeth most strange effects in the hearer...especially the skillful auditor." Byrd's motets seem to have found skillful auditors in his own lifetime. Although he could not resist the occasional dig at the inaccuracy of private manuscripts (which he bluntly called "untrue copies"), they show how hard some of his contemporaries worked at collecting and preserving his music. The Oxford don Robert Dow, fellow of All Souls, was a musical connoisseur and scribe who died young in 1588, just before Byrd published his first book of *Cantiones*. Dow left a substantial set of handwritten partbooks—all five of which, in an astonishing stroke of good luck, have survived to our own day. These partbooks, which include nineteen of Byrd's motets, are an eloquent testimony to the social circles in which they were used: beautifully copied sacred songs alternate with learned epigrams on the joys of wine and music. John Sadler, an older scribe who had been educated in music before the Reformation, copied a large number of Byrd's motets in a group of nostalgic and lavishly illuminated manuscripts. In the Paston anthologies, assembled for use in a Catholic household, many of the same pieces rub shoulders with Continental sacred music by the likes of Lassus and Victoria. John Baldwin gave Byrd's motets pride of place in his own collections. He went a step further by copying some unpublished pieces that would otherwise have been lost. It is hard to know why Byrd did not include an eloquent and expressive piece such as *Peccavi super numerum arenae maris* (Figure 8.1 shows Baldwin's copy of the tenor part) in any of his motet books, but we are fortunate that other Elizabethan musicians recognized its value and chose to rescue it from oblivion.

Byrd's motets went in and out of fashion after his death. Playford was still advertising them for sale in the 1650s. He singled out *Ne irascaris* as the most noteworthy of the 1589 set, and gave *Infelix ego* special mention among the 1591 set. A few of the more popular motets were adapted to English texts for use in seventeenth-century church services, but most of them were soon forgotten by all but a handful of antiquarians. The eighteenth-century Madrigal Society sent a transcription of a Byrd motet to

FIGURE 8.1 *Peccavi super numerum arenae maris*, in the handwriting of John Baldwin
(Oxford, Christ Church MS 981)

the Italian composer Antonio Lotti, best remembered in English choral
circles for his luxuriously dissonant setting of the *Crucifixus.* They made
an apt choice by giving him the equally anguished and lugubrious
Tribulationes civitatum. (Lotti's reply is not recorded.) The first published
score of the 1589 motets was prepared by the officious Victorian editor
William Horsley, who added some patronizing notes on the "awkward
and unmelodious" part-writing and the "vague and timid" harmonies.
Many of these pieces remained in obscurity, unheard and largely undis-
cussed, until very recent years. Some of this was doubtless due to their
curious status (curious at least to post-Enlightenment eyes) as sacred
chamber music: it was, and still would be, very hard to shoehorn a piece
such as *Deus venerunt gentes* into any sort of respectable church service.

The 1591 collection marked the end of an era for Byrd's Latin-texted
music. Beginning with his mass for four voices, printed perhaps eighteen
months later, he set himself a new task. Setting the well-known Ordinary
of the Mass, with its repetitions and almost complete lack of overt emotional content, had little in common with setting the sort of text found
in the *Cantiones,* whether of one variety ("let every living thing on earth
sing Alleluia") or of the other ("miserable am I, bereft of all help"). The
task intensified over the following decade as he began to compose his
Gradualia, a large collection of ritual music for various feast days. He
faced some joyful texts, a handful of bittersweet ones, and a majority that

seemed, at least on the surface, to have little room for his favorite expressive techniques. Eventually his approach changed to meet these new requirements. It became more contemplative, more reserved, more like the older Byrd we hear in pieces such as *Iustorum animae* or *Retire my soul*. He never published another motet collection, but his two books of *Cantiones* are still among his finest and best-loved works.

CHAPTER NINE

My Lady Nevell's Book

...desirous to delight thee with variety, whereof (in my opinion)
no science is more plentifully adorned than music.
—*Songs of Sundry Natures*, 1589

I N SEPTEMBER 1591, THE SCRIBE JOHN BALDWIN COMPLETED A LARGE manuscript of Byrd's keyboard music. The original binding, still intact after more than four centuries, is stamped with the title *My Lady Nevell's Book*. The Nevell manuscript contains forty-two pieces, more than a third of Byrd's surviving keyboard works. It seems to have been a systematic effort at compiling his most important keyboard music up to that point, an instrumental equivalent to his songbooks and motet books. He had found ample time during the 1570s and 1580s to compose for the keyboard. His Chapel Royal duties included that of organist, and he must have done a lot of playing (and, one imagines, improvising) in official services, but most of his explorations at the keyboard happened outside of church. The music in Nevell is all secular. The book includes ground-bass compositions, variations on popular tunes, free fantasias, and numerous dance forms—most notably the typical Elizabethan sets of pavans and galliards, which Byrd transformed from clichéd dance-hall fare into some of the most refined instrumental music of the late Renaissance.

There is no other sixteenth-century keyboard source quite like Nevell. It is a carefully ordered volume of music by a single composer, almost certainly put together under his own supervision. Elizabethan printing technology was not able to handle elaborate keyboard music, so Byrd chose the best calligrapher he knew and gave him what he needed to produce a monumental compilation. The result is one of the most arresting of all sixteenth-century music manuscripts. The personalities of both composer and scribe leap off the page. (A richly detailed electronic facsimile of Nevell can be found on the website of the British Library, where the manuscript now resides. It is required viewing for any admirer of Byrd's keyboard music.) Among Baldwin's elegant and slightly fussy diamond-shaped notes, we can see occasional corrections in an informal, fluent, self-assured hand (Figure 9.1). These marginal corrections almost always solve internal problems in the music or bring it into line with more accurate sources. There is little doubt that Byrd added them himself.

The "Lady Nevell" of the title has recently been identified as Elizabeth Nevell, half-sister of the Renaissance polymath Francis Bacon and wife of Henry Nevell of Billingbere, whose coat of arms appears on the original frontispiece. She was approximately the same age as Byrd, born around the year 1540. When the manuscript was presented to her, she was about fifty years old—far from the stereotypical young keyboard dilettante associated with the Elizabethan "virginals." Four pieces in the collection refer to her by name: the *Fancy* and the *Voluntary for my Lady Nevell, My Lady Nevell's Ground*, and *Qui Passe for my Lady Nevell*, the last a setting of the popular Italian song *Chi passa per questa*

FIGURE 9.1   Marginal correction in *My Lady Nevell's Book*

strada. Little is known of her character, although it was apparently a strong one. Henry Nevell remarked wryly to a friend in 1590 that she "wore the breeches" in the family. Morley dedicated his 1595 *First Book of Canzonets to Two Voices* to her, by then on her third marriage and known as Lady Periam. He wrote in the preface that his own wife, who had served in the Nevell household, had herself chosen to offer the collection of canzonets as a musical tribute to her former mistress. Lady Nevell seems not to have kept her Byrd manuscript for long. By the end of the 1590s it had been presented to Queen Elizabeth, who gave it away and sent it on the long journey that led, via a succession of owners, to its present home in the British Library. Elizabeth Nevell died in 1621, leaving behind an extensive correspondence and the school (still existing today) she had founded in the town of Henley-on-Thames. Her life-sized monument in the Henley parish church shows a formidable older woman sculpted in white marble, holding a book in her hand.

Perhaps the most surprising thing about the Nevell manuscript is how little precedent there was for it. Early Elizabethan keyboard sources are notoriously few and far between. The English manuscript now known as the Dublin Virginal Book, compiled around 1570, is closest in spirit to Nevell. It is a completely secular collection featuring numerous dances and arrangements of popular songs, many of them showing a strong Italian influence. The Mulliner Book, a slightly earlier anthology, is made up largely of liturgical organ music and polyphonic song transcriptions, with some lighter pieces added near the end. Mulliner is a precious document of sixteenth-century English keyboard music, but most of its contents would already have sounded quite archaic by 1591. It is hard to exaggerate what a new achievement Nevell really was. If it were not for a single manuscript copied in the 1560s that included two of Byrd's organ works, youthful settings of the plainsong *Miserere*, we would have absolutely no earlier sources of his keyboard music. When the first real source appears more or less *ex nihilo* in the form of the Nevell book, it becomes clear just how quickly and decisively Byrd had been transforming Elizabethan keyboard style.

The core of the Nevell manuscript is a series of pavans (stately duple-time dances) and galliards (lively triple-time dances), almost all of them in matched pairs. By the 1570s, when Byrd started writing this sort of piece, the pavan itself was considered rather old-fashioned. He took its musical form—"a kind of staid music," as Morley described it, "ordained for grave dancing"—and poured a whole variety of innovations into what had already become a somewhat stylized mold. The galliard, what Morley called the "lighter and more stirring" counterpart to the pavan, was still fashionable in the late sixteenth century. We are told by a gentleman of Queen Elizabeth's privy chamber that her "ordinary exercise" in 1589 was "six or seven galliards in a morning," no mean feat given the galliard's quick tempo and athletic leaps. The pavan and galliard were most often performed as a set, and Byrd usually composed them as such, each pair sharing the same tonal center and the same basic dimensions. Like the contrasting slow and fast dances of Baroque instrumental suites, the two forms were perfect foils to each other.

Unlike Byrd's other keyboard works, the Nevell pavans and galliards do not all have titles: many of them are simply given numbers. The first pavan is an early work which another source calls "the first that [Byrd] ever made." The tenth and last pavan-galliard pair is a late addition to Nevell, copied just before the end of the book. Its unusual place in the manuscript, almost as an afterthought, and its dedication to William Petre (who was only fifteen or sixteen when the manuscript was copied) both suggest that it had been very recently composed. The rest of the pavans and galliards are carefully arranged in an unbroken sequence. Minor modes alternate systematically with major modes, shorter forms with longer forms. The whole series is typical of Byrd's taste for long-range organization and symmetry, and the numbering is almost certainly the composer's own.

The Elizabethan pavan and galliard first gained their popularity as consort music, performed by groups of instruments rather than a solo keyboard player. Byrd's first Nevell pavan can be traced back to that tradition. It is his own keyboard adaptation of a consort piece he had probably written in the early 1570s. The version in Nevell betrays its polyphonic origins with rich five-voice writing in a serious C-minor mode, not too different from the vocal counterpoint he was composing around the same time. His original consort pavan falls into three sections, three "strains" of sixteen measures. Each strain ends with a decisive cadence and a repeat sign: it is designed to be played twice. When Byrd reworked this early pavan for the keyboard, he added a smattering of typical adornments—running sixteenth notes and cadential diminutions—to be played when each strain was repeated. The result was the basic structure of the keyboard pavan or galliard: A A' B B' C C', three self-contained phrases, each with an ornamented reprise. During the next four decades, Byrd would explore this form (and adjust its boundaries) in all possible directions, from his tiny, jewel-like Salisbury pavan to massive edifices such as the *Quadran* and the *Passing Measures*.

If the imitative polyphony of Byrd's Latin motets is essentially a prose style, recalling the grave and magnificent sentences of Elizabethan oratory, his pavans and galliards are reminiscent of poetic forms. The musical measures are set out in couplets of eight, sixteen, or, in a couple of extraordinary cases, thirty-two bars. (Some other English keyboard composers took liberties with these traditional binary phrase lengths, but Byrd almost never did.) Each strain ends with a cadence and is often punctuated partway through by a harmonic caesura. The succession of phrases is tied together by harmonic "rhyme" and, in some cases, blurred by musical enjambment. The effect, like that of the best Renaissance poetry, is one of elegantly varied symmetry. Byrd's admiration for poetic form is clear in his English songs, but it finds one of its greatest expressions, rather surprisingly, in the structure of these textless pieces. In many ways the pavan and galliard was to him what the sonnet was to Shakespeare: a strict set of prescriptions within which he found expressive liberty.

The pavan-galliard pair soon became one of Byrd's favorite vehicles for large-scale harmonic and textural exploration. His third Nevell set, probably one of his first mature keyboard works, is a typical example of his procedure. The pavan, like many others by Byrd, starts modestly and lets its musical interest unfold bit by bit. The first strain begins in a grave, largely simultaneous style with slow-moving harmonies. The ornamented repeat brings a flurry of dotted figures and running scales in both hands. The tonal horizons broaden in the second strain, which begins on F and then takes a strong turn to the sharp side, bringing in prominent major chords a tritone away on B. By the time the equally adventurous third strain begins, the voices have begun to engage in real counterpoint, which becomes even clearer to the ear as little imitative themes are brought out one by one in the varied reprise. Byrd uses a different approach to part-writing in the rhythmically lively galliard—this is already obvious from the shameless left-hand parallel fifths all through the first strain—but the harmonic paradoxes are there to stay.

The tenth and final pavan-and-galliard set in Nevell, dedicated to William Petre, was almost certainly the last of the series to be written. Here Byrd takes a more sober and restrained view of the form. The harmonic scheme is tightly controlled, departing from the central G-minor mode only for brief periods, and there is a remarkable economy of material throughout. The beginning of the second strain (Example 9.1) is characteristic of what surrounds it: tiny but expressive musical ideas (including one inevitably reminiscent of Dowland's *Lachrimae*) that work their way through the texture; a plangent raised note in the bass, creating a brief first-inversion chord; a carefully calculated turn to what we would now call the relative major. Byrd must have recognized the quality of this pavan and galliard: they were the only keyboard pieces he ever reworked in print. In his early seventies, near the end of his musical career, he made a beautiful new version of them to open the keyboard anthology *Parthenia*.

A special case in Nevell is the ninth pavan and galliard, the *Passing Measures*, an unusually large-scale set based on the fashionable Italian chord changes of the *passamezzo antico*. Its name was immortalized by Sir Toby Belch in Shakespeare's *Twelfth Night*:

Ex. 9.1 Pavan and Galliard in g, no. 2 (Sir William Petre; BK 3a), mm. 34–38

> *Clown:* O, he's drunk, Sir Toby, an hour agone; his eyes were set at eight in the
> morning.
>
> *Toby:* Then he's a rogue, and a passy-measures pavan. I hate a drunken rogue.

Sir Toby's addled brain could still summon up the fact that the traditional passamezzo pavan was indeed "set at eight," composed as a regular series of eight-bar phrases. Byrd's own "passy-measures pavan" is actually set at thirty-two. Each pitch in the *passamezzo antico* bass (G – F – G – D – Bb – F – G/D – G) is sustained or at least implied for four measures, which makes it more of an underlying cantus firmus than an obvious ostinato of the sort Byrd uses in pieces such as the *Bells* or his various "short grounds." The bass is not always audible, but it is always present on a structural level. To create a work on so massive a scale, Byrd abandons the usual structure of doubled strains in favor of what is essentially an unbroken set of variations: six in the pavan, nine in the galliard. The result has much in common with older traditions (both English and Italian) of keyboard improvisation, each variation introducing a set of characteristic new figures that soon take on a life of their own. Imitative counterpoint, when it occurs, is almost invariably at the unison or the octave, as suits a piece with such a slow harmonic rhythm. It was an experiment Byrd would revisit later with his *Quadran* pavan and galliard, an equally ambitious composition based on the *passamezzo moderno*.

The Nevell book includes a number of variation sets, most of them on well-known Elizabethan tunes. Byrd was always sensitive to the appeal of popular song. Even his most serious instrumental pieces contain their share of references to English ballads, dance tunes, and popular melodies. Much of the material he chose for his Nevell variations was rustic, or at least pseudo-rustic: titles such as *The Woods so Wild, All in a Garden Green, The Hunt's Up,* and *The Carman's Whistle* speak for themselves. These pieces show his talent for free musical elaboration and ornamentation. They offer him almost unlimited space to do what he loved doing in the embellished repeats of his pavans and galliards. Like many other variation sets, from the Renaissance and from later eras, they tend to start in a deceptively easy vein and become more virtuosic as they go on. The melody usually begins in the top voice and migrates through the musical texture. Byrd's last variation almost always embellishes the tune with an ornamental descant in the highest register of the Elizabethan keyboard.

Byrd's twenty-two variations on the popular song *Have with you to Walsingham* are perhaps the finest of the variation sets in Nevell. He begins simply, with an unadorned statement of the melody alternating between the hands, which soon becomes a little two-part arrangement. The harmonic scheme (like the eight-bar tune it supports) does not admit much change, and Byrd does not force it. Instead he uses the form as an opportunity to build up a compendium of keyboard textures and techniques. The details are filled in slowly: in a piece on this scale, there is no need for hurry. Ornamental figuration starts to appear in the fourth and fifth variations. The eleventh variation is a little imitative ricercar on the opening notes of the melody. By the fourteenth, there are running parallel thirds in the left hand. (Will Forster, an early seventeenth-century admirer and perhaps a pupil of Byrd, recopied this passage with some helpful hints on fingering.) Variations 15 through 17 bring in the triple-time antics characteristic of earlier Elizabethan keyboard music, but it is clear that this piece is more than just an exercise in progressive diminution: the real high point begins only later, when the melody returns deep in the bass at the beginning of the splendidly resonant variation 20. After the final variation 22, with its descant soaring to top A, Byrd does not abandon the project. He adds a much-needed counterweight in the form of a gradually unwinding plagal coda, the same technique he had developed in his larger keyboard fantasias. The whole thing is an apt illustration of what Byrd meant when he addressed himself to the listener in his 1589 songbook—just two years before Nevell was completed—as "desirous to delight thee with variety."

There are a few freely composed pieces in Nevell. They go by various names: "voluntary," "lesson," "fancy," "fantasia." One of the Nevell fantasias, the *Lesson of voluntary*, is in fact a keyboard transcription of a five-voice consort piece. The others seem to be new works, perhaps even written specially for the manuscript, a speculation bolstered by titles such as *A fancy for my Lady Nevell* or *A voluntary for my Lady Nevell*. Many of these pieces are in a thoroughly up-to-date style, avoiding excessive metrical embellishments and featuring an ornamented reprise of the final section—a very Italianate touch. The D-minor fantasia, like its A-minor forerunner from the early 1560s, begins in a serious vein with the traditional *Salve Regina* theme and picks up energy and flexibility as it goes along. Shortly before the end, it runs headlong into a deceptive cadence, followed by an unexpectedly bold rhythmic canon (Example 9.2) and an eventual resolution. Here it is hard not to recall the very similar process (Examples 3.1 and 3.2 above) near the end of Byrd's youthful A-minor fantasia. A lot has changed in twenty-five or thirty years: the extra music before the *real* final cadence, what Byrd interrupts the harmonic flow to impress on our ears, is now no longer an archaic tribute to Tallis and Redford but a positively Baroque explosion of cross-rhythms worthy of Monteverdi or Gabrieli.

The Nevell fantasia on *Ut re mi fa sol la* is in a category of its own. Although it is one of Byrd's most ambitious keyboard pieces, it is built on the simplest and most ancient theme of all. The hexachord ("six notes") described in the title was the basic building block of Renaissance music theory and sight-reading. It is equivalent to the first six notes of the major scale: an orderly series of whole tones with one crucial semitone in the middle, between the third and fourth pitches, *mi* and *fa*. When Morley's novice pupil in his *Plain and Easy Introduction* asks to "begin at the very beginning," his first lesson is in singing the hexachord. This series of intervals never changes, but it can migrate to different places in the tonal system. The harmonic explorations of an unusually emotive piece such as Byrd's *Vide Domine afflictionem nostram* could (briefly) take

Ex. 9.2 Fantasia in d (BK 46), mm. 63–66

in a hexachord beginning on A♭ and including the note D♭. The system may seem archaic and cumbersome in retrospect, but it offers a surprisingly high level of flexibility: with a little preparation, you can establish or reestablish your tonal center almost anywhere.

Unlike the pavans and galliards in Nevell, with their recurring binary patterns, *Ut re mi* is conceived entirely around a series of odd numbers. There are seventeen statements of the hexachordal theme. The theme itself, as used by Byrd, is also uneven: six semibreves (whole notes) up the scale, one semibreve of rest, and six back down again, making thirteen in all. The short rest at the center is the natural pause inherent in its origins as a sight-singing exercise, the breath taken before heading back down the scale from *la* to *ut*. This small gesture transforms what could be an uncomfortably square subject and gives it a different sort of symmetry, closely related to that of the piece as a whole. The uneven theme is itself employed in an irregular way. There is no set distance between successive statements of the hexachord—the gap can be anything from one to six semibreves—and each entrance, often on an unexpected pitch, has its own element of surprise.

Even in a tonally uniform series such as the set of *Walsingham* variations, where the basic key never changes, Byrd takes the opportunity to spread the melody through the musical texture and bring it out in different octaves. The theme of *Ut re mi* is at home just about anywhere on the keyboard, and he takes full advantage of its flexibility. Until the very end of the piece, it never appears in the same exact place twice in a row. As Byrd enters deeper into the structure of the fantasia, he abandons his largely conventional harmonic scheme based on the circle of fifths and begins a steady march up the scale with successive hexachords built on F, G, A, B♭, and C. The crux of the hexachord itself is of course the central semitone between *mi* and *fa*. When Byrd reaches the exact center of the piece, the ninth variation of seventeen, he has to negotiate the same narrow passage with two hexachords a semitone apart (Example 9.3) on A and B♭. It is nearly as jolting to modern ears as it must have been to Elizabethan ears. The two scales have only one pitch in common, the note D, which undergoes a transformation from *fa* into *mi*. Byrd softens the blow by using this D as a sort of pivot, but the effect (Example 9.4) is still swift, dramatic, and unexpected. It may well be the boldest chromatic gesture he ever made—more so than the queasy local color in

Ex. 9.3 Ut re mi (BK 64), transition between hexachord 8 and hexachord 9

Ex. 9.4 Ut re mi (BK 64), mm. 70–77

Come woeful Orpheus or the final refrain of the Lamentations. The rest of the piece, though delightful in its own right, is in many ways no more than a process of unwinding from this central moment of dislocation. The seventeenth and last variation is a majestic coda that moves, quite fittingly, through the various tonal spaces explored earlier in the piece.

Byrd's approach to the hexachord fantasia is even more striking when we compare it with a piece such as the *Ut re mi fa sol la* by John Bull preserved in the Fitzwilliam Virginal Book. Bull takes the concept one step further by following the hexachord through a series of relentless whole-tone modulations that eventually take in all twelve degrees of the chromatic scale—including a full enharmonic respelling at one point, almost certainly the first of its kind in English instrumental music. The effect is brilliant, but it is arguably achieved at the expense of large-scale coherence. Byrd never pursues excessive chromaticism for its own sake, although he brings the enharmonic pitches of G♯ and A♭ (by no means interchangeable in Renaissance tuning systems) almost as perilously close as Bull does.

It is also worth recalling that Byrd himself gave the hexachord a lighter treatment on another occasion. His *Ut re mi fa sol la* with "plainsong breves to be played by a second person" is a keyboard work for three hands, two presumably belonging to the teacher and one to the beginning pupil he has entrusted with the cantus firmus. Under the slow, repetitive, unswerving march of the major scale, he entertains his student with arrangements of well-known tunes such as *The Shaking of the Sheets* and *The Woods so Wild*. Even in Byrd's role as stern pedagogue, the delights of popular song were never far from his mind.

Spending time with Byrd's keyboard music, it is impossible not to be caught up in the atmosphere of musical freedom, play, and sheer joy in invention. Even in serious, carefully constructed pieces such as the hexachord fantasy or the large-scale pavans, he shows the natural fluency of someone who spent his life at the keyboard and worked out so much of his music there. In the course of his own career, he saw English keyboard style—especially in secular genres—evolve from a basically improvisatory process to a serious school of composition in its own right. Much of that transformation was his own work. His mature keyboard music is so appealing because it never loses the ease and spontaneity he acquired with the best of the older tradition. In some ways, it brings us closer to a real glimpse of Byrd's musical personality than even his most expressive vocal works can. In a poem appended to one of his anthologies, Baldwin praised Byrd as an unrivaled keyboard composer: "With fingers and with pen he hath not now his peer." As the copyist of the Nevell book, he would have known that best of all.

CHAPTER TEN

The Three Masses

I will not sing shut in a cage

—John Sadler, ca. 1590

BYRD WROTE THREE SETTINGS OF THE LATIN MASS, ONE EACH FOR THREE, four, and five voices. He published them discreetly as small pamphlets, with none of the elaborate prefatory materials found in his other books. There are no title pages, no dedications, and no dates: the only identifying mark is the name *W. Byrd* printed at the top of each page. The dates were finally sorted out with some admirable detective work in the mid-twentieth century. Byrd's printer Thomas East created ornate initial letters (Figure 10.1) with reusable blocks of wood, which were carved in crisp detail and wore out gradually over the years. By studying East's

FIGURE 10.1 Soprano part of the five-voice mass

other publications with the same wood-block initials, we can arrive at an approximate chronology for the three masses. The four-voice mass was printed first, in 1592–93, followed by the three-voice mass in 1593–94 and the five-voice mass in 1594–95. (They seem to have enjoyed considerable popularity: East had already produced second editions of the two smaller masses by 1600.) This was the last music Byrd published before leaving the familiar surroundings of the royal court and retiring to rural Essex to live out the final decades of his career.

When Byrd set the mass to music in the early 1590s, he was doing something no English composer had done for thirty years. Given the political and cultural risks involved, it is surprising that he managed to do it at all. The 1559 Act of Uniformity strictly forbade the celebration of the old Catholic liturgy in England. Those who went on cultivating it could be punished with fines, imprisonment, or, in exceptional cases, even death. What had taken place daily at every pre-Reformation altar, from the humblest parish church to the greatest cathedral, was now a rare and dangerous luxury. William Allen, an Elizabethan cleric living in exile in Rome, saw the absence of the mass as the greatest difficulty facing his fellow Catholics back in England: "the universal lack of the sovereign Sacrifice and Sacraments catholicly ministered, without which the soul of man dieth, as the body doth without corporal food." The small group of Catholic priests who worked secretly in Elizabethan England did their best to provide regular masses for their flock. These were clandestine and closely guarded events. Altar furnishings were designed to masquerade as secular household goods, and hiding spaces were built to conceal the priest and his assistants in the event of a raid. An unexpected knock on the door could put everyone's life at risk. The circumstances were, to say the least, not ideal for complex polyphony.

For Byrd's colleagues across the English Channel, the mass meant something very different. It was the most prestigious musical genre of sixteenth-century Catholic Europe, in great demand among patrons and singers. A successful Renaissance church composer could expect to write many polyphonic masses in the course of his career. Palestrina wrote more than a hundred. He assured his patron Duke Guglielmo Gonzaga in 1578 that he could, if necessary, produce one every ten days. Duke Guglielmo was an enthusiastic and experienced amateur composer—he had even composed masses himself—so it is unlikely that Palestrina was lying or trying to deceive him. Later documents show that Palestrina eventually finished the commission at a rate of one mass every three weeks, which is still a remarkable feat.

Such a level of productivity depended on a set of time-honored methods. Almost all the polyphonic masses of the Renaissance were based on pre-existing material of some kind: ecclesiastical chants, secular tunes, polyphonic motets or songs. Most late sixteenth-century composers used the so-called "parody" technique, taking a piece of polyphonic music and reworking it wholesale into a new setting of the mass. The late Renaissance parody mass was essentially a set of musical variations wedded to the somewhat unwieldy composite text of the Roman liturgy. Anyone who had to set the same words a hundred times, or even a dozen times, must have welcomed this sort of outside assistance. Composers advertised their source material openly in their titles, even when it was risqué (*Entre vous filles de quinze ans*), debauched (*Vinum bonum*), scatological (*Je ne mange point de porc*), or worse. By the end of the sixteenth century, most new polyphonic masses were parody masses of some sort.

The parody technique seems never to have caught on fully in England, despite the pioneering efforts of a few Tudor composers. Many English mass settings were doubtless lost in the disarray and vandalism of the Reformation years. Those which do survive vary widely in style. Some of them are complex cantus-firmus works, featuring long stretches of rich and elaborate six-voice writing. Taverner's *Missa Gloria tibi Trinitas*, a small part of which was eventually immortalized in the instrumental In Nomine, is typical of the early Tudor mass at its most ornate. Fayrfax, Ludford, Sheppard, Tye, and Tallis all composed masses in an equally luxurious vein. Many of the same composers also wrote short masses for only four or five voices, with straightforward counterpoint and clear declamation of the text. Taverner's *Mean Mass* is a good example of the type. ("Mean" refers to the understated mezzo-soprano of the top line, in contrast with the flamboyant high treble parts so popular in pre-Reformation England.) Some of these short masses, such as Sheppard's *Plainsong Mass for a Mean*, are little more than harmonized plainchant. There are almost no English masses based on secular songs: the only surviving examples are the three *Western Wind* masses and some "masses upon the square" which use a fifteenth-century courtly tune.

Even if Byrd was familiar with these precedents, he did not follow them very closely. By the time he started writing masses, he was a fifty-year-old composer who had already developed a mature Latin polyphonic style of his own. He seems not to have been in great need of outside help. The Taverner *Mean Mass*, with its lucid counterpoint and graceful melodic lines, was apparently the most promising model he could find. He composed his four-part Sanctus around a substantial quotation from it, which was the closest he ever came to the techniques of the parody mass. Otherwise he was on his own. In all the other musical genres he cultivated—keyboard and string music, courtly songs, vernacular church music, even Latin motets—he could draw some direct inspiration from his English contemporaries. He did not have that option with his three masses. When he sat down to write them in isolation, he set himself a task faced by no other Renaissance composer.

Byrd clearly enjoyed working multiple times through a single musical problem: we can see this habit in pieces as diverse as the five-part In Nomines, the Nevell pavans and galliards, and the big imitative motets based on semitonal figures. Here he took the full Ordinary of the Mass, the unchanging group of texts prescribed by the Roman liturgy, and set it to music three times. In some places the result sounds uncannily like the same mass written three times over; in other places the differences from one mass to the next, the shifts in technique and atmosphere, can be almost shocking. He appears to have undertaken the composition of his masses as a deliberate and limited series of experiments. He wrote almost a hundred five-part songs and nearly as many five-part motets, but only one five-part mass. Once he had used each particular set of voices (Example 10.1), he never came back to it. Some of his more eccentric scoring decisions in the masses (like those in his *Gradualia* a decade later) may even have been inspired by the talents and vocal ranges of particular singers in his community.

His three-voice mass was, by its very nature, the most experimental. Nobody else in the late Renaissance was writing whole masses for three voices. Composers certainly included trio sections in larger works, and textless three-part music was in considerable demand, but Byrd's three-part mass was unique. He may have been responding to the practical needs of Elizabethan Catholic worship—there must have been occasions when just a few singers were available. He was also setting himself

Ex. 10.1 Total ranges in the three masses

a purely musical challenge. When only three voices are in play, not a single note can go to waste, and some sleight of hand is needed to create a convincingly full texture. Byrd seems to have developed a new interest in serious three-part writing during the early 1590s. His elegant and concise three-part string fantasias are projects in a similar vein, and some of the three-part penitential psalms in the 1589 English songbook can be heard as sketches for the large-scale project he would take on in the three-voice mass.

The scoring of the four-voice mass may appear more normal at first glance, but it has rather little in common with the standard four-part arrangement cultivated by other late Renaissance composers. The voices have vast and substantially overlapping ranges, some covering almost two octaves. Byrd's four-part ensemble was not the same as Victoria's or Palestrina's. Modern editions have done their best to solve the problem with various mixtures of transposition, voice-swapping, and editorial disclaimer. There is some evidence that the whole thing should in fact be taken down a fourth and sung by a group of low voices. Byrd tried out yet another experimental sonority in the five-part mass, the last of the set to be published. Instead of creating a five-part texture by adding a second countertenor line (as so much Elizabethan cathedral music did), or using a terraced scoring with five different ranges (the traditional English solution), he wrote two tenor parts. It was a rather Italianate way to compose for five voices. If he studied the masses of his Counter-Reformation contemporaries, he may well have picked up the idea from them.

The text of the mass falls into five major sections: Kyrie, Gloria, Credo, Sanctus (including the Benedictus), and Agnus Dei. Each section offers a different challenge to the composer. The first is, at least in principle, the most straightforward. It consists of just six words (*Kyrie eleison / Christe eleison / Kyrie eleison*), a threefold plea for mercy that was generally set as a series of three brief and distinct musical passages. The handful of Byrd's English contemporaries who copied or catalogued his masses generally called them "Kyries," if only to avoid the taboo word "mass." Byrd was in fact the first English Renaissance composer to include the Kyrie consistently in his polyphonic masses. The Sarum rite, which had been followed in most of pre-Reformation England, used special chanted settings of the Kyrie with interpolated texts (known as tropes) that changed from day to day. Tudor composers avoided the obvious complications by starting with the Gloria, and the older English tradition of the four-movement polyphonic mass went on until the Sarum rite was abolished for the last time in 1559. When Byrd chose the Roman five-movement form, he revealed something about his own attitude. His masses were clearly not intended as works of nostalgia for a lost English past. They were his distinctive contribution to what he recognized as an international musical tradition. They were also intended for use in real acts of underground Catholic worship, most likely presided over by English Jesuits, who were militantly Roman in both their politics and their rubrics.

The Kyrie plays a crucial role in the structure of the five-movement polyphonic mass. Most sixteenth-century masses are unified by a shared melodic idea, a head-motive, which begins every movement—a precedent Byrd must have known well, although he did not follow it slavishly. The head-motive generally appears in its purest form at the beginning of the mass. In some parody masses, the Kyrie begins as a more or less straight transcription of the source material, which is then developed further as the music progresses. Even in a more freely composed mass, the Kyrie still reveals the subject matter, the tonality, the texture, and the general mood of what is to come. It is the exordium of the piece, designed

Ex. 10.2 Three-part Kyrie

to capture the listeners' attention and draw them into the musical argument. (Composers seem to have understood what was at stake and lavished some of their best efforts on their first pages. It is not uncommon to find a Renaissance mass that starts with a thoroughly convincing Kyrie and lapses into mediocrity later on.)

The opening gambit of Byrd's three-part mass (Example 10.2) is probably the most austere polyphonic Kyrie of the whole Renaissance—if it can even be called polyphonic. It is little more than a brief series of chords. The real head-motive is a texture rather than a tune: parallel tenths between the outer voices, surrounding a free inner part. Even in the later movements of the three-part mass, which unfold into a more imitative style, the same basic sonority is still discernible beneath the surface. Decorated parallel tenths were a common device in impromptu counterpoint and a staple of keyboard improvisation. It is no coincidence that Byrd chose this exact texture to represent organ playing (*alta sacri resonent organa*) in his 1591 motet *Laudibus in sanctis*. John Dowland was still recommending it in the early seventeenth century: "The most famous manner of the counterpoint ... is if the bass go together with the mean, or any other voice, being also distant by a tenth, while the tenor doth go in concord to both." There was no easier way to write pleasing three-voice music, and Byrd took full advantage of it.

His four-voice Kyrie is more reminiscent of its European cousins, with four imitative and fully independent parts. The melodic themes pass among the voices with very little change. The only real adjustment is in the initial motive, which appears in two slightly variant forms, one when it begins on G and the other (what later came to be called a tonal answer) when it begins on D. The mood is still far from untroubled high Renaissance serenity. There are plenty of suspended dissonances—most notably in the second Kyrie, which begins with a pair of trenchant major sevenths—and the atmosphere of restrained intensity hints at some of the more expressive moments to come in the mass. The head-motive itself, or in any case its imitative framework, turns out to be an important building-block of the whole mass: it recurs at the beginning of every other movement but the Sanctus, stripped down to the elemental form of a soprano–alto duet.

Although the four-part mass was the first to be printed and almost certainly the first to be composed, Byrd began it with a remarkable sense of authority and self-assurance. The only hint that he was not familiar with the whole tradition appears as a detail of text-setting. He could not decide whether "Kyrie eleison" should be pronounced with five syllables or with six, and he fluctuates uneasily between the two—sometimes in the same measure, as at the beginning of the second Kyrie. (Earlier Tudor masses were of course no help, and most of Byrd's literary and theological forebears had simply written *Kyrieleison*.) By the time he published his other masses, he had solved the problem.

The five-voice Kyrie is also fully imitative, but the material is conceived and developed in a rather different way. Byrd had begun the four-voice mass with a meticulously crafted, somewhat high-strung first movement. Here he unbends toward a less formal style—the final section is little more than repeated falling figures around a pedal point—and cuts the overall length of the movement by nearly a third. The head-motive of the five-voice Kyrie is more ambiguous and more expressive than its counterpart in the earlier mass. It features the rising and falling semitone that has by now become a familiar figure in Byrd's music. He introduces it as the beginning of a complex trajectory (Example 10.3) through the upper part of the octave, taking in all the chromatic notes along the way. The theme does not remain intact for long: it appears in half a dozen

Ex. 10.3A Five-part Kyrie, mm. 1–9

Ex. 10.3B

different guises in the nine-bar first Kyrie, bending and reshaping itself to the flow of counterpoint, although the basic contour (and the underlying gesture) never changes. Like the head-motives of Byrd's other two masses, it reappears in some form in most of the other movements, and it tacitly sets the mood of much of the piece.

For a composer writing his first polyphonic mass, turning to the Gloria and Credo must have been something of a shock. They are the most challenging texts because they are by far the longest. The Nicene Creed is a complex statement of faith hammered out by fourth-century theologians who could hardly have imagined it as a candidate for elaborate musical setting. The Gloria is a hymn of praise that was certainly intended for singing, but its length and its complex structure of varied repetitions still made it difficult to set in polyphony. Composers in pre-Reformation England spent much of their time handling long, unwieldy texts of this sort, and they developed a number of different techniques for dealing with them. In their more luxurious mass settings, the long movements were broken up into many small pieces. Duets, trios, and quartets, sometimes of breathtaking virtuosity, alternated with climactic full sections. When the musical style was simpler, a long text could be dispatched in a few minutes with terse homophony. English composers also took more radical measures. By the early sixteenth century, most of them had cut the Gordian knot of the polyphonic Credo by leaving out large sections of the text. The surviving settings by Tallis, for example, simply skip from *sedet ad dexteram Patris* to *et exspecto resurrectionem mortuorum*, ignoring almost a third of the whole Creed—including the clauses having to do with the Holy Spirit and the Church, cuts that Byrd was in no position to make.

Byrd divided his Gloria and Credo settings into a dozen sections each, and he varied the scoring as much as his modest group of voices would allow. Some of the reduced-voice passages are among the loveliest moments in his masses. Even his three-part mass features a few strategically placed duets. The only signs of awkwardness or uncertainty appear in the latter stages of the four-part Credo, where important cadences start to fall in some odd places. This may be a result of early experimentation. It may also reflect the absence of any initial help from Byrd's older contemporaries, who had avoided the challenge by discarding the last part of the text. Byrd himself tackled the full Nicene Creed in all three masses, and, not surprisingly, he took every opportunity for direct illustration of the words. Much of it is the sort of word-painting that Morley recommended to his students as little more than common sense:

> Moreover, you must have a care that when your matter signifieth ascending, high heaven, and such like, you make your music ascend: and by the contrary where your ditty speaketh of descending lowness, depth, hell, and others such, you must make your music descend, for as it will be thought a great absurdity to talk of heaven and point downward to the earth, so will it be counted great incongruity if a musician upon the words *he ascended into heaven* should cause his music to descend, or by the contrary upon the descension should cause his music to ascend.

Descending figures duly appear at *descendit de caelis*, rising figures at *et resurrexit* and *resurrectionem mortuorum*, and the Ascension is marked by gleeful disregard for normal vocal ranges: Byrd follows Morley's advice in the four-part Creed by taking the tenor up to a top C. Some of the text-setting in these movements is more understated and imaginative. The moment of incarnation, the word becoming flesh, is depicted in the five-part mass by a spare, ethereal, oddly halting trio of high voices. The

Crucifixus follows with an unexpected and beautiful harmonic fall into the flat side. The invocation of "one holy, catholic, and apostolic church"— the words *Catholicam, Apostolicam,* and *Ecclesiam* are always capitalized by Byrd's printer—is given a suitably grand setting in all three masses.

Most of the Credo text, like almost all of the Gloria, is much more abstract ("begotten, not made, of one substance with the Father …") and unsuited to dramatic illustration of the words. Byrd could not rely on a series of madrigalian tricks, even subtle ones, to carry him through these long movements. He had to draw on deeper musical resources. This was a task he had already faced before in other genres: several of the motet texts he used in his *Cantiones* were as daunting as anything he would ever deal with in a polyphonic mass, and he was no stranger to compositions—vocal or instrumental—on such a large scale. He knew that he needed a strong tonal and structural plan as well as a sensitive response to individual phrases of text. It is in the course of the Gloria and Credo that we realize Byrd's three masses were much more than spontaneous outpourings of piety or creativity. These substantial movements were planned and executed down to the smallest detail.

The Sanctus belongs to a different world. It was sung just before the critical moment of the consecration, and many Renaissance composers set its hieratic and slightly mysterious Old Testament text in a deliberately old-fashioned style, with long-held notes and solemn statements of the cantus firmus. Even the most frivolous parody mass was apt to dissolve into clouds of incense at this point. The convention must have been familiar to Byrd. This is the place in each of his masses where the familiar head-motive gives way to new material, all of it alluding in various ways to older traditions. The four-part Sanctus begins and ends with direct quotations from its early sixteenth-century model, the Taverner *Mean Mass.* The three-voice and five-voice Sanctus allude to an even more venerable technique: polyphonic writing around a leisurely cantus firmus. The cantus firmus in both cases is an imaginary one. In the three-voice Sanctus it is simply a very long note in the top voice—the longest single note anywhere in the masses—under which the other two parts sing rising scales reminiscent of the head-motive borrowed from Taverner. In the five-voice Sanctus, it is a more developed idea, a three-note figure in breves that begins in the soprano and passes through the musical texture. This three-note figure has nothing to do with real chant, although its stately pace and lowered seventh degree give it a suitably old-fashioned air.

Given Byrd's reliance on Taverner in the four-part Sanctus, it is possible that he started his whole project of setting the Latin mass with this particular movement. If he wanted to supply ritual music for the English Catholic community, it was certainly a logical place to begin. The Elizabethan recusant author Laurence Vaux described the Sanctus as the focal point of the sung mass, where "all the people, or such as supply their place, do sing in honor of the blessed Trinity three times, Holy, Holy, Holy, the Lord God of hosts, blessed is he that cometh in the name of the Lord, Osanna in the highest." Here we see the Sanctus singled out by one of Byrd's Catholic contemporaries as a moment when congregational or choral singing (by "all the people, or such as supply their place") was not only tolerated but expected.

The last movement of the mass is the Agnus Dei, a threefold appeal for mercy and peace. These are probably the most familiar parts of Byrd's masses. It is easy to forget how untypical they were of their age. For most Renaissance composers, the Agnus—despite the pathos of the text—was *not* seen as an occasion for highly expressive writing. If anything, it was a showcase for clever canons and other feats of technical skill. Settings of the Agnus Dei achieved their effect with canonic virtuosity (as in the formidable last movements of the Josquin *L'homme armé* masses) and richness of scoring. Even sober Counter-Reformation figures such as Victoria and Palestrina routinely added an extra canonic voice for the last Agnus. Byrd was no stranger to canons and complex textures, but he avoided that sort of display in his masses. The Agnus, for him, was an opportunity to bring out his most intense and emotionally charged music.

Byrd sets the stage in these final movements with careful control of texture, especially in the two larger masses, where the singers begin with a modest duet or trio in the first section and gradually work their way up to a full ensemble in the third. The five-part Agnus shows its expressive character from the very beginning, with some ravishing dissonances in the trio and quartet sections. The final appeal is a simultaneous outcry in all five voices, repeated a fifth higher for effect, which unwinds at length into a marvelously peaceful setting of *dona nobis pacem*. The four-part Agnus is more extreme. It starts out with quiet, orderly counterpoint and

dissolves into an onslaught of pungent suspensions in the final pages—
one on almost every strong beat, nearly thirty in all, a seemingly endless
chain (Example 10.4) that is broken only by the final cadence and the
unexpected G-major glow of the last chord. The effect is uncanny, quite
unlike anything else in sixteenth-century sacred music. It is certainly a
moment of emotional crisis, but Byrd is also reveling (one could even say
wallowing) in the beauty of dissonance and the hypnotic effect it creates
when taken to such extremes.

More than four centuries after they appeared as a handful of unmarked
pamphlets, Byrd's three masses have become his best-known works, standard fare for church choirs and recordings of Tudor music. They occupy
an honorable but slightly odd place in the canon of Renaissance
polyphony. They have few real precedents and no real successors. Byrd
never even gave them names—or, if he did, the names have long been
lost. It is hard to imagine him producing half a dozen more freely-composed masses, as his friend and colleague Philippe de Monte (who himself spent some time in England) did in his own career. It is all but
impossible to imagine him writing a parody mass on *Ne irascaris*, or *Haec
dies*, or *Though Amaryllis dance in green*, or on whatever Italian trifle may
have been in fashion during the early 1590s.

Byrd's masses were cut off from the European tradition by an accident
of geography, and from the English tradition by an accident of politics.
Despite his isolated situation, he still appears to have been trying his hand
at concise imitative polyphony in the best Counter-Reformation style.
He picked the most Continental of mid-Tudor mass settings as his initial
model. Although his masses seem never to have found their way into any
European libraries, he went to some trouble to make them sound cosmopolitan and up to date. There are absolutely no dissonant progressions of
the "English cadence" type (simultaneous or narrowly avoided false relations) that were so common in his Latin motets. This was not just a
matter of maturing style: the mannerism returned in his early seventeenth-century *Gradualia*, where there are dozens of prominent false-
relation cadences. Their characteristic sound was not so much provincial
as old-fashioned. It was beloved in continental Europe by the generation
of Gombert and Clemens, but avoided by the more disciplined Counter-
Reformation composers of the late sixteenth century. When Palestrina
wrote a parody mass on an older Franco-Flemish motet (Jean Lhéritier's

Ex. 10.4A Four-part Agnus, mm. 41–end

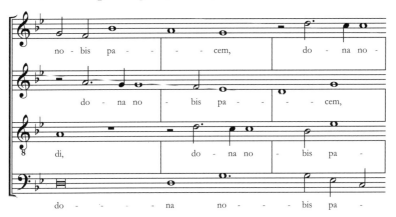

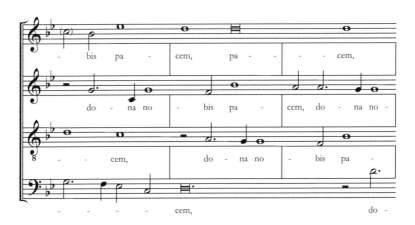

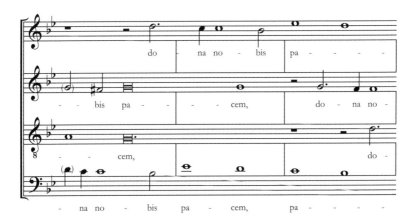

Ex. 10.4B

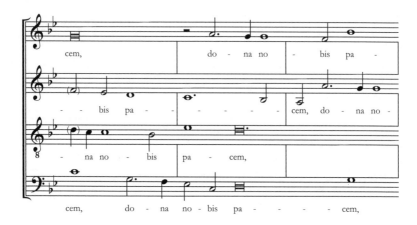

Nigra sum) featuring numerous cadential false relations, he carefully bowdlerized them all. Byrd did exactly the same with his own polyphonic style in the course of writing his masses.

He did something else new by deciding to write for such small vocal groups. He had not composed any Latin-texted music for three or four voices since the utilitarian experiments of his late teens. His masses seem to have been a deliberate exercise in musical asceticism, in accomplishing as much as possible with limited resources. It is a long journey from the opulent sounds of the six-part *Domine salva nos* to the tense precision of the four-part Kyrie, but those two pieces were separated by no more than a couple of years. Byrd was preparing to enter a different cultural world in middle age, and the transition can be heard in his music. He had spent almost two decades in the most luxurious situation any Elizabethan composer could have hoped for, surrounded by hand-picked musicians, fluent copyists, and eager audiences. English court circles were full of skilled amateur performers, along with a steady stream of young professionals who found their way to London to sing for a living. These were people who could put on an expert performance of a harrowing twelve-minute motet as after-dinner entertainment. Byrd was about to turn his back on that milieu and begin a new life among devout rural Catholics for whom sacred music in Latin meant something very different (and, in many cases, something more dangerous). That is the real paradox of his masses: they reveal both a broadening and a narrowing of musical horizons.

There is little evidence of how Byrd's masses were put to practical use: secret celebrations of the mass were—for obvious reasons—not often documented in writing. This music was probably sung by small groups rather than large choirs, and some sort of instrumental participation seems likely. Organs and viols were ubiquitous in Catholic households, and we are told that the resourceful widow Lady Magdalen Montague presided over a domestic chapel where "on solemn feasts the sacrifice of the mass was celebrated with singing and musical instruments." At least some recusant household choirs appear to have been of mixed gender, which is not at all surprising given the important role played by women in Elizabethan domestic music-making. William Weston's account of a week-long musical gathering held in 1586 to welcome his Jesuit colleagues Henry Garnet and Robert Southwell—an event at which Byrd himself was present—refers matter-of-factly to "singers, male and female."

One unusual clue in Byrd's original edition of the masses may point to how they were actually performed in clandestine services. Printers and scribes of sixteenth-century polyphony almost invariably used a small sign called a *custos* or "direct" at the end of each line of music, pointing the singer to the next note. The *custos* was also used to smooth the transition between sections of a multi-part motet, or other pieces intended to be sung in immediate sequence. In Byrd's three-part and four-part masses, the end of every movement in every voice is marked with a *custos* for the following movement. This is true even between pairs of movements, such as the Gloria and the Credo, which would normally be separated by a good deal of additional music and liturgical action. (The sign is absent a few times in the rather crowded upper parts of the four-voice mass, for what appears to be simple lack of space. Byrd's five-voice mass, the last to be printed, also uses it between movements, though more sparingly: the transitions between Credo, Sanctus, and Agnus are entrusted only to the soprano, who is the first to sing.)

This is an absolutely unique use of the *custos*. No other sixteenth-century polyphonic mass, in print or in manuscript, employs it in this way. It is difficult to avoid the conclusion—however surprising to modern ears—that Byrd may have intended, or at least tolerated, having these works sung straight through during a silent celebration of low mass, much as a French Baroque organist would have played steadily as the liturgy took place *sotto voce* in the background. In any case there are very few other Renaissance masses that could stand up as well to such treatment.

As the last of his three masses was going to press, Byrd made the definitive turn away from court and city. In July 1594, he was still signing himself as a resident of Harlington, a western suburb of London not far from Windsor. He sold his property there at some point in 1595. By July 1595, he and his family had moved to the village of Stondon Massey in the Essex countryside, where they were already being noticed as Catholic dissidents who refused to attend services at the local parish church. He seems to have published his masses as a final testament of sorts before he withdrew (at least partially) from the public eye. Given the lack of prefaces and dedications, we may never know what he was thinking as he put them together, but we can be sure that they came at a crucial point of transition. He was taking all the resources available to him as part of the London publishing world—the busy print shop of Thomas East, the musical font and elegant woodblock initials, the complex political connections—and using them in the service of the underground Catholic diaspora. His three masses were the product of unusual and unrepeatable circumstances in his own life. They also marked a new chapter in his development as a composer.

CHAPTER ELEVEN

Court and Country

What pleasure have great princes

more dainty to their choice

than herdsmen wild who careless

in quiet life rejoice,

and Fortune's fate not fearing

sing sweet in summer morning?

—*Psalms, Sonnets and Songs*, 1588

BYRD AND HIS FAMILY LEFT HARLINGTON IN LATE 1594 OR EARLY 1595 and resettled in the rural Essex parish of Stondon Massey, some thirty miles northeast of central London. The location would have been particularly attractive for a Catholic musician and his household. Byrd's wealthy patron Sir John Petre, whose family owned two houses at nearby Ingatestone and West Horndon, had already assembled a like-minded religious and musical community around himself by the time they arrived. Byrd's new home, Stondon Place, was itself a good-sized manor house on two hundred acres of land, including a working farm with multiple barns, an orchard, a "brewhouse, milkhouse, and buttery," and an ample supply of "timber trees"—an arrangement that seems to have brought him considerable profit over the years. He had already had his eye on Stondon Place by 1593. Once he was settled there, he began a long series of legal battles with various neighbors and tenants, asserting his right to full ownership and use of the land.

He was fiercely possessive of his new property. His first undertaking when he moved to Stondon Place was to evict the current tenant, a man named Denis Lolly who still occupied part of the house and insisted on "free egress and regress into the kitchen for baking, brewing, and roasting of meat at his pleasure," as well as free use of the great hall and the various bedchambers. (Despite Byrd's efforts to remove him, he stayed until his lease ran out in 1597.) By the late 1590s, Byrd was closing up the public roads that ran across his land, including "a common highway both for footmen and horsemen, carts and carriages" that he eventually reopened "by the persuasion of Lord Petre."

Jane Shelley, whose late husband had owned Stondon Place for many years, soon began her own campaign to regain the estate. Shelley shared Byrd's religious convictions: she had been imprisoned for her Catholic faith, worse treatment than Byrd ever suffered, and her husband had been sentenced to execution at Tyburn for his involvement in the Catholic plots of the 1580s but had managed to escape with confiscation of his property, including Stondon Place, which was turned over to the Crown for safekeeping. Their common experience of persecution could not keep Shelley and the composer from a prolonged and bitter conflict that went on until her death in 1610. The documents of the case include a detailed list of her "grievances against William Byrd." They do not make edifying reading. She complains that Byrd

> hath practiced to disgrace her with divers her honorable friends, and others of great quality, persuading them that she was a woman of no conscience, and that she went about to put him out of his living without any just cause or title thereunto. And being told by [Shelley's] counsel in her presence that he had no right to the said living, he both then and at other times before her said that if he could not hold it by right, he would hold it by might, which course he hath pursued ever since.

There were other conflicts with the neighbors in Stondon Massey. Almost as soon as Byrd and his family had settled there, they attracted attention for their refusal to go to church. The Elizabethan parish was a center of social life as well as religious observance, and in the close and gossipy atmosphere of a small rural village, complete absence from church would not have gone unnoticed for long. (Denis Lolly, the unwelcome tenant at Stondon Place, was the local churchwarden in the mid-1590s. It was his official duty to report the Byrd family's recusancy, a situation that would quickly have become obvious to anyone sharing a house with them.) By the late sixteenth century, church attendance in England had become more than a matter of piety or social engagement: it was compulsory under Elizabethan civil law in a way it had never been compulsory during the pre-Reformation years. The head of the English state was also the head of the English church, and lack of outward religious conformity was punished as an act of disobedience to the government. Queen Elizabeth famously declared that she had "no desire to make windows into men's souls," but she and her ministers were very much interested in suppressing visible dissent, and recusancy laws were a simple and effective method of surveillance. The practice found an even fiercer expression in places such as the English colony of Jamestown in Virginia, whose 1607 founding documents prescribed the death penalty for the third absence from common prayer.

After Byrd moved to Stondon Massey, his absence from services on Sundays and holidays could no longer be excused by his regular attendance at the Chapel Royal. Although he had acquired a certain degree of legal protection during his last years in residence at court—a recusancy case brought up against him in 1592 ends abruptly with a note saying "let the trial cease by order of the Queen"—he and his family were not spared the attention of local authorities in Essex. In July 1595, they were accused of not having attended services for the previous six months. In March 1596, it was further noted that they "do not and have not come to church since they came to our parish to dwell." (Combined with the earlier document, this may imply that they moved there in January 1595.) The family soon gained a reputation as "papistical recusants which utterly refuse to come to the church." The investigation was gradually extended from Byrd's children and grandchildren to his servants and neighbors, some of whom appear to have been influenced by his family's beliefs. He was cited in May 1605 as the "chief and principal seducer" of a local recusant John Wright and his daughter Anne. The same document adds that Byrd's wife

appointed business on the Sabbath day for her servants of purpose to keep them from church, and hath also done her best endeavor to seduce Thoda Pigbone her now maidservant to draw her to popery, as the same maid hath confessed; and besides hath drawn her maidservants from time to time these seven years from coming to church; and the said Ellen refuseth conference; and the minister and churchwardens have not spoken with the said William Byrd, because he is from home.

Byrd seems to have become something of a legend in English recusant circles for his stubbornness and his tenacity in the face of harassment. The Jesuit William Weston claimed that he "had been attached to the Queen's chapel" but had "sacrificed everything for the faith—his position, the court, and all those aspirations common to men who seek preferment in royal circles as means of improving their fortune." It may have been an attractive story, but it was patently not true. Byrd managed to retain his court position (though most often *in absentia*) until the end of his life. Even the damning May 1605 indictment described him matter-of-factly as "a gentleman of the King's Majesty's Chapel." In the 1605 and 1607 *Gradualia* he called himself "Royal Organist"; in the 1611 *Psalms, Songs and Sonnets*, and on the title page of *Parthenia* a year or two later, he was still named as a member of the Chapel. He received livery allowances for the funerals of Queen Elizabeth in 1603 and Queen Anne in 1619. Two decades' worth of tax documents, dating from 1601 through 1621, list him as "abiding here at court at the time of taxation and for the most part of the year before." That was doubtless a convenient fiction meant to preserve his financial privileges, but it proves that he remained a member of the royal household, with all the benefits that entailed. It is also clear from other sources that he spent time in London during his later years. He had a "lodging" in the Earl of Worcester's house in the Strand, and a surviving fragment of a household account book belonging to Magdalen Herbert, the mother of the poet George Herbert, shows that Byrd was a dinner guest at her nearby London house several times in a single month in 1601.

During his years in Stondon Massey, Byrd appears often to have enjoyed the best of both worlds: the benefits of close connections at court and the familiar comfort of a local Catholic community. He often visited the Petres, who kept a feather bed and a "country coverlet" in "Mr. Byrd's chamber"; their guest reciprocated with an annual gift of two turkeys at Christmas. Byrd was already describing John Petre, the patriarch of the family, as his "very good friend" in the early 1580s. There was ample reason for him to feel at home there. The Petres cultivated a serious musical life to an extent unusual even among cultured and well-to-do Elizabethans. Their accounts are full of expenditures for the purchase and maintenance of various musical instruments, a steady supply of harpsichord, viol, and lute strings, and the hire, sometimes at considerable cost, of professional musicians from London. By 1590 they even had an organ (made by Byrd's brother-in-law Robert Broughe) installed at home. An early seventeenth-century inventory of musical books in the Petre household shows an impressive collection of both sacred and secular music. Their steward John Bentley was a fluent music copyist who prepared a manuscript anthology of nearly 130 pieces for domestic use; these partbooks included such substantial works as Tallis's *Gaude gloriosa* and *Salve intemerata*, music that required performers of great skill and stamina.

The Petre family was well known for its Catholicism, although John Petre himself was willing to make some compromises for the sake of political expediency. One eyewitness account shows him encouraging a reluctant Catholic servant "to go to the church for fashion sake, and in respect to avoid the danger of the law," but adding that the servant should "keep [his] own conscience" in the matter. The informant added that "I verily think Sir John, although he goeth to the church, doth not receive the communion." John's wife Mary was a more strictly observant Catholic whose prosecution for recusancy was at one point halted—like Byrd's own—in the name of the Queen herself. Visitors to Ingatestone Hall can still see a tiny, carefully constructed underground chamber near the center of the house, designed to conceal priests in the event of an unexpected search. Clergy seem to have been harbored and masses celebrated at Ingatestone with some regularity. Byrd wrote in the dedication to his second book of *Gradualia* that his liturgical music "proceeded from [Petre's] house, most generous to me and mine," and there is no reason not to take that statement literally: in fact his visits most often coincided with Christmas, Pentecost, and the other principal feasts of the church year, which were celebrated lavishly in the Petre household.

Another recusant group linked to Byrd was the distinguished Paston family, whose house in Norfolk was known as a center of musical culture and Catholic worship. Edward Paston was a well-traveled gentleman who compiled many books of lute intabulations "pricked in ciphers after the

Spanish and Italian fashion." He had a substantial group of musical scribes working for him. Over the years he accumulated no fewer than fifty sets of partbooks, a library of well over a thousand pieces, including numerous songs by Byrd (a number of them reset to topical texts of Paston's own making), Continental masses and motets, and some remarkably old-fashioned English repertory. Like the Petres, to whom they were related by marriage, the Pastons managed to avoid the worst of the Elizabethan religious persecutions and live a more or less undisturbed life as rural Catholic gentry. Edward Paston died at the age of eighty, leaving his formidable collection of music to his son William and his grandson Thomas. His epitaph commemorates him as a man "most skillful of liberal sciences, especially music and poetry, as also strange languages."

A number of Byrd's mature consort songs show the influence of the recusant milieu in which he spent so much of his later life. *With lilies white* is an elegy on the death of the Catholic matriarch Lady Magdalen Montague in 1608. *Though I be Brown*, a wedding ode composed in the same year, celebrates the marriage of Lady Magdalen's granddaughter Mary Browne to Edward Paston's eldest son. *My mistress had a little dog* belongs to the same group of songs: it is a satirical piece depicting a mock trial on the death of a beloved dog at the Paston estate of Appleton Hall. There is doubtless some private message or political in-joke behind the whole thing. Even if it was no more than an occasional piece written to commemorate a long-forgotten event in the Paston family, Byrd put a great deal of care and creativity into it: it is a substantial song, mostly through-composed, with a wide variety of musical textures and some remarkably witty text-setting. (The poem itself, with its wry references to "coneys" and "tumbling," may be one of Byrd's few excursions into the world of Elizabethan bawdry.)

Other songs are concerned with public events and public figures. Penelope Rich, the notorious courtier immortalized as the heroine of Sidney's *Astrophel and Stella*, is commemorated in several of Byrd's late songs; she may even be the unnamed "mistress" who lost her little dog at Appleton Hall. *Wretched Albinus* is a sardonic commentary on the fall of Robert Devereux, earl of Essex, the military leader and erstwhile royal favorite who was executed for treason in 1601 after an unsuccessful attempt to overthrow the English government. The title character of Byrd's song is the ancient Roman governor of Britain who led a rebellion against the emperor and lost his head for his trouble. The allegorical parallel with Essex, whose downfall is attributed here to the machinations of "a silly woman," is all too clear. Byrd sets the text with unmistakable echoes of his more serious funeral elegies. Judging by satirical works of this sort, the older Byrd was not only close to events at court but still comfortable making musical commentary on them.

Byrd's ongoing involvement with the court also extended to the Chapel Royal, which he continued to enrich with occasional pieces of sacred music. A few of his surviving English anthems are obviously later works, written long after he had left his cathedral post at Lincoln and most likely after he had withdrawn from his daily duties as a court musician. He kept up ties with his Chapel colleagues through the early seventeenth century, and the handful of demonstrably late English church music by him still shows an atmosphere of great musical inspiration and enthusiasm. The six-voice *Sing joyfully*, balanced on the narrow edge between Anglican decorum and madrigalian exuberance, is perhaps the most memorable of his late anthems. The matched pair of soprano lines, an Italianate arrangement Byrd grew to love later in life, gives the music a suitable air of rejoicing. *Sing joyfully* was well received at court: it was sung at the baptism of King James's short-lived daughter Mary in 1605, and it begins and ends with prominent references to "the God of Jacob" that may well be a tribute to the Jacobean monarch himself.

The list of real church anthems by Byrd is a modest one—not much more than a dozen pieces—especially when compared with his formidable legacy of Latin-texted music and instrumental works. Some of them are composed for full choir throughout; others include an independent organ part and accompanied solo passages of various kinds, in the manner of his Verse Service. A number of pieces transmitted as verse anthems seem to be adaptations of sacred songs originally written for household ensembles of viols and voices. We know rather little about the circumstances in which this music was composed. A younger composer such as Orlando Gibbons could produce anthems in response to quite particular commissions: *This is the record of John* at the request of the ill-fated Archbishop Laud during his time at St. John's College, *Behold thou hast made my days* written in a single day for the dean of Windsor just before his death. If Byrd was doing the same sort of thing, he left no evidence of it.

The Great Service, the most elaborate of all Byrd's English church works, is inextricably linked to his later anthems and shares a number of their musical characteristics. It includes music for a full day's worship in the reformed English rite: Matins, Eucharist, and Evensong. A manuscript produced at York Cathedral in the late 1590s calls it "Byrd's new suit of service," and there is no real reason not to take "new" at face value. (The scribe who made this comment, a vicar choral named John Todd whose distinctive hand reappears in other sources, was in residence at York in 1597–99 and must have copied the music during that time. A scrawled date of 1618 was a later addition to the manuscript.) The indefatigable Baldwin had also acquired and copied some excerpts of the Great Service by 1606. In any case Byrd must have written it by 1603, because its text is taken from the Elizabethan edition of the Prayer Book rather than the Jacobean edition. The surviving evidence appears to point to it as a product of the mid-to-late 1590s, during what would otherwise have been a fallow period between the last of Byrd's Latin masses and his compilation of the two books of *Gradualia*. Some stylistic traits, not least its broad harmonic flexibility, also point to the 1590s as the most likely decade. It is surprising to think of Byrd's Catholic and Protestant liturgical music coexisting at such close quarters, but it all appears in some ways to be part of a single project: producing large-scale liturgical works (and no other single work of his is as formidable as the Great Service) with consistent rhetorical power and formal unity.

The word "Great" was a scribal designation rather than Byrd's own; it seems to have referred originally to quantity rather than quality. Most Elizabethan service music is in five parts, including two countertenor lines. Here Byrd duplicates the entire arrangement, creating a ten-voice double choir. The two five-part choirs do not merely sing back and forth in turn, joining together for reinforcement at crucial moments, as in the standard *decani/cantoris* arrangement of English cathedral music: there are ten real parts, each with a distinctive role to play. Byrd uses them to create a kaleidoscopic variety of sounds, with the voices constantly weaving in and out, combining, doubling, and dividing to create new effects. It is hard to imagine that many Elizabethan choirs other than the Queen's own would have had the necessary forces to do this work justice. Byrd certainly never wrote anything else for ten voices. Perhaps because of its somewhat profligate vocal scoring, the service was forgotten not long after the composer's death. (It was rediscovered in the early twentieth century by Edmund Fellowes while sifting through manuscripts in the library of Durham Cathedral. He later recalled this unexpected find as the high point of a long musical career.)

By the 1590s there was already a growing tradition of more elaborate English services, reaching back as far as Parsons and even Sheppard, whose Second Service was a clear influence on Byrd's Great Service. Although the style of the Great Service is well removed from the Protestant austerity Byrd had known as a young cathedral musician, it shares a number of techniques with the rest of the Elizabethan Anglican repertory. The basic ideal is still that of declamatory writing, one note per syllable, which was a quite practical approach considering the scale of the texts Byrd was setting: the Te Deum, the whole Nicene Creed (as in the Latin mass), and a number of long biblical canticles. Perhaps the most striking piece of declamation is an unusual syncopated five-note figure that brings out a quick alternation of strong and weak syllables: "if ye will hear his voice" in the Venite, "of an infinite majesty" and "day by day we magnify thee" in the Te Deum, "according to the scriptures" and "who proceedeth from the Father" in the Creed, and a number of more subtle appearances. That particular figure also surfaces (at the words "great in kindness and truth") in the conclusion of his anthem *O God the proud are risen*, a piece very likely written at the same time and for the same singers.

Like the larger movements of Byrd's Latin masses, the individual parts of the Great Service all begin with short opening sections for reduced voices and bring in the full choir as they go along. Much of the elaboration is vertical rather than horizontal—a fitting approach given the embarrassment of riches at hand, including four separate countertenor lines. In some places there are eight or even nine actual parts in play. There are a few stretches of more sustained polyphony, such as the splendid setting of "Let me never be confounded" at the end of the Te Deum (Example 11.1), which are worked out as extensively as anything in Byrd's instrumental music or his Latin liturgical music.

Ex. 11.1A Te Deum from the Great Service, mm. 190–end

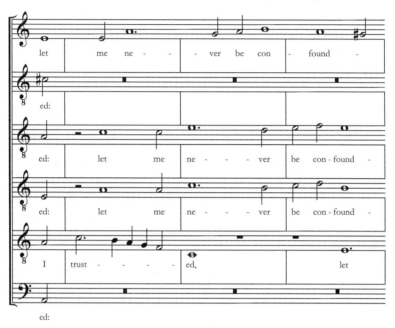

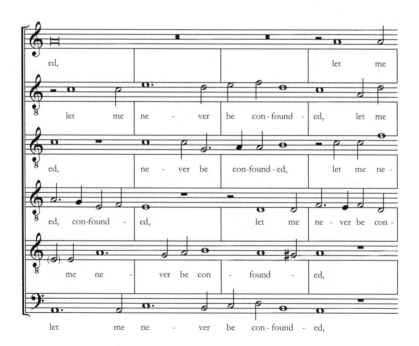

Ex. 11.1B

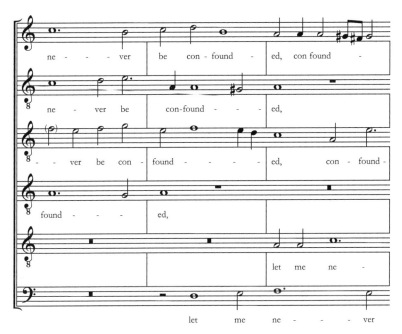

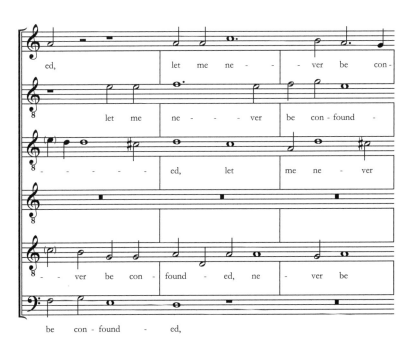

Ex. 11.1C

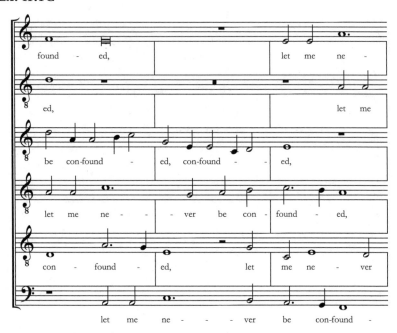

Ex. 11.1D

The doxologies that end four of the movements are all singled out for special elaboration. The text is formulaic and unchanging:

> Glory be to the Father, and to the Son, and to the Holy Ghost:
> as it was in the beginning, is now, and ever shall be, world without end.
> Amen.

Byrd generally starts each doxology with simple declamation and lets it develop into real counterpoint by the time he has reached "world without end." (In the two books of *Gradualia*, his next big liturgical project, he faced the Latin version of this text a dozen times and treated it in more or less the same way.) These concluding phrases become more extravagant as the work unfolds. By the end of the Nunc Dimittis, the last movement in the Great Service, Byrd has gone into full-blown polyphony with some grand double augmentation in the bass part. The final pair of canticles, to be sung together at Evensong, are the most complex and expressive of all. A passage such as the six-part "He hath showed strength" in the Magnificat (Example 11.2), which even takes in some leisurely melismas in the outer voices, has come a long way from the textual clarity prescribed by mid-sixteenth-century English reformers.

By the time Byrd had finished composing the Great Service, he was probably well removed from the regular routine of the sung English liturgy. A few small details, such as missing pieces of text in the Te Deum, suggest that he may even have been relying on memory rather than ongoing daily experience. Given his persistent connections with the musicians of the Chapel Royal, it is not too surprising to see him still engaged in this sort of musical exploration after his full-time residency there had come to an end. Court and country had never been entirely separate spheres for him: that much is already clear in his 1588 *Psalms, Sonnets and Songs*, the most courtly of Elizabethan songbooks, some of whose texts appear to have reached Byrd via copies made in the provincial Petre household. It is easy to underestimate the close ties between the great recusant houses—where the Catholic gentry lived their own private version of courtly life—and the court circles that treated religious dissidents such as Byrd (and the Petres, and the Pastons, and nearly every other Catholic patron of his) with a peculiar mixture of surveillance and tacit tolerance. These were two worlds between which Byrd moved with great ease.

Ex. 11.2A Magnificat from the Great Service, mm. 81–92

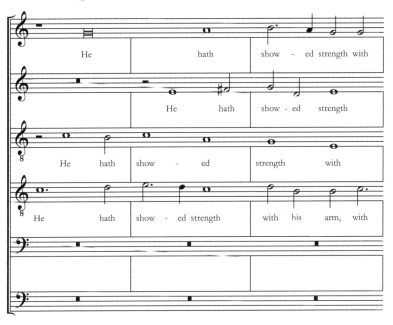

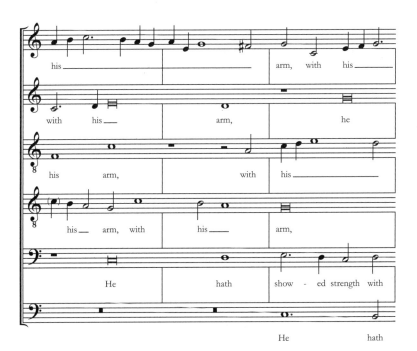

Ex. 11.2B

By the end of the sixteenth century, the Chapel Royal finally seems to have been ready for the style of Byrd's mature English church works. The last years of Elizabeth's reign saw, at least in some circles, a gradual rejection of Calvinist liturgical principles and a growing tolerance of elaborate worship. This was the generation of the influential theologian Richard Hooker, whose *Laws of Ecclesiastical Polity* included a passionate defense of the Anglican liturgy against Puritan detractors. (It was also the generation of Shakespeare's *Twelfth Night*, whose comic villain Malvolio, a scathing caricature of the sour arch-Puritan, could reliably be expected to raise a laugh from audiences.) In the fifth book of his *Laws*—published in 1597, just as John Todd was first copying out "Byrd's new suit of service"— –Hooker wrote that "the house of prayer is a court beautified with the presence of celestial powers; that there we stand, we pray, we sound forth hymns unto God, having his Angels intermingled as our associates." He went on to describe church music as

> a thing which delighteth all ages, and beseemeth all states; a thing as season-able in grief as in joy...there is [music] that draweth to a marvellous, grave, and sober mediocrity [moderation]; there is also that carrieth as it were into ecstasies, filling the mind with a heavenly joy, and for the time, in a manner, severing it from the body.

This is not too far from Morley's own declaration, made in the same year, that the purpose of sacred music is "to draw the hearer, as it were, in chains of gold by the ears to the consideration of holy things." Both of these sentences could easily have been written with the Great Service itself in mind.

CHAPTER TWELVE

Later Instrumental Music

The oftener you shall hear it, the better cause of liking you will discover.
—*Psalms, Songs, and Sonnets,* 1611

BYRD WENT ON WRITING INSTRUMENTAL MUSIC UNTIL THE END OF HIS career. His mature keyboard and consort works, like his mature vocal works, still show a lively interest in new musical possibilities. Most of these pieces never made it into print: the only exceptions are the eight items in *Parthenia* (1612/13) and the two fantasias he printed in the 1611 *Psalms, Songs and Sonnets.* The rest we owe to the labor of enthusiastic scribes, including Thomas Weelkes and Will Forster, both Jacobean admirers of Byrd who recognized the value of his keyboard music and preserved it in manuscript. His consort music also enjoyed an unexpected revival of sorts when the English tradition of viol playing (which had been somewhat eclipsed by the recent vogue for Italian-style music) regained favor during the reign of King James.

When the older Byrd is mentioned by foreign colleagues—something that does not occur very often—it is almost always in the context of instrumental rather than vocal music. The handful of Byrd's works that found their way into early seventeenth-century Continental manuscripts are without exception instrumental pieces. A young Frenchman named Charles de Ligny, visiting England in 1605, reported on a meeting of Jesuits and Catholic gentlemen, including "Mr. William Byrd, who played the organ and many other instruments." If the gathering was hosted by the Petres at Ingatestone or Thorndon Hall, as seems quite likely from the existing evidence, the "many other instruments" would at the very least have included viols and a variety of keyboard instruments. (When Ligny returned to London, he was promptly arrested and thrown into prison on suspicion of being a Catholic spy: the incriminating evidence was his possession of a set of "certain books which Mr. William Byrd had composed and dedicated to Lord Henry Howard of the Privy Council." This was a clear reference to the first volume of *Gradualia*, which had appeared in print only a few months earlier. Ligny's recusant friends seem to have sent him on his way with a valuable but dangerous musical gift.)

In 1610 Luis de Groote, a diplomat serving the Brussels court of the Archdukes Albert and Isabella, consulted Byrd on the value of an organ he hoped to acquire from John Bull: he wrote that "I learned from a famous musician named Byrd, who was the teacher of Peter Philips, that the organ was by no means worth a thousand florins." By this point Philips was director of music at the archducal court, and Byrd's status as his former teacher was doubtless a strong endorsement. Byrd also seems to have enjoyed a good working relationship with Bull, who had joined the Chapel Royal in 1586 and quickly established himself as one of the leading keyboard virtuosos of northern Europe. (Much like Byrd, he had begun his career as a provincial cathedral organist who was at one point suspended by the dean and chapter for musical insubordination.) In 1597 Bull was appointed Gresham Professor of Music. He praised Byrd, who was apparently present for the occasion, in his inaugural lecture: "My master liveth, and long may he live, and I his scholar not worthy in your and his presence to speak of this art and science." When Bull took a leave of absence from the Gresham professorship in 1602, it was "ordered and agreed that Thomas Byrd, professor of the same science of music and the son of William Byrd one of the gentlemen of her Majesty's chapel, shall hereafter begin and continue the reading of the same public lecture in Gresham house." Byrd himself continued to engage with Bull's compositional style (quite critically at times) in his later keyboard works.

Byrd must have been well acquainted—not least through the work of his brother-in-law Robert Broughe—with the Elizabethan trade in musical instruments and the contemporary world of instrument building.

Broughe was described in 1598 as a "maker of organs, virginals, and other instruments of music." His workshop was in London, and much of his business took place there, but he also built and maintained various instruments for the Petre household, including their "new wind instrument" (an organ that was delivered to Thorndon Hall in 1590, wrapped in "four bed mats" for the journey) and a "pair of small virginals for Mr. John Petre." Broughe was hired regularly to tune and maintain the instruments. This sort of maintenance often occurred just before Byrd's visits to Thorndon and Ingatestone, and music-making at the keyboard must have been an important part of his residence there.

There are some two dozen apparently mature keyboard pieces by Byrd which were not included in the Nevell book. Given Nevell's status as what seems to be a systematic compilation of his keyboard music at the time, it is likely that most (if perhaps not all) of these remaining works were indeed composed after 1591. Some kinds of music are absent from the later sources. Byrd appears not to have written any fantasias or grounds after the 1590s, and the cantus-firmus settings of his younger years had long since faded into obscurity. What remains is still a colorful and diverse selection, including pavans, galliards, preludes, and variations on popular songs. Byrd kept up a lifelong interest in the instrumental music of his contemporaries, and several of his later keyboard pieces are creative adaptations of other people's works. When he arranged John Dowland's well-known *Lachrimae* or the lutenist John Johnson's *Pavan to Delight*, he came as close as he ever would to the Elizabethan tradition of lute music.

Dowland's *Lachrimae* was published in lute tablature in 1596, as a lute song (*Flow my tears*) in 1600, and as a consort pavan (*Lachrimae Antiquae*) in 1604. It became a classic of English Renaissance music in a way few other works ever did. Byrd's version is one of almost a hundred surviving arrangements. He starts by transposing the whole piece up a fourth, which creates a lighter and more translucent sound; this also takes the climactic high E of Dowland's last line and relocates it to the A at the top of Byrd's keyboard, the note he so often reserved for the final phrases of his own compositions. The arrangement begins as a more or less direct quotation of Dowland and quickly goes its own way. After a brief unadorned phrase at the beginning, Byrd starts to add new layers of rapid ornamentation, effectively doubling the number of notes in each measure. Most of the empty space in Dowland's original texture is filled in with these running figures, or, increasingly as the piece goes on, with little flurries of imitation on whatever new subject presents itself. (Byrd's emphasis on counterpoint seems to have been inspired by Dowland's slightly more dense and complex 1604 consort setting—further evidence that he made his arrangement late in life.)

For a performer or listener used to Dowland's exquisitely understated original, there is some sense that Byrd is gilding the lily here. His version of *Lachrimae* is still an attractive enough work, and a valuable glimpse into his musical personality: it gives us a chance to look over his shoulder as he improvises on a contemporary art song (a long way from his usual popular tunes) and explores its musical possibilities. The scribe of the Fitzwilliam Virginal Book calls it a piece "by John Dowland, set forth by William Byrd." The effect is more reminiscent of hearing a great jazz pianist play a standard than of an "arrangement" in any traditional sense of the word.

Byrd was also in the habit of revisiting and reworking his own music. Not surprisingly, he did more of that as he grew older. In a few places, such as the Petre pavan he revised for *Parthenia*, there is real evidence of a change in musical taste or compositional strategy. Some later instrumental works, such as his three settings of *Monsieur's Alman*, seem to be successive approaches to the same musical problem. Other pieces are arrangements or adaptations of various kinds. One particularly interesting case is a keyboard version of Byrd's own motet *O quam gloriosum*, a piece he published in the 1589 *Cantiones*. In this intabulation, the basic structure of the motet and of the individual vocal lines is kept intact, but it is overgrown with running figures, cadential ornaments, and filler of all imaginable sorts. Whoever the arranger was, he abhorred a vacuum. If the piece is really an arrangement by Byrd himself—which seems quite likely from internal evidence—it is another rare document of the composer at the keyboard, this time playing one of his own polyphonic works and adorning it as he saw fit. (Is it possible that Elizabethan singers also indulged in some version of this practice when they performed Byrd's vocal chamber music?)

Byrd's *Quadran* pavan and galliard are the longest and most ambitious of his later keyboard pieces. They are settings of the Italian *passamezzo moderno* bass, the major-mode cousin of the G-minor *passamezzo antico*

Byrd had set in the 1580s in his *Passing Measures* pavan and galliard. The "quadran" of the title is the square sign indicating B♮, the major third that gives the *passamezzo moderno* its distinctive harmonic flavor. Byrd manages to reconcile this simple bass pattern—another well-worn set of chord changes that began life in Italian Renaissance dance bands (and was arguably something of an ancestor to the twelve-bar blues)—with his taste for pervasive and intricate counterpoint. As in the *Passing Measures* set, Byrd continues each note of the ground bass (or at least implies it) for a full four measures of music, far beyond anything heard in the traditional *passamezzo*: in fact it is possible to listen to, and enjoy, the whole piece without being conscious of the pre-existing harmonic framework. The very first bass pitch, the opening G, is host to a little imitative exposition of its own, with a theme developed in canon at the unison and octave through the three upper voices. The rest of the piece continues on a similar scale.

Thomas Morley, who composed a *Quadran* setting himself, still seems to have been convinced that it was low popular music: he wrote with evident contempt that "this Quadrant pavan . . . walketh among barbers and fiddlers more common than any other." Byrd set himself a hard task by pushing a basically improvisatory form to such large proportions. He had already done something similar in the *Passing Measures*, but the *Quadran* is in almost every way the more extreme piece, with a persistently irregular phrase structure, a high concentration of diatonic dissonance, a number of hair-raising false relations, and some melodic sequences that are pushed beyond what any reasonable ear might expect. One four-note figure makes its way down the keyboard in the second reprise; by the time Byrd is done with it, it has been repeated verbatim sixteen times in a row. A few of his melodic ideas build up such strong momentum that they simply continue, in a sort of breathless enjambment, over what should be a break between sections of the piece. The result is an audacious, eccentric, and ultimately very satisfying quarter-hour of music. When Tomkins listed the *Quadran* settings of Byrd and Bull in his early seventeenth-century list of "lessons of worth"—admirable keyboard pieces—he wrote that the Bull was "excellent for the hand" and the Byrd was "excellent for matter." "Excellent for matter": those three words sum up much of what is appealing in Byrd's larger keyboard works, the unfailing drive to explore and develop new musical material.

Not all Byrd's reworkings of popular forms were so complicated or difficult. He was equally at home with a more light-hearted approach. We can see this side of his personality in a variety of pieces: in his *French Corantos*, a suite of three song arrangements including the well-known *Belle qui tiens ma vie*; in the irresistibly playable *Callino Casturame*, a setting of an Irish tune; or in the *Queen's Alman*, a group of variations on an old Italian song. The original version of the Queen's Alman, *Madre non mi far monaca*, is the protest of a young woman who refuses to take the veil. ("Mother, don't make me a nun / because I don't want to be one: / don't sew me my habit / because I don't want to wear it.") The song's Elizabethan title may conceivably have been a backhanded tribute to a virgin queen who found it politically inexpedient to marry. By the time Byrd set it for the keyboard, it had achieved the status of popular song in England: one particularly trenchant broadside ballad from the late 1560s, an allegorical account of "the horrible and woeful destruction of Jerusalem," was written to be sung "to the tune of the Queen's Alman." Byrd's setting mixes English keyboard figuration with Italianate harmonic drive, taking full advantage (Example 12.1) of the familiar circle of fifths that would become so ubiquitous in the later seventeenth century. Byrd's twenty consort variations on *Browning* (the folk tune also known as *The leaves be green*) make up an equally delightful work, on a level with the best of his keyboard variations: an exuberant study in perpetual motion, passing the melody through all five parts in turn.

Even the most serious of Byrd's mature instrumental works owe something to popular music, or at least reflect his interest in the full range of English Renaissance musical styles. The clearest example of his versatility is probably found in another piece for viol consort, his first six–part G-minor fantasia. It begins with a grave imitative exposition of the sort that would be entirely at home in a Latin motet. Little by little, the music is taken over by a series of antiphonal exchanges, trading the same material back and forth between small groups of instruments. These exchanges become more urgent and more compressed until they finally turn into something unexpected: a rollicking version of the chorus to the famous Elizabethan tune *Greensleeves* (Example 12.2), passed between the two upper parts with the most rustic of accompaniments. (This is not very far from the fictional street scene in William Cobbold's early seventeenth-century song *New Fashions*, where one of the characters launches into an

Ex. 12.1 The Queen's Alman (BK 10), mm. 67–end

almost identical rendition of *Greensleeves*.) Once the tune has run its course, the fantasia goes on to something equally unexpected, a full three-strain galliard complete with the customary repetitions. It ends with a sweeping coda over pedal tones in the lower parts, descending to a resonant low D in the bass viol.

Some contemporary scribes seem not to have known what to do with this piece. One manuscript stops abruptly at the end of the quotation from *Greensleeves*, and another at the end of the galliard. These may even have been early versions (or later changes?) made by Byrd himself. There is some evidence that he felt ill at ease with the unconventional structure of this fantasia: when he decided to publish a selection of consort music in his 1611 songbook, he chose his other six-part fantasia in G minor, a shorter, more conservative, and, at least in some ways, less impressive

Ex. 12.2 Consort fantasia in g, 6v, no. 1, mm. 84–87

Ex. 12.3 Consort pavan, 6v, mm. 13–16

work. The larger fantasia is perhaps less unified, at least on a superficial level, but much of its beauty is in its disunity. It follows a complex trajectory through a number of styles—from high to low, broadly speaking, and back again—and handles them all with great skill. Once again there is a striking parallel with the plays of Shakespeare, where courtly and homely forms of speech often coexist in a single narrative, sometimes even in the same character.

Byrd did not write many other pieces for six viols. One memorable exception, his six-part consort pavan and galliard in C, seems to be a thoroughly mature work: it may even have been the last consort music he ever composed. There was no real English tradition of six-part consort dances until the early seventeenth century, and the only surviving manuscript source of this pavan and galliard is a very late one. It is an especially notable pair because both pieces are built around a single shared musical theme, a sort of head-motive, which recurs in various guises at the beginning of each strain. (The theme itself, a dotted four-note rising figure, is simple and flexible enough to admit half a dozen variations.) Byrd did not take that exact approach in any of his other pavan–galliard pairs. Most of them show ample musical signs of belonging together, and of course each set shares a common mode, but there is no precedent—even in his harmonically fixed *passamezzo* pairs—for this sort of pervasive thematic unity.

The Renaissance pavan was, in its original form, little more than a stylized procession: a measured walk designed to show the dancer's poise and elegance in slow motion. Byrd's six-part consort pavan could hardly have been intended for actual dancing, but its classically simple lines capture the essence of the form. Although the piece is based on C, Byrd includes a flat in the key signature, which makes room for the beautiful harmonic excursions of the second strain (Example 12.3). The reserved but expressive mood is entirely characteristic of his later instrumental style. This particular pavan-and-galliard set was also a kind of homage to his earlier years as a composer for viols. It recalls nothing more than his five-part C-minor pavan—whose keyboard adaptation became the first pavan in the Nevell book, commemorated by a scribe as "the first that he ever made," the origin of his magisterial cycle of keyboard pavans and galliards. With his late pair of six-part consort dances, he brought that aspect of his career full circle.

CHAPTER THIRTEEN

Gradualia

I must therefore with silence build
the labyrinth of my delight…
—*Where fancy fond,* consort song by Byrd

Byrd's *Gradualia* is a large collection of music, 109 pieces in all, for the major events of the Catholic calendar. It includes the famous and ancient holidays (Christmas, Easter, Pentecost), some pointedly Roman observances (Corpus Christi, All Saints' Day, the Assumption of Mary), and a good deal of assorted music for various liturgical times and seasons. Byrd published it in two volumes, the first in 1605 and the second in 1607. He worked on it through a violent political crisis in England and the oncoming rush of modernity: his *Gradualia* was finished in the same year that saw Shakespeare's *King Lear,* Monteverdi's pioneering opera *Orfeo*, and the founding of the Jamestown colony in America. He offered it to the public with an air of finality and called it his "swan song," although he went on composing and publishing for nearly a decade longer.

The whole project was more or less unique in its time. Byrd's three masses, written during the 1590s, used the familiar and unchanging words (Kyrie, Gloria, Credo, Sanctus, Agnus) of the Latin liturgy. They were intensely practical works, designed for regular use in the English Catholic community. His two books of *Gradualia* are different because they use a series of special Latin texts, the so-called Propers of the Mass, which change from day to day. Polyphonic settings of the Propers were luxury items, to be sung just once a year on the appropriate occasion. Given the hard work of composing, the cost of distribution, and the limited useful-ness of (say) an elaborate mass for Ascension Thursday, there were under-standably only a few musicians who produced systematic collections of this kind. The handful of previous attempts had mostly been sponsored by powerful musical establishments such as the cathedral of Notre-Dame in Paris or the court of the Holy Roman Emperor. It is all the more sur-prising to see Byrd doing this sort of thing in a provincial backwater of Jacobean England, where it was strictly illegal to use the music as he intended it.

Byrd knew that he could not accomplish such a task on his own, so he solicited help from some powerful friends and patrons. He obtained per-mission to publish both volumes of *Gradualia* from Richard Bancroft, Bishop of London and later Archbishop of Canterbury, who served as an official censor of printed works: all of this music was registered with the Stationers' Company "under [Bancroft's] hands." As a staunch supporter of the Elizabethan ecclesiastical settlement, Bancroft could hardly have approved of Byrd's Latin liturgical works, but he was persuaded to allow them into print, probably with some encouragement from Byrd's asso-ciates at court. Bancroft's own rule in dealing with the troublesome English recusant community was to divide and conquer. He actively encouraged the internecine quarrels among various factions of the English Catholic clergy, and he tolerated the printing and circulation of polemics by Catholic authors, by means of which (as he himself said) "schism between them was nourished." His acceptance of Byrd's new work, with its implicit connections to the Jesuit order and the houses of the rural Catholic gentry, may well have arisen from the same Machiavellian attitude: anything likely to cause controversy—as the *Gradualia* indeed did—was, in the end, a victory for the establishment.

The first volume of *Gradualia* was dedicated to Henry Howard, earl of Northampton. He was an exact contemporary of Byrd, born in 1540 and marked for life by the violent political upheavals of mid-sixteenth-cen-tury England. When he was seven years old, his father was executed on a charge of treason and he was turned over to the care of John Foxe, com-piler of the famously bloodthirsty Protestant *Book of Martyrs*. Howard retained a lifelong sympathy for the Catholic cause, and he was at least tangentially implicated (as Byrd was) in various popish plots during the

1580s, but he settled down by middle age into a more or less stable compromise with the establishment. He was also a keen amateur musician who took lute lessons, peppered his correspondence with musical puns, and negotiated an increase in salary for the Gentlemen of the Chapel Royal, for which Byrd thanked him effusively in his dedicatory preface. By the early seventeenth century, Howard had become part of the inner circle at court and an intimate advisor to the king, a position that earned him the unflattering nickname of "his Majesty's earwig." It is hard to discern his real religious views at a distance of four hundred years; he seems to have been unsure of them himself. He flirted with recusancy, furthered his career by persecuting Jesuits (including some of Byrd's associates), wrote fulsome and contradictory letters to King James and Cardinal Bellarmine, and left a collection of handwritten devotional books that have almost nothing to do with the official liturgy of any church, Anglican or Roman. This eccentric, opportunist, and somewhat tortured character was in his own way a remarkably good choice for the dedication of such an unusual work.

Byrd intended the 1605 *Gradualia* to be the first installment in an even larger collection of music. His plan soon ran into unexpected trouble. The preparation of the second volume was already underway when England was stunned in November 1605 by the discovery of the Gunpowder Plot. This brought a predictable wave of anti-Catholic sentiment, and Byrd must have realized it was not the right moment for another book of Latin liturgical music. The next volume had to wait for almost two more years: he complained in 1607 that the contents of *Gradualia* II had been "long since completed and delivered to the press." The new book was dedicated to his friend John Petre, who seems to have been actively involved in the production and performance of the music. Byrd described it as a selection of fruits and flowers cultivated in the mild climate of Petre's household, offered to him "as a tithe."

Figure 13.1 shows Byrd's two-page index to the first book of *Gradualia*. It gives some idea of the scope of the project. This first volume alone was the largest single collection of polyphonic music ever printed in Renaissance England: there are sixty-three pieces, many of them with detachable alleluias or divided into different sections, sometimes as many as six or seven under a single heading. It was a formidable and expensive undertaking for Byrd and his printer; John Petre appears to have eased the process by offering them a loan. One of the surviving copies of *Gradualia* II was presented to the lawyer and music-lover Ralph Bosville, who inscribed it as "Mr. William Byrd his last set of songs given me by him." Also written on the title page is a note of the original price: *6s. 6d.* (A good pair of Elizabethan boots "with three buckles apiece" went for *6s. 8d.* This music would have been a substantial purchase.)

Like most other collections of English Renaissance polyphony, the two books of *Gradualia* are organized broadly by number of voices: three-part, four-part, and five-part pieces are printed together in separate sections. The second set of *Gradualia* even includes music for six voices, something Byrd had not cultivated since the early 1590s. Whenever possible, he assembled all the music required for a single day and printed it as a group. Most of these groups share a common scoring and a common tonal center. The music for All Saints' Day is based on F and written for five singers; the music for Corpus Christi is based on G and written for four singers; and so on throughout the year. This meant, among other things, that Byrd had to reject the long-standing practice of composing polyphonic Mass Propers around their traditional Gregorian chant melodies, which are in an essentially random series of modes and have little or no musical relationship to each other. Byrd's settings of the Proper were all (with a very small handful of exceptions) composed from scratch, and he did his best to give each day its own distinctive musical atmosphere.

Byrd's system of modal and expressive unity was stretched to its limits in the five-voice section of *Gradualia* I, most of which is dedicated to various commemorations and feast days of the Virgin Mary. This part of the *Gradualia* is made up of dozens of small parts to be rearranged, substituted, and grafted onto one another. It can be used to construct the liturgy for the major Marian holidays (the Nativity on 8 September, the Annunciation on 25 March, Candlemas on 2 February, and the Assumption on 15 August), along with a wide variety of minor feasts and other seasonal observances. Some pieces of music are intended for just one specific day of the year; others are used again and again (the three-part verse *Eructavit cor meum* would have been heard at least once a week in any household that made regular use of the Marian *Gradualia*); still others are made up of various detachable phrases to be sung or omitted according to the occasion at hand. The result is more like a set of Lego bricks than

Index Cantionum quinque Vocum.

1 SVScepimus Deus.
  Magnus Dominus.   Versus.
2 Sicut audivimus.
3 Senex puerum.
4 Nunc Dimittis.
   Quia viderunt.   Versus.
   Lumen ad reuelati : versus.
5 Responsum accepit Simeon.

6 Salue sancta parens.   Alleluia.
   Eructauit   versus.
7 Benedicta & venerabilis.
8 Virgo dei genitrix.
9 Fælix es.   Alleluia.
10 Beata es virgo.   Alleluia.
11 Beata viscera.   Alleluia.

12 Rorate cæli.
   Benedixit Domine.   Versus.
13 Tollite portas.
   Quis ascendit.   Versus.
14 Aue Maria. Alleluia.
15 Ecce Virgo. Alleluia.

16 Vultum tuum.   Alleluia.
17 Speciosus forma.
   Lingua mea.   versus.
18 Post partum.   Alleluia.
19 Fælix namque.   Alleluia.

20 Alleluia.   Aue Maria.
   Virga Iesse.   versus.
21 Gaude Maria.

22 Diffusa est.
   Propter veritatem.   Versus.
   Audi Filia.
   Vultum tuum.   versus.
   Adducentur Regi.   versus.
   Adducentur in lætitia. versus.

23 Gaudeamus omnes in Domino.
   Assumpta est.   versus.
24 Assumpta est.
25 Optimam partem.

26 Adoramus te Christe.
27 Vnam petij.   1 pars.
   Vt videam.   2 pars.
28 Plorans plorauit.   1 pars.
   Dic Regi.   2 pars.

29 Gaudeamus omnes in Domino.
   Exultate Iusti.   Versus.
30 Timete Dominum.
   Inquirentes autem. Versus.
31 Iustorum animæ.
32 Beati mundo corde.

Finis.

Index Cantionum quatuor Vocum.

1 CIbauit eos.
   Exultate deo.   Versus.
2 Oculi omnium.
   Aperis tu manum. Versus.
3 Sacerdotes Domini.
4 Quotiescunq;.

5 Aue verum.
6 O salutaris.
7 O sacrum.   Alleluia.
8 Nobis natus.   1 pars.
   Verbum,caro.   2 pars.
   Tantum ergo.   3 pars.

9 Ecce

FIGURE 13.1   *Gradualia* I (1605), full index

a normal book of Renaissance motets. Here Byrd took his cue from the old chant tradition: he was sparing with his rubrics and expected his singers to be in control. Anyone who wanted to make practical use of this music had to be well-trained in the intricacies of the Roman rite and ready to leaf back and forth through a large book at a moment's notice.

Index.

Finis.

Index Cantionum trium Vocum.

FINIS.

E.ij.

It is no great surprise that early seventeenth-century scribes, even the Catholic ones, ignored Byrd's ambitions and instead mined the first book of *Gradualia* for attractive trios and other simple musical goods. Some parts of his scheme were not fully deciphered—at least not in print—until the twentieth century.

The rest of the *Gradualia* is less confusing. Byrd generally wrote four or five pieces of music for each mass: these were designed to accompany the opening procession, the meditative pause between Scripture readings, the offertory, and the communion. Sometimes he also included a few extra items for singers to add as they saw fit, but they were secondary to the larger plan. When he described his settings of the Mass Proper in his 1605 preface, he called them "notes as a garland to adorn certain holy and delightful phrases of the Christian rite." He was well aware that the "holy and delightful phrases" came first. In his motet books and songbooks, he had sought out expressive or politically potent words; in the *Gradualia*, as in his three masses, he was simply following the dictates of the Roman missal and setting an ancient cycle of texts to new music. These constraints seem to have driven him, at least in some cases, to rethink his whole compositional process. His elegant little offertories and communions—some of them are barely a minute long—could hardly be further removed from the leisurely Latin motets of the 1570s. Even in the more elaborate parts of the *Gradualia*, it is clear that his style has been refined and stripped down by the demands of such a large project.

Some individual feast days stand out from the others. The music in honor of St. Peter and St. Paul in *Gradualia* II is set apart from the rest of the collection by its sumptuous six-part scoring. With its (at least implicit) commemoration of Peter as the first pope and the head of the universal church, it must also have raised some political suspicion in Jacobean England, especially in the aftermath of the Gunpowder Plot. Byrd, or perhaps his printer, responded by censoring it: every non-scriptural text having to do with Peter is simply left out of the book, resulting in long stretches of music with no words at all. (Byrd did the same thing in a few other places, most notably by leaving out a line of the Ascension hymn *Iesu nostra redemptio* that referred to the freeing of prisoners.) This unusual gesture seems to have attracted some attention: one of the most important seventeenth-century manuscript copies of the *Gradualia* includes all of the six-part pieces except the three that Byrd censored, and the bass partbook owned by Ralph Bosville has two of the three torn out.

Of course Byrd was more concerned with the quality of his music than with its latent political dangers, and he spared no effort in composing an impressive set of Mass Propers for St. Peter and St. Paul. The six-part texture gave him a chance to indulge in complex imitative processes and unexpected moments of dissonance. The major mode and rich sonority might recall the smooth Counter-Reformation triumphalism of a piece such as Palestrina's *Tu es Petrus*, but the resemblance stops there. Byrd's own version of *Tu es Petrus* is anything but smooth and well-proportioned: a rather perfunctory beginning is followed by a massive setting of *aedificabo ecclesiam meam*—"upon this rock *I will build my church*"—as Byrd builds a towering edifice of rising and falling melodies over long-held notes in the bass. To drive the point home, this passage makes its way systematically through the traditional series of hexachords on G, F, and C, the ancient foundation stones of Western music that Byrd had explored at length in his keyboard fantasia on *Ut re mi fa sol la*. (Any musical devotee of St. Peter would also have known that the foundational pitches of these hexachords were known in Latin as *claves*, the eponymous "keys" with which the saint was always depicted—not least in each of the three masses published by Byrd in the 1590s, where Peter and his keys adorn the woodcut initial *K* for *Kyrie*.) This unusual piece may well have been a special tribute to John Petre, who would have appreciated the complex pun on the saint's name, his own name, the Latin *petra* or "rock," and his country estate of Ingatestone, which the family themselves referred to as "Ginge Petre."

Byrd faced a different challenge when he composed the Mass Proper for Easter, the most important day in the Christian calendar and in the life of the English recusant community. His response was not a predictable one. The atmosphere of his Easter mass is restless, almost disjointed in places; he chose a minor key for this most festive of occasions, rejecting sweetness and light for the dramatic chiaroscuro of an early Baroque Resurrection. His opening gambit, the rising melody on the all-important word *Resurrexi* (Example 13.1), is a complex, twisting journey rather than an unimpeded shot toward the heavens. He has come a long way from his 1591 *Haec dies*, that most cheerful and madrigalian of Easter motets—although he does allow himself some naïve text-painting in the

Ex. 13.1 *Resurrexi*, **second soprano, mm. 1–4**

Re - sur - re - - - - - - - - xi

Easter *Gradualia*, most notably in the tiny offertory *Terra tremuit*, which takes its performers through an earthquake (and its aftershocks) in forty-five seconds. Even a more straightforwardly joyful set such as the Ascension mass, the next to be sung after Easter, is leavened by small touches like the brief rhythmic irregularity at the beginning of the communion *Psallite Domino*. The initial four-beat measure before a succession of three-beat groups is an almost imperceptible gesture, but it deftly saves the piece from the cliché of triple-time rejoicing so common to seventeenth-century sacred music.

A number of pieces in the *Gradualia* must have had special significance for Byrd and his Catholic associates. The early-summer feast of Corpus Christi, which falls two months after Easter, was cultivated with fervor among English recusants. Medieval parishes had celebrated it with lavish floral displays and elaborate outdoor processions, and this sort of activity continued even after Catholic worship became illegal in England. One household near Byrd's in rural Essex showed a remarkable mixture of piety and audacity by leading a Corpus Christi procession around their gardens in 1605, the year of the first *Gradualia* volume—"the house being watched," as they later reported, "which we knew not till the next day." Byrd provided a dozen pieces of music for Corpus Christi and associated observances, including the well-known motet *Ave verum corpus*. The rest of the set is less familiar, but it contains some of Byrd's most radiant and melodious writing. The first measures of *O quam suavis* (Example 13.2) are a rare moment of real Italianate chromaticism in his music, a gust of warm air from the south.

The festive season of Christmas was especially treasured by English recusants, so it is something of a surprise to see the Christmas *Gradualia* scored for only four singers. Could this have had to do with the difficulty of travel over unpaved roads in midwinter? It may also have been an early and cautious experiment in setting the Mass Proper to music. There are some signs that the Christmas music was the very first composed: it is inconsistent in vocal scoring and mode, and it begins, unusually for Byrd, by quoting the Gregorian chant for the day (*Puer natus est nobis*) in three of the four voices. This gesture seems to have been a brief nod to the old tradition of chant-based polyphonic Mass Propers, something that Byrd never took up again in quite the same way.

Ex. 13.2 *O quam suavis*, mm. 1–8

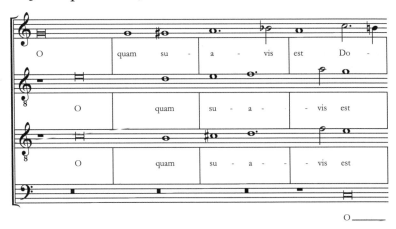

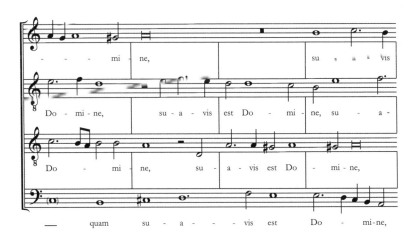

The closely related feast of Epiphany, on January 6, was celebrated by the Elizabethans as Twelfth Night: a holiday immortalized on stage by Shakespeare ("If music be the food of love, play on…") and marked by household revelry, singing, dancing, gift-giving, and a fair amount of mischief. Byrd's music for Epiphany is really a continuation of his Christmas music. It shares the same basic tonal center, the same musical atmosphere, and the same eccentric choice of singers, who may simply have been the voices available for the occasion: two mezzo-sopranos, a high tenor, and a bass. Like the Christmas set, it is sweet, melodious music which often creates the illusion of being in more than four parts. It is less overtly expressive (and less moody) than many of his other Mass Propers, although he could not resist some creative illustration of the text here and there: a whiff of exotic dissonance when the Magi see the star "in the East," or the splendid falling cadence at "all the nations shall serve him."

Byrd's music for feasts of the Virgin Mary, as we have seen, is a special case. Because of the elaborate cut-and-paste scheme of this part of the book, he was limited to a single modal center (he chose D) and a uniform set of singers (he chose a terraced arrangement of five different voices.) Within these strict guidelines, he managed to produce a diverse and colorful collection of music. The Candlemas set is notable for using a modified cantus-firmus technique in several places, with a chant-like melody sustained in long notes. Although Byrd is certainly alluding to the relevant melodies from contemporary chant books—Example 13.3 shows his alto part side by side with the chant from the 1596 Giunta Gradual, which we know from other evidence that he owned or at least consulted—he recalls them in an imprecise way, using them to create a mood and not as a strict compositional device. His Candlemas pieces are

Ex. 13.3 *Nunc dimittis* and *Responsum accepit* **from the Giunta Graduale (1596), compared with Byrd's alto lines**

spun out at some length, with what seems to be a wistful glance back at a more expansive tradition of sacred music.

Byrd did his best to treat each Proper set as a self-contained cycle, and he often saved the most striking musical ideas for the communion antiphon at the end of the set. One memorable example is the communion *Optimam partem,* the final piece in the Assumption mass and the last in the whole Marian series. The text is a single brief sentence from the gospel of Luke:

> *Optimam partem elegit sibi Maria, quae non auferetur ab ea in aeternum.*
> Mary has chosen the best part for herself, which will not be taken from her in eternity.

Everything in Byrd's setting is perfectly judged: the brief sting of the augmented triad in the opening bars; the careful use of high vocal ranges to intensify the musical texture; the remote and slightly unearthly figure at *quae non auferetur;* and the final reflection on eternity (Example 13.4) with its ecstatic rising scales in the bass. *Optimam partem* was a familiar verse in the recusant world. It was quoted by a number of young Catholic emigrants who made the difficult choice to renounce their homes and seek a better life in seminaries and monasteries on the Continent. One of them was William Taylor, an Oxford scholar who traveled to Rome at the age of twenty-three and made his application to enter the English College there. In his contribution to the *Responsa Scholarum,* the entrance questionnaire for new seminarians, he states his own case: "I confidently hope that I have, with Mary, chosen the best part." For Byrd, choosing the best part meant something quite different. He was a family man, an owner of property, and unlikely by temperament to have lasted long in the hothouse environment cultivated by pious English Catholic exiles. He chose to exercise his talents in another way. The result, in *Optimam partem*, is one of the most beautiful pieces he ever wrote.

In his preface to the first book of *Gradualia*, Byrd spoke about the process of composing:

> In the words themselves (as I have learned from experience) there is such obscure and hidden power that to a person thinking about divine things, diligently and earnestly turning them over in his mind, the most appropriate musical phrases come, I know not how, and offer themselves freely to the mind that is not lazy or inert.

Ex. 13.4A *Optimam partem*, mm. 30–end

Ex. 13.4B

It is no coincidence that Byrd used the language of meditation—
"thinking about divine things, diligently and earnestly turning them over
in his mind"—to describe his own work as a composer. It is also no coincidence that he wrote this way about the *Gradualia* rather than any of his
equally expressive songbooks or motet books. By the early seventeenth
century, the recusant community was steeped in just this kind of reflection. There was a lively trade among English Catholics in books of private
meditation: guided imaginative tours through the stations of the liturgical year and the lives of the saints, written for people who had little or
no chance to commemorate such things in public. Byrd's two books of
Gradualia are a musical embodiment of the same practice. The listener,
and especially the singer, is invited to re-imagine and experience the
event at hand—from the wild-eyed wonder of Easter to the quiet reverence of Christmas, through as many facets as the calendar has red-letter
days.

One especially popular method of meditation in English recusant
circles was the thirty-day series of *Spiritual Exercises* designed by Ignatius
of Loyola, the early sixteenth-century founder of the Jesuit order. The

Exercises are an imaginative journey through the life, death, and resurrection of Christ. They are organized as reflections on a series of short
texts, taking in much of the same material as the complex cycle of Mass
Propers in the *Gradualia*. In his colorful memoir of recusant life, the
Elizabethan Jesuit priest John Gerard describes the years he spent
traveling in secret from one country house to the next, guiding various
people through these meditations. A month spent with the Ignatian
Exercises quite often resulted—at least among eager young men without
family obligations—in a sudden desire to emigrate to Europe and join
the clergy being trained for the English Catholic mission. The fellow-
student who accompanied Byrd's son Thomas to Valladolid, and who
shared his recommendation from Gerard, mentioned in his interview
(as many other novices did) that he had been drawn to the seminary by
the *Exercises*. It is hard to imagine that Thomas did not follow a similar
path, doubtless with his father's encouragement. It is quite likely that the
composer went through the *Exercises* himself at some point in his forty-
year association with the Jesuits.

The process of deep reflection and "thinking about divine things"
would have been second nature to Byrd by this point in his life, but it is
still rather surprising to hear him speak in such glowing terms about
textual inspiration, given the self-imposed constraints under which he
composed the *Gradualia*. He had already spent much of his musical career
on a hunt for expressive words. The search led him through Savonarola,
Augustine, the more obscure corners of the Scriptures, and, when it
suited him, the rituals of the Roman church. When he decided later
in life to use fixed liturgical texts, he simply gave up his choice in the
matter.

Rossini once claimed—the story may be apocryphal—to be able to
set his laundry list to beautiful music. Byrd has attracted some (perhaps
misplaced) sympathy from modern critics who saw him spending his
mature years working over an endless series of arbitrary Latin fragments.
From the musical evidence of the *Gradualia*, he seems to have enjoyed
writing almost every note. He was following in the tradition of those
English Renaissance artists (Nicholas Hilliard is the first to come to
mind) who made exquisite miniatures: paintings, embroideries, poems,
musical works. As with a portrait gallery or a book of sonnets, visitors can

dip into the *Gradualia* for occasional favorites or lose themselves in its complex byways. Although the English recusant world was a culturally rich one, the constant danger of discovery and persecution kept it from producing very many artifacts of lasting value. Byrd's *Gradualia* may well be the greatest exception to this rule.

CHAPTER FOURTEEN

1611

Some solemn, others joyful, framed to the life of the words
—*Psalms, Songs and Sonnets*, 1611

BYRD PUBLISHED HIS LAST SONGBOOK IN A YEAR THAT SAW A NUMBER of other artistic triumphs, including Shakespeare's *Tempest* (the last and arguably the most musical of his plays) and the King James version of the Bible. He called the book *Psalms, Songs and Sonnets*. As the title suggests, it is a rather eclectic collection. He put it together as a retrospective of sorts, with a broad variety of musical styles ("to content every humour") and a mixture of new and old material. Some of the songs can be traced back as early as the 1590s, but many others appear to be quite recently composed; there are thirty-two pieces in all, only half a dozen of which occur in earlier sources. The 1611 songbook is arguably the most diverse of all Byrd's publications. It even includes some undisguised music for stringed instruments, something he had never dared to print in earlier years. Despite the elegiac and slightly weary tone of Byrd's 1611 preface ("these are like to be my last travails in this kind"), his enthusiasm for composition seems to have been undimmed as he entered his eighth decade:

> The natural inclination and love to the art of music, wherein I have spent the better part of mine age, have been so powerful in me, that even in my old years which are desirous of rest, I cannot contain myself from taking some pains therein.

He went on to describe the book as his "last labors" and "final farewell"—
much as he had done a few years earlier in his collection of *Gradualia*—
and quoted a line from the Stoic philosopher Seneca which his European
colleague Lassus had also used in his last musical publication: "The sun's
light is sweetest at the very moment of its setting."

Byrd had not published any music of this kind since his 1589 *Songs of
Sundry Natures*. The landscape of English vernacular song had changed
almost beyond recognition in the intervening two decades. His earlier
songbooks had appeared at more or less the same moment as two pioneering madrigal anthologies, Nicholas Yonge's 1588 *Musica Transalpina*
and Thomas Watson's 1590 *Italian Madrigals Englished*. Byrd made a brief
appearance as the sole English composer in both collections, which were
otherwise devoted to adaptations of Italian originals. In the wake of those
two books, Elizabethan composers began producing a large quantity of
madrigals in their own language. The English madrigal soon developed a
distinctive musical idiom of its own, although it never lost sight of its
origins in the tuneful, light *madrigale arioso* and the dance-like forms cultivated by late sixteenth-century Italians. In 1601, at the height of the
new fashion, the composer Richard Carlton summed up its contradic-
tions in the preface of his *Madrigals to Five Voices*: "I have labored somewhat to imitate the Italian, they being in these days (with the most) in
high request, yet may I not nor cannot forget that I am an Englishman."

The same year, 1601, saw the appearance of the *Triumphs of Oriana*, a
collection of madrigals (bearing a politically astute dedication to Queen
Elizabeth) whose index was a roll-call of Byrd's distinguished young contemporaries: Weelkes, Gibbons, Morley, Wilbye, and a host of others. Byrd
himself was conspicuous by his absence. By the time he published his
new English songbook in 1611, the madrigal craze had largely run its
course, although some notable late examples (such as Gibbons's *The silver
swan* and Tomkins's *Too much I once lamented*) were still to come.

There is not much in the 1611 *Psalms, Songs and Sonnets* to suggest the
sweeping changes that had taken place in English song over the previous
twenty years. Byrd included one bona fide madrigal in the collection, a
four-voice setting of *This sweet and merry month of May* that he had first
published in *Italian Madrigals Englished*. Some other four-part pieces, such
as *Awake mine eyes* and *Come jolly swains*, also owe a good deal to the tradition of light Italianate music. The five-part and six-part music is

generally more serious, with a few notable exceptions. *Sing we merrily* is the most madrigalian of sacred songs, full of breezy and virtuosic word-painting. The garish (and very skillful) modulations in *Come woeful Orpheus*, reflecting the "strange chromatic notes," "sourest sharps," and "uncouth flats" of the text, may well be a dig at the chromatic excesses of some early seventeenth-century English madrigalists. As a younger composer, Byrd was driven to a similar display in his penitential motet *Vide Domine afflictionem nostram*—down the circle of fifths to A♭ and D♭, back again to pungent sharp-side chords—by sheer emotional involvement with his work. The atmosphere of *Come woeful Orpheus* is decidedly less earnest. Some other naïve illustrations in the 1611 book, such as the "warbling throats" of the "sylvan choir" in *Awake mine eyes*, seem also to have been written with tongue in cheek. Byrd must have sympathized in many ways with his fellow-musician Thomas Campion, who began his 1601 *Book of Ayres* with a withering attack on the prevailing madrigalian ideal:

> where the nature of every word is precisely expressed in the note, like the old exploded action in comedies, when if they did pronounce *memini* [I remember], they would point to the hinder part of their heads, if *video* [I see], put their finger in their eye. But such childish observing of words is altogether ridiculous.

Even in the most up-to-date parts of the 1611 songbook, Byrd is often revisiting musical genres he has cultivated before: the consort song, the large-scale polyphonic psalm, the introspective elegy. Sometimes he interprets them in a new way. More than two-thirds of Byrd's 1588 songs had extra verses printed alongside the music; only two of his 1611 songs do. Here we can see Byrd finally moving away from the Tudor song tradition, which had been almost medieval in its adherence to repetitive fixed forms, and turning consistently to the more direct rhetoric of the through-composed song. Now there is only a single journey through the text, although many of Byrd's late songs still call for a repeat of the final section—another traditional characteristic of sixteenth-century English song that had become deeply ingrained in his formal imagination. (This device resurfaces in some unusual places over the years, including his Latin motet *Ave verum corpus*, whose jog-trot rhyming text seems to have inspired him to set it as he set so many English devotional poems.)

In his *Psalms, Songs and Sonnets*, Byrd generally avoids the in-jokes and political allusions of his unpublished songs—which were clearly intended for a select audience—in favor of subject matter with a wider appeal. There are quite a few moralizing or sententious pieces. Byrd still enjoyed that sort of poetry, and Jacobean audiences seem to have been prepared at least to tolerate it. One three-voice song, *In winter cold*, is a musical retelling of Aesop's fable of the grasshopper and the ant. Like much of the three-part music in the 1611 collection, it uses a text from Geoffrey Whitney's *A Choice of Emblems*, a book of proverbs illustrated with elaborate woodcut images and didactic poems. One of the "emblems" set by Byrd, *In crystal towers* (Figure 14.1), was dedicated in its original form to Edward Paston—who was himself the author of another 1611 text, *Crowned with flowers I saw fair Amaryllis*, adapted from a Spanish courtly poem by Jorge de Montemayor. As an aficionado of Spanish culture who

FIGURE 14.1   *In crystal towers*, from Geoffrey Whitney's *Choice of Emblems* (1586)

read and wrote the language fluently, Paston was in an ideal position to supply Byrd with foreign poetry of that sort.

Some of the most memorable songs in the 1611 collection are written on anonymous texts. *Retire my soul* uses the imagery of accounting and money-lending to capture the speaker's troubled state of mind. He is looking back on a long life, taking stock as he nears the end:

> Retire my soul, consider thine estate,
> and justly sum thy lavish sins' account:
> time's dear expense, and costly pleasure's rate,
> how follies grow, how vanities amount.
> Write all these down in pale Death's reckoning tables:
> thy days will seem but dreams, thy hopes but fables.

This is several cuts above most English Renaissance madrigal verse, especially in the arresting final couplet. Byrd gives it a suitably introspective and elegiac setting, with a plangent conclusion (Example 14.1) on the final word "fables." It is not difficult to hear the voice of the aging composer himself in these lines, reflecting on the ambitions and compromises of his own life.

Byrd chose to end the *Psalms, Songs and Sonnets* with a group of six-part consort songs. Here he adds an extra viol to the traditional scheme, surrounding the singer (invariably a mezzo-soprano or high alto voice) with an unusually complex accompaniment: three viols below, one in the same general range, and one above, functioning almost as a descant. With so many parts in play, even the straightforward ending of a vocal phrase can develop into a riot of ornamentation. One particularly elaborate six-part song, *O God that guides the cheerful sun*, is subtitled "A carol for New Year's Day" and includes a chorus of singers as well as a viol accompaniment. Like Byrd's other seasonal songs, it was doubtless part of the fabric of holiday celebrations in the houses of his friends and patrons: recall John Petre's engagement of five professional string players during the twelve days of Christmas. Some other songs go to opposite extremes of texture. The simple alternating duets of *What is life, or worldly pleasure?* (Figure 14.2) make up what may be the most naïve and artless of all Byrd's compositions. If it were not in print with Byrd's name firmly attached to it, we might suspect it was by a quite different sort of composer.

Ex. 14.1 *Retire my soul*, mm. 35–end

Ex. 14.2 *What is life, or worldly pleasure?*, mm. 1–8

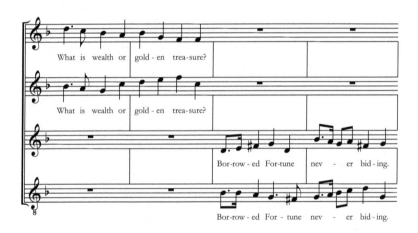

Byrd's first two songbooks had included nineteen metrical psalms of the sort so popular in post-Reformation England. There is not a single one in his last songbook. By the end of the sixteenth century, Byrd seems to have rejected homely metrical paraphrases in favor of the greater flexibility, and the greater decorum, of biblical prose. (The dour Calvinist associations of metrical psalmody may also have rankled as he grew older.) Although he had recently written some elaborate church anthems on psalm texts, not a single one of those anthems—no piece that ever appears in an Elizabethan or Jacobean ecclesiastical source—was included in the 1611 book. Here, as elsewhere, he kept his church works strictly separate from his chamber works. There is not much else that can explain his decision to withhold a splendid late anthem such as *Sing joyfully* from a starring role in the six-voice section of *Psalms, Songs and Sonnets*. His published songs, even those set to unmistakably sacred words, were clearly meant to be sung in a private, domestic context, "for the recreation" (as he said) "of all such as delight in music."

Two-thirds of the nine psalm settings in the 1611 songbook (along with the related Christmas piece *This day Christ was born*) are in fact taken directly from a Catholic source, Richard Verstegan's *Primer or Office of the Blessed Virgin Mary*. The Verstegan Primer was a bilingual book of hours for English Catholic laypeople, with a series of devotional texts in both English and Latin. It was first published in Antwerp in 1599 and was being smuggled across the Channel in substantial quantities by the early seventeenth century. Although Byrd eventually printed his Verstegan settings for the most general of audiences, they seem to have begun life—just like his *Gradualia* and his three masses—as Catholic domestic music. Their texts are bluntly literal versions of the Latin Vulgate that would have sounded rather odd to any singer accustomed to the usual translations and paraphrases circulating in Renaissance England.

The actual music of Byrd's late psalm settings is a different matter: it has rather little to do with the practical needs of the recusant community. In these English sacred songs, especially the five-voice and six-voice ones, there is not much sign of the pared-down new style he had been cultivating in his Latin ritual music. A serious piece like *Turn our captivity*, with its leisurely and beautiful imitative exposition (Example 14.3), is much closer to the old expressive laments of the *Cantiones* than it is to anything he wrote for recusant liturgical use. The elaborate rejoicing of *This day Christ was born*, or the lengthy final *Amen* of *Praise our Lord all ye Gentiles*, has almost nothing in common with the tense concision of Byrd's masses: what these late songs most recall are pieces such as *Haec dies* and *Laudibus in sanctis* and the other grand constructions of his younger years.

By the early seventeenth century, Byrd was writing larger-scale music in English than he was writing in Latin. It was a remarkable shift of perspective, and one that reflected broader trends in Jacobean sacred music. These new vernacular motets—no other term describes them as well—were in a style widely appreciated by the next generation of English musicians. The connection is perhaps clearest in the extraordinary group

Ex. 14.3A *Turn our captivity*, mm. 1–18

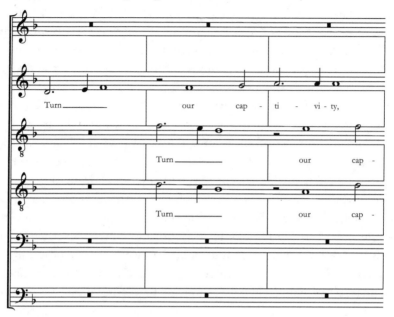

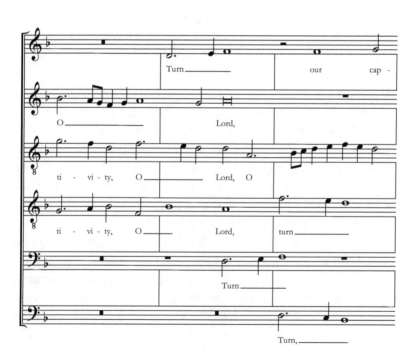

Ex. 14.3B

Ex. 14.3C

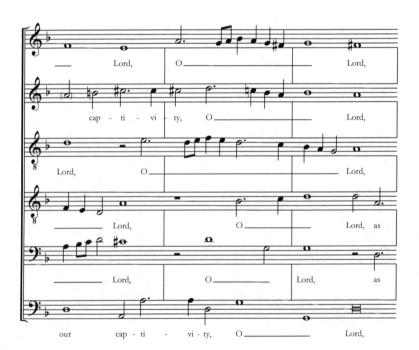

(a dozen in all) of Jacobean musical laments on the death of the biblical Absalom, pieces such as the Tomkins and Weelkes settings of *When David heard that Absalom was slain*, which were in many ways the real heirs to the melancholy and gravitas of the Elizabethan motet. If Byrd had gone on composing a little longer, he would surely have written one of his own.

The same grave vernacular style was reflected through a different lens in a book such as Orlando Gibbons's 1612 *First Set of Madrigals and Motets*. The title itself is noteworthy: in fact these are all English-texted pieces, and all in principle secular, although the moods of Gibbons's individual songs range from moralizing (*I weigh not Fortune's frown nor smile*) to pastoral (*Now each flowery bank of May*) to amorous (*Ah dear heart, why do you rise?*) and, perhaps inevitably for a composer of this generation, elegiac (*Nay let me weep, What is our life?, The silver swan*). The music varies in style from one song to the next, but much of it is consistently polyphonic, with imitative points worked out at length: a dignified, somewhat abstract musical edifice. Gibbons was not at all amiss in using the word "motet" to describe such pieces. He could hardly have produced this sort of book without the example set by Byrd in recent years. He underscored the connection by dedicating his *First Set of Madrigals and Motets* to the nephew and namesake of Byrd's patron Christopher Hatton; he even devoted a full page to exactly the same printed emblem (the Golden Hind) Byrd had used a quarter-century earlier in his first songbook.

Unlike Byrd's earlier songbooks, the *Psalms, Songs and Sonnets* only went through one edition. By this point in life, he seems to have been relatively unconcerned with matters of reputation and profit. There was also not much need for musical revision. The 1611 book is almost flawlessly edited, with just a handful of tiny errors, most of them fixed in the printer's shop with pasted-in cancel slips. Byrd says as much himself while discussing his songs in the preface. He hopes the reader will devote as much care to their performance as he has to their preparation:

> Only this I desire, that you will be but as careful to hear them well expressed, as I have been both in the composing and correcting of them. Otherwise the best song that ever was made will seem harsh and unpleasant, for that the well expressing of them, either by voices or instruments, is the life of our labours, which is seldom or never well performed at the first singing or playing.

He goes on to say something more profound:

> Besides, a song that is well and artificially [skillfully] made cannot be well perceived nor understood at the first hearing, but the oftener you shall hear it, the better cause of liking you will discover: and commonly that song is best esteemed with which our ears are most acquainted.

Anyone who listens to music will recognize the truth of that statement: "the oftener you shall hear it, the better cause of liking you will discover." It is a moving insight from a seventy-year-old composer who had lived through so many changes in musical practice and style.

The year 1611 is now best remembered as the year of the vastly influential Authorized Version of the Bible, the so-called King James Bible, commissioned by the monarch to serve as the official Anglican version of the Scriptures. Byrd must have had at least indirect contact with some of the fifty translators—Richard Bancroft, who licensed the *Gradualia*, oversaw the whole process of translation—but he never set a word of their Bible to music. If he ever owned a copy, there is no trace of it now. His own favored translations, as we have seen, generally came either from Catholic sources or from venerable English liturgical texts such as the Coverdale psalter. The diplomatic, irenic, and very stylish King James Bible had little in common with the projects undertaken by Catholic translators such as Richard Verstegan, who lays out his method clearly in the introduction to his 1599 *Primer:* "In the translation of the Psalms, and other parts of holy scripture, the sense (as is most requisite) hath more been sought to be observed than any phrases in our language more affected and pleasing."

Substance over style: that was an aim shared by the translators of the Douai–Rheims Bible, who were also English Catholic exiles working on the Continent. Their basic goal, like Verstegan's, was to produce a version of the Latin Vulgate that could be read by people who were educated only in the vernacular. The translators of the Authorized Version complained about that principle in their own preface, and hinted at more sinister motives: "We have shunned the obscurity of the Papists," as they said, who "darken the sense, that since they must needs translate the Bible, yet by the language thereof, it may be kept from being understood." (They also gave examples of what they considered to be offensively obscure terms in the "Papist" versions. Among them are the words "rational" and "holocaust": the English language did not always develop in the ways they predicted.)

One particular quirk of these English Catholic translations is featured prominently in Byrd's 1611 songbook: the habit of always rendering the Latin *Dominus* or the Greek *Kyrios* as "our Lord" rather than "the Lord," whatever the literary context might be. (Verstegan's version of the Magnificat—which Byrd must have known well—duly begins "My soul doth magnify our Lord".) The phrase occurs in most of Byrd's Primer psalms, sometimes early enough to appear in the index of titles: *Sing ye to our Lord, Come let us rejoice unto our Lord, Praise our Lord all ye Gentiles*. It was widely recognized as a Catholic shibboleth in his day. George Abbot, who was appointed Archbishop of Canterbury in 1611, spoke from fifty years of experience:

> This they [Catholics] make to be a mark of difference between themselves so speaking, and us saying after the Scripture, *The Lord*. And accordingly our English people do practice it if they savor of Popery: so much that in all my life I have scant heard any in common speech always saying *Our Lord*, but that party hath more or less been tainted that way.

No educated singer would have missed the connotations. Byrd clearly had no trouble finding public approval for whatever music he chose to publish—even his fiercely Catholic books of *Gradualia* were given a pass by a Church of England censor—but these songs still offer a surprising hint of their origins in what was still very much a cultural in-group, with its own distinctive habits of speech and devotion.

Like so many other seventeenth-century musical collections, Byrd's 1611 book has a colorful subtitle: "Psalms, songs and sonnets, *some solemn, others joyful, framed to the life of the words*." "Framed to the life": it is an elegant way of describing good musical setting, or good representation in general. It has the ring of cliché, of a Renaissance commonplace, but it was not at all a common phrase. It does appear somewhere else, only two years before Byrd used it, in one of the first instances of what we might call literary criticism of Shakespeare: the anonymous 1609 preface to *Troilus and Cressida*, which praises Shakespeare's plays, "especially this author's comedies, that are so framed to the life, that they serve for the most common commentaries of all the actions of our lives, showing such a dexterity and power of wit that the most displeased with plays are pleased with his comedies." Whatever this anonymous editor was thinking when he (apparently) classified *Troilus and Cressida* as a comedy, it is clear what he was saying about Shakespeare's comic genius: the characters are "so framed to the life" that we recognize ourselves in them, we see the foibles and absurdities of our own lives, and even the most jaded can hardly resist smiling. They are funny precisely because they are a visible and audible manifestation of an underlying reality.

It is attractive to imagine Byrd reading that line in a copy of Shakespeare and finding that it applied just as well to musical wit and creativity. Whether or not he ever did, he described his own English songs two years later as "framed to the life of the words." The phrase is worth a bit more reflection. The life of the words, what Byrd says is being repre-sented in his music, is something more than just the words. The life of the words is also their signification, their associations, their subtext. In many ways this is a secular gloss on Byrd's 1605 statement about meditating and pondering on sacred texts. We have already seen his rather skeptical atti-tude toward the conventions of Italianate word-painting (and, by extension, toward the school of Petrarchan or pseudo-Petrarchan mad-rigal verse that all but demanded it.) That sort of text-setting could be defined easily enough as "framed to the words." What really lies behind Byrd's mature idea of musical representation is the *life*, that elusive middle term: there is an inner life to the text that it is the composer's duty to reveal, as we can see and hear so well in a splendid late song such as *Retire my soul*. This is not too distant from the eloquent words of the preface to the Authorized Version, written in the same year:

> Translation it is that openeth the window, to let in the light; that breaketh the shell, that we may eat the kernel; that putteth aside the curtain, that we may look into the most holy place; that removeth the cover of the well, so that we may come by the water.

The task of the interpreter—textual or musical—is to use all his skill to make the underlying reality more perceptible. Byrd himself could hardly have said it better.

CHAPTER FIFTEEN

Last Works

The natural inclination and love to the art of music, wherein I have spent the better part of mine age, have been so powerful in me, that even in my old years which are desirous of rest, I cannot contain myself from taking some pains therein.

—*Psalms, Songs and Sonnets*, 1611

DESPITE BYRD'S CLAIM THAT THE 1611 SONGS WOULD BE HIS "LAST labours," he went on writing music, though on a limited scale, for several more years. He himself said that he was reluctant to stop composing as old age approached, and he seems to have enjoyed some renewed fame in his last years as an elder statesman of English musical life. Almost all of his very late works appear to have been commissioned or assembled by special request.

Byrd's musical style was certainly old-fashioned by the early seventeenth century, but his continuing popularity during the Jacobean years should not come as a great surprise. The English Renaissance, like many other progressive cultural movements, was overtaken by occasional waves of nostalgia for the glories of a real or imagined past. We can see this tendency in Spenser's elaborate invocations of medieval chivalry, or in the work of the antiquarian collector Robert Cotton, to whom we owe the preservation of such medieval treasures as *Beowulf*, *Sir Gawain and the Green Knight*, and the Lindisfarne Gospels. We can also see it in a different guise in the Anglican penchant—considered highly suspect by the more puritanical churchmen of Byrd's day—for elaborate altar furnishings and other trappings of past religious practice. The translators of the King James Bible were themselves surprisingly conservative, even archaizing in places, producing a new version of the Scriptures that reflected the mood of the sixteenth-century reformers as much as it did current Jacobean literary taste. The antiquarian impulse was also alive and well among musicians. This was the same generation that saw a sincere revival of interest in viol playing and consort songs, as well as a spate of new cathedral music with ostentatiously high treble parts (up to a written high A in some cases) which recalled the last flowering of the English choir schools before the Reformation.

Of course this sort of archaism and conservatism was only one trend among many. The early seventeenth century was also a time of great musical innovation in England. At least some Jacobean composers were perfectly well informed about recent musical developments in Italy and elsewhere on the Continent, and it was not long before those developments made their way into English musical life. By 1617, the royal carnival celebrations could include a "whole Masque...sung (after the Italian manner) *Stylo recitativo*, by Master Nicholas Lanier." The Jacobean court hosted a great number of masques, festive pageants of song and dance that were produced on the most lavish scale possible. The popularity of the masque made its mark on English art and culture: it is hard to imagine an achievement such as Shakespeare's *Tempest* without the growing influence of English music-drama all around it.

This was an era in which Baroque musical forms and frankly Italianate monody came to coexist with the old polyphonic ideal. Byrd never wrote in any of the newer styles, although his name was mentioned at least once in conjunction with them. When an ambitious group of entrepreneurs drew up a proposal in 1620 for a new 12,000-seat royal amphitheater in London that would host extravagant stage productions (including "sea fights, nocturnals, fire, and waterworks"), they made plans to solicit musical help from Byrd, as well as Lanier, the younger Ferrabosco (son of the Elizabethan composer), "and other great masters in music." What they had in mind was doubtless theatrical music of the sort already being cultivated at court. They must have known that Byrd had almost nothing in common with the composers who wrote songs and recitatives "after the Italian manner," but his name was apparently still one to conjure with as the Jacobean era drew to a close.

A 1622 inventory of music books in the Earl of Worcester's London household—made by his son Charles Somerset in the same year Byrd mentioned his "lodging" there in his will—includes Monteverdi's fourth and fifth books of madrigals. Those two great collections, perhaps more than any other two documents of early seventeenth-century music, illustrate between them the shift from what was still an essentially polyphonic style (though highly colored by the extended dissonance treatment of the *seconda pratica*) to a new way of writing that can truly be called Baroque. Charles doubtless had some idea of this watershed when he catalogued the fifth book as "cum Basso continuo." Byrd must have been well acquainted with the Somerset music library, and it is tempting to imagine him in his last years reading through Monteverdi's madrigal books (the fifth was printed in the same year as his second set of *Gradualia*) and realizing what had eventually become of the Italian secular style he was so reluctant to embrace. His very last pieces, those which appeared between 1612 and 1614, were all in genres already familiar to him: devotional partsongs, consort songs, keyboard pavans and galliards. Despite a few unexpected adjustments in style, they are still quite recognizable as Byrd's music.

William Leighton's 1614 anthology *The Tears or Lamentations of a Sorrowful Soul* featured four songs by Byrd. It was one of the more unusual musical publications to come out of early seventeenth-century England. Leighton was an amateur poet and musician who rose quickly to social prominence during the last years of Elizabeth's reign. He was appointed a Member of Parliament in 1601, named a Gentleman Pensioner in 1602, and knighted in 1603. His success did not last long: he spent much of the following decade in and out of prison for debt. His misfortune seems to have been due to some mixture of financial improvidence, petty dishonesty, and bad luck. He passed the time in prison by writing devotional and penitential poems, most of them quite lugubrious even by Jacobean standards. He published a large collection of them in 1613, assuring his readers that a volume of musical settings would follow—which duly happened just a year later.

Leighton's table of contents is a roll-call of familiar musical names, "famous artists" (in his own words) "of that sublime profession." He was

not exaggerating. There is almost no distinguished Jacobean composer—
Tomkins and Campion are the only notable exceptions—who did *not*
contribute something to the book. The full roster includes Byrd, Dowland,
Gibbons, Bull, Weelkes, Ferrabosco, Lupo, Coperario, Peerson, Giles, and
Wilbye, along with a number of lesser figures. Leighton must have been
aware of his remarkable skill in recruiting such composers, notwithstanding the mixed quality (at best) of his poetry. He said as much in his
own preface:

> Since Music's rarest artists cheer my muse,
> I care not who my want of skill accuse.

He promised these songs in 1613 and delivered fifty-three of them to
the press in 1614. There was doubtless some manuscript circulation of
Leighton's poetry going on alongside the official printed edition, but the
surviving evidence shows that the whole process must have happened
very quickly. It seems to have been, above all, a vast exercise in public
relations by a man who had fallen out of favor (much more spectacularly
than Byrd ever did in the 1580s) and wished to restore his own reputation
through an elaborate show of penitence and artistic patronage. There are
several flowery prefaces—including a dedication to King James's son
Prince Charles—and a dozen commendatory poems from Leighton's
friends and colleagues. Some of them seem to show genuine sympathy
for him in his recent troubles, while others are mostly taken up with
banal literary conceits and bad puns on Leighton's name. The book is
adorned in several places by a large emblem (Figure 15.1), specially
engraved for the occasion, with a five-voice perpetual canon printed in
a circle and surrounded by the names of all the musical contributors.
Byrd's name is featured prominently above the beginning of the
melody.

Byrd must have brought some degree of personal interest—for whatever reason—to Leighton's project. By his mid-seventies he was clearly
not the sort to be easily persuaded, much less coerced, or to follow a
crowd of younger composers for fashion's sake. (Some of their contributions, such as Dowland's *A heart that's broken and contrite*, are elegant trifles
that might have been written in an hour. Other Leighton songs, such as
those by Peerson, Lupo, and the lutenist Robert Jones, are more demon-
strative and experimental.) It is somewhat disappointing to discover that

FIGURE 15.1   Emblem from the title page of William Leighton's *Tears or Lamentations of a Sorrowful Soul* (1614)

Byrd's four songs are of uneven quality, with their share of uninspired or even dull passages. The opening of *Look down O Lord* is certainly a sound piece of word illustration, but he rarely wrote such an ungrateful or unvocal line; there is also the occasional fleeting moment, as in the latter part of *I laid me down to rest*, where the part-writing simply seems to go awry. Byrd is more successful elsewhere in the 1614 collection. He had always been inspired by texts in a melancholic vein, and Leighton's poem *Come help O God* clearly appealed to that side of his temperament. He chose a striking minor mode—G with two flats—which he had favored in some of his most intense and earnest works. The text is typical of Leighton's style and mood:

> Come, help, O God,
> for Christ's sweet bloody sweat:

> I seek thy love, and fear thy rod,
> for mercy I entreat.
> My griefs remediless
> if mercy merciless.

The simplicity of Byrd's setting is an apt foil for the naïve text. The beginning phrase is hardly more than a murmur; repetitions of "my griefs" pass through the voices in an artless sequence (Example 15.1), and the crucial word "mercy" is set as a quiet syllabic plea. These are not the same expressive techniques Byrd would have used for this sort of penitential text thirty or forty years earlier, although there are still plenty of beautiful details—some brief chromatic inflections in the bass, the final cadence unfolding gracefully in the alto—that set *Come help O God* apart from the bulk of Jacobean devotional songs. The result is effective and ultimately quite moving; it certainly does not sound as if it was wrung from an unenthusiastic elderly composer by an ambitious gentleman poet eager to include the best names in his anthology. It was almost certainly the last sacred music Byrd ever wrote.

Leighton's book was the first English source of any kind to use the term "consort song." He used it to describe his opening set of seventeen songs, vocal pieces accompanied by the fashionable English broken consort—a group that combined viols with instruments such as lute, bandora, cittern, and recorder or flute. Byrd never composed for broken consort, or for mixed instrumental ensembles of any kind, but he did continue to write songs for solo voice and viols (what we would call consort songs in modern parlance) until the end of his career. Perhaps his last consort song of all was the elegy *Fair Britain isle*, on the death of the eighteen-year-old Prince Henry, elder son of James and heir to the throne. It is one of the relatively few consort songs by Byrd that can be given a more or less precise date. Henry died in November 1612, and his funeral took place in December. The song was probably written during the first wave of public grief in late 1612 and early 1613. Henry's unexpected death elicited a large number of artistic responses: there were elaborate sermons, prose elegies, poems (including one from Sir Walter Raleigh, whom Henry himself had tried to save—unsuccessfully in the end—from imprisonment and execution), and numerous works of music. Tomkins responded to the news with the poignant verse anthem *Know*

Ex. 15.1 *Come help O God,* mm. 40–48

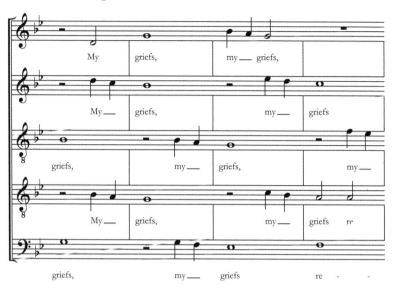

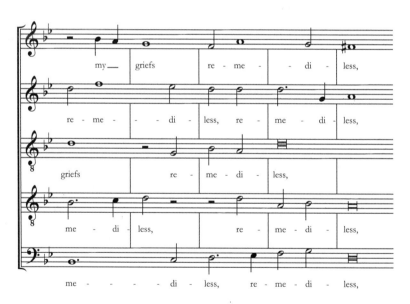

you not, which one of the manuscript sources calls "Prince Henry his Funeral Anthem." Not long after, Campion and Coperario published their 1613 "Songs of Mourning, bewailing the untimely death of Prince Henry," a collection of music for solo voice and lute. Thomas Vautor, John Ward, and a number of other composers also wrote songs in the prince's memory. Byrd's musical contribution was only one among many.

We owe the survival of *Fair Britain isle*, like that of many other Byrd consort songs, to the tenacity of the Paston scribes, who loved to collect elegies on the death of distinguished figures—and indeed on the death of royalty, as in *Crowned with flowers and lilies*, Byrd's lament for Queen Mary I, or *The noble famous Queen*, another Byrd song adapted by Edward Paston to words commemorating Mary, Queen of Scots. Although *Fair Britain isle* is demonstrably a very late work, it shows Byrd turning to a number of devices he had used in earlier songs of a serious nature. First among these techniques was the consort-song form itself, which by now was associated with several generations' worth of laments and elegies. Byrd made the distinctly old-fashioned choice to write a strophic song: two verses, both set to the same music. He seems to have kept both verses in mind as he composed, at least given the remarkably effective ending of the second stanza, the plangent upward leap to the top D (Example 15.2) on "the *hope* of age of gold," the hope that had been dashed at Henry's untimely death. (It is hard not to recall the almost identical wail of grief— "and Music dies"—that concludes *Ye sacred Muses*, Byrd's 1585 elegy for Tallis.) Byrd also makes free use of other expressive devices—most notably the brooding semitonal figure that begins each instrumental part and defines the contour of the first vocal phrase.

The closest parallels to this song are probably Byrd's laments in the late 1580s on the death of Sidney, another popular figure who died young and was mourned widely in poetry and song. Byrd may well have had some contact with Sidney through their shared courtly and literary connections: a piece such as *O that most rare breast* shows signs of being a sincere tribute paid by one artist to another. Given Byrd's gradual withdrawal from court circles late in life, it is hard to know whether there was much, if any, element of personal grief in *Fair Britain isle*. He may well have felt a twinge of relief at the passing of Henry, who had already acquired something of a reputation as a staunch young Protestant who would clear up the maddening ambiguities of the Jacobean church and

Ex. 15.2 *Fair Britain isle*, mm. 33–39, second verse

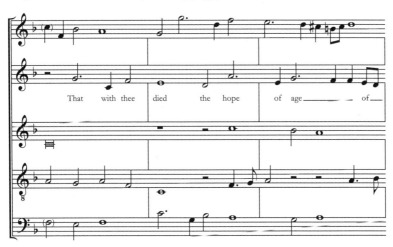

lead England into a new golden age of reform. He might also have felt genuine regret at the death of a prince who was already known as a patron of the arts and a young man of some artistic promise. (If Byrd ever met him in person, it may have been as a guest of the musical Petre family at Thorndon Hall, where the prince made an overnight visit in 1608.) Henry was tutored privately in music by Ferrabosco, who dedicated a volume of lute songs to him. His court was the scene of some impressive musical achievements: it is worth recalling that Tallis's great forty-part motet *Spem in alium* has only survived because of an English adaptation, *Sing and glorify*, made for Henry's investiture as Prince of Wales in 1610.

Byrd's very last instrumental works were also connected with the English royal family. The keyboard anthology called *Parthenia*, first published in late 1612 or early 1613, includes eight pieces by Byrd, alongside seven by Bull and six by Gibbons. The collection was assembled as a wedding gift for James's daughter Princess Elizabeth (later immortalized as the "Winter Queen" of the Thirty Years' War) and her German fiancé Frederick V, Elector Palatine. "Parthenia" means "maiden songs," and the full title—*Parthenia, or the Maidenhead of the first music that ever was printed for the Virginal*—was a complex pun on the book's pioneering role as the first printed keyboard music in England, the status of the young bride to whom it was offered, and the English practice of referring to plucked keyboard instruments as "virginals." (The same play on words was made in a less delicate way by George Abbot, the Archbishop of Canterbury, who said in 1613 of the recently disgraced Bull that "the man hath more music than honesty and is as famous for marring of virginity as he is for fingering of organs and virginals.")

Parthenia was indeed the first collection of its kind: it broke new ground in English music publishing. It was printed from engraved copper plates rather than old-fashioned moveable metal type of the sort used by printers such as East and Vautrollier. Moveable type was well suited to polyphonic music in individual parts, but it was inconvenient to adapt to keyboard music on multiple staves. The new practice of music engraving, which finally came into its own in England in the early seventeenth century, was a perfect match for complex Jacobean keyboard styles. The result (Figure 15.2) is a compact, elegant and efficient presentation of a sort of music that until then had been preserved only in manuscript. *Parthenia* brought English keyboard music almost overnight into circulation on the Continent. Nearly all the surviving seventeenth-century European sources of Byrd's music appear to be copied, directly or indirectly, from this single book.

Byrd published several pavans and galliards in *Parthenia*, interspersed with two brief preludes of the sort he had been cultivating since his years

FIGURE 15.2 Byrd's pavan for the Earl of Salisbury, from *Parthenia* (1612/13)

as an organist in Lincoln in the 1560s. The first pavan-and-galliard pair is, rather surprisingly, a revision of an older work: the tenth Nevell set, dedicated in 1591 to the fifteen-year-old William Petre (by now Sir William Petre, as he is called in the printed book). It is not surprising that he wanted to make a final musical tribute to the Petres, who had supported him so assiduously through his career. The original version of the Petre pavan included a flamboyant ending with syncopated figuration in the right hand and a bass line plunging to the low C at the bottom of Byrd's keyboard. When he revised the piece twenty years later, he stripped down the final cadence to a much simpler form. That did not keep him from some gleeful shows of virtuosity elsewhere in *Parthenia*, most notably in the bounding figuration of the *Brownlow* galliard (Example 15.3), a piece that irresistibly recalls the musical language of Byrd's younger contemporaries.

Ex. 15.3 Galliard in C, no. 4 (Mistress Mary Brownlow; BK 34), mm. 41–42

Byrd's contribution to *Parthenia* ends with a group of three pieces dedicated to Robert Cecil, first earl of Salisbury. It is unlike any other pavan-and-galliard group he ever wrote. There are three items—one pavan followed by two related galliards—instead of the usual matched pair. The pavan and the first galliard have just two separate strains rather than the usual three, each strain only eight bars long, and Byrd does not write out any ornamented reprises: he simply puts repeat signs around each section. The almost shocking concision and reserve of these three pieces confirms what already seems likely from their dedication: they were unusually late works composed as a memorial for Salisbury, a patron and supporter of Byrd, who died just a few months before *Parthenia* was printed.

The Salisbury pavan (Example 15.4 shows it in full) is one of the very rare pieces by Byrd—the 1611 song *What is life, or worldly pleasure?* is another—that we might suspect not to be his work at all if it were not attributed to him in a reputable printed source. The harmonic plan is curiously modern: the first half ending on the dominant, the second half beginning with a quick sequential turn to what we would now call the relative major before reverting gracefully to the original minor mode. Any composer of the late seventeenth or early eighteenth century would have been content with a similar process. (This distinctly un-archaic tonal scheme may well have contributed to the popularity of the Salisbury pavan in later centuries, even at moments when most of Byrd's keyboard music was not widely known or appreciated. It made its way into the standard piano repertory, was arranged for orchestra by enthusiasts such as Stokowski and Barbirolli, and was even reworked by an enterprising Edwardian cleric named Alfred Whitehead into the four-voice anthem *I have longed for thy saving health*—which, if nothing else, underscores how firmly the pavan was grounded in real four-part counterpoint.)

Byrd never wrote a simpler or more lucid keyboard piece. Although the texture is sparse and unadorned, there is no lack of expressive detail, such as the single F$\sharp$ giving a brief modal tinge to the first phrase, or the nostalgic descending tetrachord in the bass (a very Baroque gesture) that concludes the first strain. Perhaps loveliest of all is the middle of the second strain, with its pungent bass G$\sharp$ under an unexpected mid-measure syncopation in the top voice, where time seems to stand still for a moment on the highly colored sonority that musicians would eventually come to

Ex. 15.4 Pavan in a, no. 2 (Earl of Salisbury; BK 15)

call a first-inversion seventh chord. (Some twentieth-century interpreta-
tions of the piece, quite unforgivably, ruined the effect by simplifying the
rhythm of this line.) Every note in the Salisbury pavan falls effortlessly
into place, from the first chord to the last. Like the tiniest *Gradualia* pieces
or the little three-part viol fantasias, it is a jewel-like miniature, a musical
epigram.

Once Byrd had completed this final group of works, he seems to have stopped composing for good. If he produced anything after 1614, it has almost certainly not survived. We hear very little from him during his last ten years. There are some scattered hints that he was still involved at least tangentially with public musical life, evidence such as the provision of mourning livery for his attendance at Queen Anne's funeral in 1619 or the extraordinary proposal made for the new royal theatre in 1620. The steady stream of recusancy citations finally dries up in Byrd's last years, although he was still named in 1619 for willfully employing a domestic servant "knowing that [he] had not been to church for three months," and the last mention of his recusancy occurs as late as 1621. He may have been too old and infirm to be considered worth prosecuting for non-attendance, even though his presence in London in January 1622 as a witness to his brother John's will is evidence that he was still active and able to travel into his eighties. In his own will, made (or at least copied out for the last time) in November 1622, he describes himself as "being of good health and perfect memory." In the same year, Tomkins called him "my ancient and most reverenced master," and Henry Peacham made his famous tribute to him in the *Compleat Gentleman*:

> For motets, and music of piety and devotion, as well for the honour of our nation, as the merit of the man, I prefer above all other our Phoenix, M. William Byrd, whom in that kind, I know not whether any may equal, I am sure, none excel, even by the judgement of France and Italy, who are very sparing in the commendation of strangers.

Byrd died on 4 July 1623. The Cheque Book of the Chapel Royal records the date and commemorates him as "a father of music." The cause of his death, unlike that of his unlucky predecessor Robert Parsons, is not known. His place in the Chapel was taken by "a countertenor of Westminster" named John Croker. His will, the last surviving document we have from his hand, reveals something about his contentious family life but nothing at all about his rich musical life. When Tallis died in 1585, he had made arrangements for his share of the music-printing monopoly, left a substantial bequest to his "company" of the Chapel Royal, and named two of his Chapel colleagues as overseers of his will. There is nothing of the kind in Byrd's will. He does not mention any of his musical colleagues, perhaps because he outlived so many of them. The most personal touch is his brief prayer "that I may live and die a true and perfect member" of the "holy Catholic Church, without which I believe there is no salvation for me." He also expressed a wish to be "honestly buried," if possible beside his wife in their home parish of Stondon Massey. (This was the same parish church they had stubbornly refused to attend or support for decades: was there some softening of convictions near the end?) There is no record of whether Byrd's request was carried out, and his grave has never been found.

CHAPTER SIXTEEN

Students and Legacy

My loving master (never without reverence to be named of the musicians)
M. Byrd . . .

　　　　　　　—*Thomas Morley, 1597*

WITH THE DEATH OF BYRD IN 1623, A GENERATION OF ENGLISH composers came to an end. The younger musicians who followed him had grown up in a very different environment: they had no living memory of pre-Reformation sacred music and barely knew the older traditions of English secular song. Although these younger composers were formed by a new musical world, surprisingly few of them escaped Byrd's influence altogether—whether they were innovative or conservative, Anglican cathedral musicians or Catholic emigrants to Europe, given primarily to instrumental music or to vocal music. Morley, Tomkins, Bull, and Philips were all students of his, and any other English musician who came of age in the late sixteenth or early seventeenth century would doubtless have been well aware of him and his work.

Thomas Morley seems to have worked quite closely with Byrd in his apprentice years. The seventeenth-century antiquarian Anthony à Wood recalled that "by this Byrd's endeavors the said Morley became not only excellent in music, as well as in the theoretical as practical part, but also well seen in the Mathematics, in which Byrd was excellent." One of Morley's very first compositions, the motet *Domine Dominus noster* (which he wrote in 1576 at the age of nineteen), is deeply indebted to the style of Byrd's *Cantiones*: in fact its last five measures are lifted note for note from Byrd's *Libera me Domine et pone me*, which had been published just the year before. (The same attitude of breezy half-plagiarism would persist in Morley's later works, the madrigals adapted from the Italian *balletti* of Gastoldi and Anerio or the Latin motets that were in fact lightly retouched versions of pieces by Philips and Rogier.) He was certainly the Byrd pupil who made the most of his connection with the old master—which was not too surprising, given his notable streak of professional ambition.

Morley had something else in common with Byrd: he was profoundly involved with the political and religious controversies of his day. Like several other musicians of his generation, perhaps most notably John Dowland, he showed serious interest in Catholicism—even to the point of converting and becoming "reconciled" to the old church—but soon found himself out of his depth and returned in panic to a respectable Anglican viewpoint. He was acquainted with the recusant Paston family, who recommended him as a music teacher in 1587 and may have helped introduce him, via their copious manuscript collection, to the repertory of sixteenth-century Italian madrigals that would influence so much of his own work. He also became entangled in the world of international espionage during these years, which made his situation all the more risky. Byrd's Catholic associate Charles Paget, himself a musician and something of a notorious double agent, tells the story in a letter sent from the Netherlands in 1591:

> There is one Morley that playeth on the organs in Paul's [St. Paul's Cathedral, where he was employed in the early 1590s] that was with me in my house. He seemed here to be a good Catholic and was reconciled, but notwithstanding suspecting his behaviour I intercepted letters that Mr. Nowell wrote to him, whereby I discovered enough to have hanged him. Nevertheless he showing with tears great repentance, and asking on his knees forgiveness, I was content to let him go. I hear since his coming thither he hath played the promoter and apprehendeth Catholics.

After this close call, Morley seems to have backed away from political engagement and turned his energies to music publishing. He obtained the royal monopoly for printing music that had originally been granted to Tallis and Byrd. In the last decade of his life, between 1592 and 1602, he produced a dozen songbooks and a textbook on musical composition. His *Plain and Easy Introduction* is a unique document of Elizabethan musical pedagogy, and there is no doubt that much of its content—as he himself said—reflects the lessons he had learned from Byrd. He dedicated it to his teacher in the warmest terms, thanking him for the gift of musical knowledge, through which "the faculties of the reasonable soul be stirred up to enter into contemplation, and searching of more than earthly things":

> The consideration of this hath moved me to publish these labors of mine under your name both to signify unto the world my thankful mind, and also to notify unto yourself in some sort the entire love and unfeigned affection which I bear unto you... Accept (I pray you) of this book, both that you may exercise your deep skill in censuring of what shall be amiss, as also defend what is in it truly spoken, as that which sometime proceeded from yourself.

Many of the technical details in the *Plain and Easy Introduction* can be traced back to Byrd's own practices. Morley seems also to have been influenced by his teacher's more general approach to music. He describes the process of musical study as "contemplation," an unmistakable echo of Byrd's views. He tells his students that "there is no way readier to cause you to become perfect, than to contend with some one or other." That sort of creative rivalry, what Henry Peacham (in discussing the music of Byrd and Ferrabosco) called "friendly emulation," was among the chief inspirations of Morley's career. He flung himself headlong into the competitive world of musical editing and publishing, and he certainly ventured further into the evolving styles of Elizabethan secular music than his teacher was ever willing to go. His last book, published two years before he died, was a collection of lute songs (including a setting of Shakespeare's "It was a lover and his lass") optimistically entitled *The First Book of Ayres*. When Byrd lamented in the introduction to his 1607 *Gradualia* that he had outlived so many of his students, he must have had Morley's recent and untimely death (just five years earlier) in mind.

Some of Byrd's pupils went on composing well into the seventeenth century. Thomas Tomkins, who described him in 1622 as "my ancient and most reverenced master," survived him by several decades. His most direct tribute to his teacher was the dedication of a five-voice madrigal called *Too much I once lamented*. This graceful, rather moody piece begins with Byrd's favored technique of rising and falling semitonal figures, which Tomkins combines to create some pungent and quite Baroque-sounding diminished sevenths. He follows them with a series of quintessentially English fa-la-la refrains, something that Byrd, even in his lightest secular works, never once indulged in. Tomkins must have been aware of the incongruity: what he writes in the end is perhaps the most melancholy fa-la-la in the whole surviving repertory of English madrigals.

Tomkins had ample reason for melancholy in his later years. He lived long enough to see the ravages of the Civil War and the wholesale destruction of much of the English cathedral tradition. The new organ at Worcester Cathedral, which had been installed through his own "industry" and "mediation," was broken up when the city was besieged in 1646. One of his last compositions was a plaintive keyboard piece, *A sad pavan for these distracted times*, written in 1649 just after the execution of King Charles I. The style is reminiscent of Byrd's most expressive keyboard works, with an added layer of wandering chromatic harmony. As in many of Tomkins's other keyboard pavans, the underlying symmetry of phrases—which had been such a stubbornly held principle in Byrd's keyboard music—is regularly sacrificed to make way for local harmonic or melodic effect.

Despite his use of some distinctly seventeenth-century mannerisms, Tomkins was at heart a musical conservative and indeed something of an antiquarian. This is clear both in the music he wrote (most notably his vast output of church anthems) and in the music he collected. He began his handwritten list of "lessons of worth" with Tallis's "offertory," the virtuosic and quite old-fashioned *Felix namque* that had made such an impression on the young Byrd in the 1560s. He owned a copy of the *Plain and Easy Introduction* in which he made his own handwritten notes, including some contributions to Morley's list of famous English composers and four new canons on one of Morley's model plainsong melodies. Even in Tomkins's last years, the Elizabethan influence was never too far out of earshot.

Other composers of this generation were linked to Byrd in less direct ways. Thomas Weelkes had access to some unusually clear and accurate versions of his keyboard works, which implies a musical connection of some kind between the two men—although Byrd did not have very much in common with Weelkes, who was a brilliant madrigalist with little patience for displays of learned counterpoint or the ambitions of court and church. He died in the same year as Byrd, at the age of just forty-seven, having been dismissed from his post as organist of Chichester Cathedral after years of habitual drunkenness and insubordination. His own preface to the book of five- and six-voice madrigals he published in 1600 (including the unforgettable *Thule, the period of cosmography*) shows a flash of defiance in the face of the cultural pretensions of his age: "many of us musicians think it as much praise to be somewhat more than musicians, as it is for gold to be somewhat more than gold."

Orlando Gibbons was a profoundly talented musician who was the youngest (by a good two decades) of the contributors to *Parthenia*. There is no real evidence that he was a student of Byrd's, but he may well have been the instrumental composer who followed most immediately in his footsteps. He wrote a number of keyboard pavans and galliards, as well as variations on *The Hunt's Up* and *The Woods so Wild* (both set by Byrd), and a group of delightful three-part string fantasias, whose upper voices seem to have been intended for violins—new and rather exotic foreign instruments that were very much in vogue in the 1620s. Gibbons also followed Byrd in his illustrious career as a favored court musician, which went on unclouded until his sudden illness and death (in the company of his Chapel Royal colleagues) while waiting to receive the new queen Henrietta Maria from abroad in 1625.

A number of Byrd's younger contemporaries decided to leave England and live out their musical lives elsewhere. Some of these émigrés were Catholics who found the situation at home difficult or intolerable. Both Peter Philips and John Bull fell into that category, though for rather different reasons. Philips was a student of Byrd, as we know from Luis de Groote's 1610 letter of recommendation, and he seems to have spent much of his youth in London under the care of Byrd's colleague Sebastian Westcote, the resourceful and staunchly Catholic choirmaster of St. Paul's Cathedral. (The Protestant bishop of London was already complaining in the 1560s that Westcote influenced his choristers with "lessons of false religion.") By his early twenties, Philips had emigrated to Rome and found work as an organist at the English College. He spent five years traveling through Europe in the service of the ubiquitous Pagets, found himself embroiled in political intrigues (which landed him in prison for several weeks, where he took the opportunity to compose a *Pavana* and

Galliarda Dolorosa), and eventually settled in Brussels at the court of the Archdukes Albert and Isabella. He spent the rest of his life there, working alongside Peter Paul Rubens and other illustrious figures of the northern Counter-Reformation. He was ordained to the priesthood after the death of his wife, and by middle age he was writing exclusively devotional music—although he never repudiated his earlier works, which included more than fifty secular madrigals and a keyboard arrangement of Marenzio's brazenly erotic *Tirsi morir volea*.

Philips lived out his career between a number of rapidly diverging musical worlds. After his voluntary exile in 1582, he appears never to have come back to England, although Peacham wrote in 1622 that "our rare countryman, Peter Philips ... hath sent us over many excellent songs, as well motets as madrigals." Peacham noted that Philips's music "affecteth altogether the Italian vein," and Morley already counted him in 1598 among the "best approved Italian authors," but he went to the trouble of identifying himself as "Inglese" or "Anglus" on all his own title pages, and he never lost his distinctly English taste for contrapuntal elaboration and musical understatement. He launched his publishing career (as Morley did) by editing and anthologizing Italian madrigals, but his most substantial musical legacy is the group of nearly three hundred Latin motets he composed over the years. Most of them feature a basso continuo part, which is something Byrd certainly never included in any of his motets: in fact Philips, in his 1613 book of *Gemmulae Sacrae*, was the first English composer to use this quintessentially Baroque device in print.

Philips's certificate of residence in Brussels, made in 1597, declares that he had left home "for the Catholic faith." That statement may have been a bit duplicitous—his original decision to travel to Rome clearly had a great deal to do with his interest in Italian music—but he was obviously in sympathy with the ideals of the European Counter-Reformation and would not have made it very far as a professional musician in Protestant England (or, one suspects, as a musical servant in an isolated recusant country house). Other Catholic emigrants seem to have had yet more complicated motives. John Bull, another pupil of Byrd, claimed in a petition to the mayor of Antwerp that he had been driven into exile because of his Catholic convictions. It had become clear by then that he was also suffering the aftermath of various scandals in England, involving forced entry into a colleague's rooms, an assault on a minister during a church service, and charges of sexual impropriety—the last of which prompted George Abbot to make his wry comment about Bull having "more music than honesty." An English ambassador in Brussels, writing to King James in 1614, took an even more cynical view of the whole affair:

> It was notorious to all the world, the said Bull did not leave your Majesty's service for any wrong done unto him, or for matter of religion, under which feigned pretext he now sought to wrong the reputation of your Majesty's justice, but did in that dishonest manner steal out of England through the guilt of a corrupt conscience, to escape the punishment, which notoriously he had deserved, and was designed to have been inflicted on him by the hand of justice, for his incontinence, fornication, adultery, and other grievous crimes.

Bull must have known that his reputation was not likely to recover. He had already left England in 1613, only a few months after his illustrious appearance in *Parthenia*, and he never once returned during the remaining fifteen years of his life. Although he did not fit the mold of the pious exiles who were (rather unquestioningly) glorified in English recusant folklore, he seems to have been remarkably well suited to the life of a European keyboard player and composer. Bull's music had a close connection to that of Sweelinck, whom he commemorated in 1621, the year of his death, with a fantasia on one of his fugal themes. Bull's own keyboard style was characterized above all by elaborate figuration and relentless virtuosity: there are entire pages of his music that could have been drawn straight from Czerny's *School of Velocity*. (Tomkins captured the essence of Bull's style when he called it "excellent for the hand.") That was not a tendency he had inherited directly from Byrd, although there are certainly passages in the older composer's fantasias and variation sets that show a similar if more disciplined exuberance. Byrd himself seems to have been influenced by Bull's style in some late works such as the *Brownlow* galliard.

Like Byrd, Bull was also a collector of books: he is among the very few composers of the English Renaissance whose libraries can be reconstructed with some degree of security. His surviving books, not too surprisingly, all have to do with music in various ways. There are handwritten copies of madrigals in score, various sixteenth-century music publications, and the venerable medieval treatises of Boethius and Guido of

Arezzo, links to a much older European musical and pedagogical tradition.

Unlike so many of the younger contemporaries discussed here, Byrd seems never even to have visited Europe, much less tried his hand at emigration. The only hint that he had any interest in travel is his ownership of a book with "certain brief and special instructions for gentlemen, merchants, etc. employed in services abroad." There is a tantalizing entry in the guest register of the English College in Rome recording a November 1616 visit by someone named William Byrd, but it is highly unlikely that this was the elderly composer, who seems to have been at home in Essex at the time, dodging the last of his recusancy fines. It is difficult to know how much direct knowledge of Byrd's music actually penetrated beyond the English Channel. Baldwin wrote as early as 1591 that "far to strange countries abroad his skill doth shine," and Peacham said that he was unexcelled "even by the judgement of France and Italy," but there is relatively little musical evidence to back up their claims, beyond the eventual appearance of a few printed collections in European libraries. His keyboard style certainly made a mark in northern Europe, where keyboard music flourished in the hands of English exiles such as Philips and Bull. We can be reasonably sure that he also intended his masses and motets to have something of an international influence, but there is no real sign that this ever happened.

Although Byrd enjoyed immense popularity in his native England, it did not last very long. By the later seventeenth century, his music had already become the province of antiquarians as much as practicing musicians. There were some scattered exceptions. *Parthenia* went through numerous reprints, the last in 1659, and copies continued to circulate among amateur keyboard players and their teachers for several more generations. Some of Byrd's Anglican church works persisted in the everyday repertory of cathedral choirs. Most of his instrumental music and virtually all of his secular vocal music was soon forgotten—as was his vast output of Latin-texted polyphony, which had outlived its immediate usefulness even in the most serious recusant circles. Rather little of the ongoing Jacobean and Caroline enthusiasm for his work survived the disasters of the Civil War and the subsequent refounding of English musical life during the Restoration. (Henry Purcell was among the noble exceptions: he knew Byrd's anthems and copied several of them into his musical commonplace book.)

Interest in Byrd's music seems to have reached a low ebb in the eighteenth century. Charles Burney could write bluntly in his 1789 *General History of Music* that "Tallis and Byrd, who were equally admirable in their musical productions and execution, are now only known and revered by the curious." A number of Byrd's works were revived by the enthusiasts of the Madrigal Society and the Musical Antiquarian Society, and by individual admirers such as Samuel Wesley (who proposed an edition of the *Gradualia* in the 1820s), but it was not until the Tudor-music revival of the early twentieth century, led by ambitious figures such as Edmund Fellowes and Richard Terry, that people finally began editing, performing, and studying a truly representative selection of his music. Much of it had to wait for nearly four hundred years before its quality was once again fully appreciated.

CHAPTER SEVENTEEN

Afterthoughts

Write all these down . . .
—*Psalms, Songs and Sonnets, 1611*

THOMAS TALLIS WAS FAMOUSLY EULOGIZED AS "MILD AND QUIET." WE have no contemporary epitaph for Byrd, but if one existed, it would certainly not include those words. What do we really know about him as a person? What inspired such admiration and loyalty among his colleagues? Before we make any attempt to canonize Byrd as a hero of the English Renaissance, we might want to call on the proverbial devil's advocate for a summary of the negative evidence. The picture this paints is not too flattering, but it offers some additional insight into Byrd's character—and perhaps even, in the end, into what made him such an attractive figure.

One of the earliest documents of Byrd's career shows a young organist locked in dispute with his cathedral chapter. When his salary was suspended, he held out for almost nine months, even though he had a growing family to support. Given the amount of energy he spent defending his legal and financial interests, it is surprising that he had time to compose at all. He was hardly lying when he wrote in his mid-sixties that "I have worn out my life in Music," but we know that much of his life was also worn out in convoluted and petty rivalries. It is no wonder that he described his musical compositions as his "night labors." In the collection of printed books he bought and signed, we see a quite different daylight personality: hungry for scandalous news, intrigued by political and religious polemic, preoccupied with legal minutiae. This is the character that emerges in Jane Shelley's "grievances" against Byrd, the ruthless landlord of Stondon Place who "said that if he could not hold it by right, he would hold it by might." When one of his associates decided to stop supporting his case against Shelley, "the said Byrd did give him vile and bitter words for doing the same."

"If not by right, by might"; "vile and bitter words." These notes were made in 1608, just a year after Byrd's touching declarations of gratitude and friendship to another neighbor in the second *Gradualia* preface. Of course Shelley's document was hardly impartial, but it is still surprising to hear of a well-loved composer speaking in such terms. The report itself was addressed to none other than Robert Cecil, earl of Salisbury. Cecil added a dismissive handwritten comment of his own that gives some hint of the irritation Byrd's patrons and associates must eventually have felt at this sort of thing: he referred the case to a group of judges "who are better acquainted with the whole proceedings than I am, and will take some leisure to hear her complaint, for I have none." Byrd was apparently willing to do whatever it took to win in court. At one point he even put words into the mouth of King James himself, supplying him (in what can only be called an extraordinary show of nerve) with a draft of a lengthy first-person letter that demanded restitution of property to "our servant William Byrd, gentleman of our Chapel."

Byrd's tendency toward "bitter words" seems to have persisted to the end of his life. After the gentle introduction to his will—a model of piety and resignation—his very first bequest, of his farm in Essex, soon lapses into complaints about "the undutiful obstinacy of one whom I am unwilling to name." There can hardly be a clearer indication, at a distance of four centuries, that he went to his grave still nursing a grudge. He was well acquainted with obstinacy, and he appears to have passed it on to his descendants along with his worldly possessions. (In the late 1590s he had outfitted his entire household in Stondon Massey with running water via "pipes of lead," which may not have contributed to the sanity or equanimity of the Byrd family.) On the next page of his will, he threatens to disown his son Thomas if he should "seek by law or other ways to disturb or trouble my executors." His wishes were not fulfilled in the end. Less than a year after his death, his children were already squabbling in court about what he had really left to whom.

The "loving Master" portrayed in Morley's *Plain and Easy Introduction* is not too many pages removed from the irascible old composer who throws a plainsong book at his colleague's head. These are clearly two sides of the same complex character. Volatile times breed volatile personalities, and we hear similar anecdotes about other distinguished Elizabethans: Philip Sidney and the Earl of Oxford exchanging schoolboy insults on the tennis court, or Queen Elizabeth threatening to fling a shoe at her unnamed "Master of Music" (perhaps Byrd himself) for allowing John Bolt, one of her prize musicians, to emigrate and leave her service. Such displays of temper were often a symptom of deeper ideological rifts. Byrd was a man of strong opinions, both artistic and political, that more or less predestined him to a life of debate and controversy. He was not the mild-mannered ecumenical figure imagined by a biographer such as Edmund Fellowes, who could brush off the composer's nonconformist activities in a short chapter on "Byrd's Association with the Catholics." By his forties Byrd was effectively flaunting his recusancy in public, which could not have been a comfortable position for a professional courtier. It is also worth recalling that his family background was (and, beyond his own household, remained) thoroughly Protestant. He was as much an outsider among his relatives as he was at court.

Some of Byrd's most sublime music can be traced back to the house chapels and secret meeting places of his fellow Catholics. Despite some recent glorifications of recusancy in CD notes and concert programs, that milieu was not all sweetness and light. A darker atmosphere can be perceived in influential Catholic texts such as the Douai–Rheims Bible, where almost every verse of the Scriptures is pressed into polemical service, "phantasy" and human imagination is something to be distrusted, and even the explanatory note on the word "Alleluia" is a grim-faced denunciation of "schism and heresy." If (as Philip Brett and others have suggested) Byrd took the Douai–Rheims annotations as his constant guide and companion while working on his *Gradualia* and later devotional songs, he was composing, night after night, in an atmosphere of interior bitterness which would rival that of any Jacobean pamphleteer. It is difficult to reconcile that image with what we know about his professional life and his all-consuming love of music. He certainly made his share of compromises as he went along. Could his more zealous recusant associates, steeped in the mythology of the exile and the martyr, have considered him a lukewarm Catholic? He must have alienated some of them by doing things that did not suit their ideals: writing a splendid new vernacular service for the Chapel Royal, acquiring the latest antipapist literature, seeking approval for his printed work from Church of England censors. He could not be appropriated fully by either side, a fact that may itself have contributed to his success and longevity.

Byrd appears to have been universally respected among his fellow musicians, although there is an occasional hint of frustration at his conservative ways, not unlike the attitude shown by some of J. S. Bach's younger contemporaries toward their old master. Of course anybody with Byrd's sheer musical skill, however repellent his temperament, would have been admired (if a bit grudgingly) by his professional colleagues. Byrd also earned admiration and respect from a wide variety of non-musicians. He moved easily in the highest social circles of Renaissance England, something a fanatic or a crank could never have done. He seems to have enjoyed hospitality wherever he went. A number of houses made provision for "Mr. Byrd's chamber" or "lodging." The Petres supplied their distinguished guest with a feather bed, the Pagets with a harpsichord, and the Somersets with access to one of the best music libraries in England. The Earl of Northumberland, recommending Byrd (his daughter's music tutor at the time) to a friend, wrote simply that "the man is honest." He was stubborn, ambitious, and quite capable of holding a grudge, but he was also known for his integrity and loyalty. One Catholic associate, a manufacturer of tapestries, defended him in the strongest terms: "of Mr. Byrd you are not worthy, and we take comfort in him as a lean-to by whom we are relieved upon every casual wreck."

The same integrity is apparent in Byrd's music, with its consistently high degree of craftsmanship and eloquence. He seems to have been almost incapable of allowing an inferior piece into print—or, if he could help it, even into manuscript circulation. A rare lapse of judgment may have been recorded by the eighteenth-century scribe John Alcock, who tells us, presumably from information in a now-lost partbook, that the pleasant but unremarkable motet *Domine tu iurasti* "in the opinion of Mr. Byrd himself is the best he ever composed." We are free to disregard this as the misguided ramblings of an antiquarian, but we should recall that Alcock is also the sole source for our knowledge of, among other things, Byrd's international musical exchange with Philippe de Monte in the 1580s. There are certainly a few places—the ridiculous C-major jangle of the *Battle*, the occasional moment of blank weariness in the *Gradualia*, some thoroughly uninspired passages in the English psalms—where Byrd falls short of his usual standard. Such lapses, when they occur, remind us of how high that standard really was.

It is almost impossible to imagine the Elizabethan or Jacobean musical world without Byrd in it. Joseph Kerman has compared his pervasive influence to that of Schoenberg in the twentieth century. Byrd was an accomplished teacher, and apparently an eager one: he even complained at one point, rather disarmingly, that his Chapel Royal duties cut into the time he had set aside for private teaching. He worked closely with a large number of other musicians. In fact the whole story of his career can be told as a series of musical collaborations. His first surviving work was part of a joint project with his older colleagues Sheppard and Mundy. His debut in print, and his entrance into the musical life of the court, was undertaken in partnership with Tallis. As a mature composer, he engaged in "friendly emulation" with European contemporaries such as Ferrabosco and Monte. Near the end of his life, he joined forces with the next generation of English musicians in *Parthenia* and the Leighton songbook. Compare the careers of Josquin or Lassus, both excellent composers and strong personalities, who (as far as we know) never collaborated with anyone in any significant way.

Byrd was unusually skilled in the art of political influence and the cultivation of friends in high places, but his success was more than a matter of politics. His music, at its best, seems to have transcended many of the ideological divisions of the time. The words of his elegy for Sidney—"Foes to the cause thy prowess did defend"—speak just as well to his own situation. Even his most overtly Catholic music was acquired, performed, and treasured by all sorts of people, many of whom did not share his religious beliefs. His work was equally appreciated by those who did not share his artistic convictions. A thoroughly modern "Englishman Italianated" such as Morley had little time, in the end, for his teacher's ideas of decorum or compositional process, but he could still speak movingly of his "unfeigned love" for Byrd and his music. Reading through

Byrd's own prefaces, it is hard not to be struck by the constant reiteration of such terms: love of music, pleasure, sweetness, delight. He was an unapologetic advocate of musical beauty, and it shows in almost every page of his work. His view is summed up eloquently in his 1605 note to the reader: *Honor quidem Dei, voluptas autem vestra sit*—let the honor be God's, but let the pleasure be yours.

Documents of Byrd's Life

1540	Birthdate according to Byrd's legal deposition (made in 1598)
1543	Birthdate according to Byrd's will (signed 1622, but perhaps drafted earlier)
1554	List made naming brothers Simon and John as former choristers (ca. 1548) of St. Paul's Cathedral, London
1555	Sister Barbara marries London instrument maker Robert Broughe
1563	Appointed organist and master of choristers at Lincoln Cathedral
1563–67	Actively involved in recruitment of choristers to Lincoln
1567	Moves into house in Minster Yard, Lincoln
1568	Marries Julian Birley of Lincolnshire, at St. Margaret in the Close, Lincoln
	Approves the appointment of Christopher Wormehall to teach choristers
1569	First son, Christopher, born in Lincoln
	Unspecified controversy with cathedral chapter; salary suspended
1570	Organ playing at cathedral severely restricted; salary restored
1572	First daughter, Elizabeth, born in Lincoln
	Robert Parsons dies; Byrd appointed Gentleman of Chapel Royal in his place
1573	Writes to Thomas Paget from Clerkenwell Close, just outside the City of London
1574	First attempts to acquire property in Essex (eventually bought by brother John)
	Awarded annual payments from Lincoln Cathedral in exchange for continued provision of new music
1575	Byrd and Tallis granted royal patent for music printing
	Byrd and Tallis publish joint collection of Latin motets, *Cantiones quae ab argumento sacrae vocantur*
1576	Second son, Thomas, born in London (Tallis's godson)
	Receives gifts, including music paper, from Paget family
1577	Byrd and Tallis complain to Queen Elizabeth about financial failure of 1575 *Cantiones*

Family living at Harlington Manor, Middlesex; wife Julian listed as a recusant

1578   Presents supplication to Privy Council on behalf of brother John, imprisoned on suspicion of financial irregularities

1579   Death of brother Simon

1580   Letter to Byrd from Richard Sugeham, asking for "certain songs" and sending greetings to Tallis, Mundy, Blitheman, "and the rest"

Acquires and signs earliest surviving book in his library, Bateman's *New Arrival of the Three Graces into Anglia*

Listed among "great friends and aiders of [Catholics] beyond the seas"

1581   Complains of onerous duties at court

Appeals for money to aid the Catholic Tempest family

Described by Catholic associate Ralph Sheldon as "a lean-to by which we are relieved upon every casual wreck"

1582   Annual payments from Lincoln Cathedral discontinued

1583   Witnesses Tallis's will

1583–84 Exchanges eight-voice motets with Philippe de Monte

1584   First indicted for recusancy in Harlington

1585   Tallis dies; Byrd composes elegy *Ye sacred Muses*

Byrd's house searched for evidence of treasonous activity

Brother John inherits fleet of merchant ships from his father-in-law

1586   Regularly visiting Petre family at Thorndon Hall and Ingatestone Hall in Essex

Composes elegies on the death of Sidney

Henry Edyall recalls singing "songs of Mr. Byrd" in Paget household

1588–90 Acquires and signs eight books, mostly anti-Catholic works of political controversy

1588   Publishes *Psalms, Sonnets and Songs*, printed by Thomas East, who will serve as his printer for the next two decades

Brother John's ships join the fight against the Spanish Armada

Byrd sets to music the Queen's verses on the English victory (*Look and bow down*; the piece survives only in fragmentary form)

1589   Publishes *Songs of Sundry Natures* and *Cantiones sacrae* I

Nephew William (John's son) dies on trading voyage to Africa

1590   Publishes two pieces in *The First Set of Italian Madrigals Englished*

1591   Publishes *Cantiones sacrae* II

My Lady Nevell's Book finished

Son Christopher marries Katherine More, great-granddaughter of Sir Thomas More

1592   Recusancy case against Byrd dropped "by order of the Queen"

1592–93 Publishes four-voice mass

1593–94 Publishes three-voice mass

1594   Final document of Byrd's residence in Harlington

Acquires and signs a legal textbook (Crompton, *L'authoritie et iurisdiction*)

1594–95 Publishes five-voice mass

Moves with family to Stondon Massey, Essex

1595   Byrd family first named as recusants in Essex

1596   Son Thomas admitted to English College in Valladolid, Spain

1597	Morley dedicates *Plain and Easy Introduction* to "his loving master" Byrd
1598	Makes legal deposition describing himself as "of the age of 58 years or thereabouts"
1599	Son Thomas expelled from English College in Valladolid
1601	Frequent dinner guest at Magdalen Herbert's house in London
1602	Acquires and signs two more books of anti-Catholic polemic
	Son Thomas back in London as Gresham Lecturer in Music
1603	Issued mourning livery for funeral of Queen Elizabeth
1604	Drafts letter for King James's signature concerning his own legal disputes
1605	Publishes *Gradualia* I
	Byrd and wife Julian indicted as "seducers" to recusancy; "they have been excommunicate these seven years"
1606	Plays "the organ and many other instruments" at clandestine Catholic gathering
	Ownership of *Gradualia* I used as evidence against suspected French spy Charles de Ligny
1607	Publishes *Gradualia* II
1608	Composes elegy (*With lilies white*) on the death of Catholic matriarch Lady Magdalen Montague
1609	Last appearance in Petre household accounts
1611	Publishes *Psalms, Songs and Sonnets*
1612	Refuses to contribute to upkeep of Stondon Massey parish church and bells
1612–13	Eight keyboard pieces published in *Parthenia*
	Composes elegy *Fair Britain isle* on the death of Prince Henry
1614	Four songs published in Leighton's *Tears or Lamentations*
1615	"summoned with his children to appear to give answer as concerning his [religious] profession"
1619	Issued mourning livery for funeral of Queen Anne, wife of King James
1621	Final indictment for recusancy
1622	Brother John dies in London; Byrd witnesses his will
	Byrd signs his own last will and testament
	Tomkins dedicates madrigal *Too much I once lamented* to Byrd
	Peacham describes Byrd as "our Phoenix" in *Complete Gentleman*
1623	Dies on 4 July; commemorated in Chapel Royal records as "a father of music"

List of Works

This list is designed to help the reader locate a full modern edition of any piece by Byrd. It is divided into four successive groups: Latin-texted music, English-texted music, consort music, and keyboard music. Each entry includes the title of the piece, the number of parts (if applicable), the collection in which it was originally printed (if applicable), and where to find the edition. Page references are to the Stainer & Bell *Byrd Edition* for the vocal and string works and to *Musica Britannica* for the keyboard works.

Example:
Ab ortu solis, 4v (1607): *BE* 7a/64
This piece is for 4 voices, was first published in 1607 in the second volume of *Gradualia*, and can be found in *Byrd Edition*, volume 7a, at page 64.

Latin-Texted Music

1575   *Cantiones quae ab argumento sacrae vocantur*
1589   *Cantiones sacrae* I
1591   *Cantiones sacrae* II
1605   *Gradualia* I
1607   *Gradualia* II

Ab ortu solis, 4v (1607): *BE* 7a/64
Ad Dominum cum tribularer, 8v: *BE* 8/50
Adoramus te Christe, 1v + 4 instruments (1605): *BE* 6a/1
Adorna thalamum tuum, 3v (1605): *BE* 6b/136
Afflicti pro peccatis nostris, 6v (1591): *BE* 3/212
Alleluia: Ascendit Deus, 5v (1607): *BE* 7b/11
Alleluia: Ave Maria, 5v (1605): *BE* 5/117
Alleluia: Cognoverunt discipuli, 4v (1607): *BE* 7a/75

Alleluia: Confitemini Domino / Laudate pueri, 3v: *BE* 8/1
Alleluia: Emitte spiritum tuum, 5v (1607): *BE* 7b/42
Alleluia: Vespere autem Sabbati, 3v (1605): *BE* 6b/117
Alma Redemptoris mater, 4v (1605): *BE* 6b/35
Angelus Domini, 3v (1605): *BE* 6b/123
Apparebit in finem, 5v (1589): *BE* 3/89
Ascendit Deus, 5v (1607): *BE* 7b/19
Aspice Domine de sede, 5v (1589): *BE* 2/156
Aspice Domine quia facta est, 6v (1575): *BE* 1/39
Assumpta est Maria, 5v (1605): *BE* 5/166
Attollite portas, 6v (1575): *BE* 1/52
Audivi vocem, 5v: *BE* 9/51
Ave Maria, 5v (1605): *BE* 5/83
Ave maris stella, 3v (1605): *BE* 6b/97
Ave regina, 4v (1605): *BE* 6b/44
Ave verum corpus, 4v (1605): *BE* 6a/82
Beata es virgo Maria, 5v (1605): *BE* 5/60
Beata virgo, 4v (1607): *BE* 7a/38
Beata viscera, 5v (1605): *BE* 5/65
Beati mundo corde, 5v (1605): *BE* 6a/53
Benedicta et venerabilis, 5v (1605): *BE* 5/50
Benigne fac Domine, 5v: *BE* 9/45
Cantate Domino, 6v (1591): *BE* 3/223
Christe qui lux es et dies, 5v: *BE* 8/14
Christus resurgens, 4v (1605): *BE* 6b/9
Cibavit eos, 4v (1605): *BE* 7a/137
Circumdederunt me, 5v (1591): *BE* 3/111
Circumspice Hierusalem, 6v: *BE* 9/84
Confirma hoc Deus, 5v (1607): *BE* 7b/49
Constitues eos principes, 6v (1607): *BE* 7b/91
Cunctis diebus, 6v (1591): *BE* 3/232
Da mihi auxilium, 6v (1575): *BE* 1/113
De lamentatione Hieremiae prophetae, 5v: *BE* 8/20
Defecit in dolore, 5v (1589): *BE* 2/1
Deo gratias, 4v (1605): *BE* 6b/82
Descendit de coelis, 6v (1591): *BE* 3/163
Deus in adiutorium, 6v: *BE* 9/12
Deus venerunt gentes, 5v (1589): *BE* 2/89
Dies sanctificatus, 4v (1607): *BE* 7a/14
Diffusa est gratia, 5v (1605): *BE* 5/136
Diliges Dominum, 8v (1575): *BE* 1/151
Domine ante te, 6v: *BE* 9/36
Domine exaudi…et clamor meus, 5v: *BE* 9/78
Domine exaudi…inclina, 5v (1591): *BE* 3/74
Domine non sum dignus, 6v (1591): *BE* 3/174
Domine praestolamur, 5v (1589): *BE* 2/15
Domine quis habitabit, 9v: *BE* 8/97

Domine salva nos, 6v (1591): *BE* 3/245

Domine secundum actum meum, 6v (1575): *BE* 1/132

Domine secundum multitudinem, 5v (1589): *BE* 2/221

Domine tu iurasti, 5v (1589): *BE* 2/124

Dominus in Sina, 5v (1607): *BE* 7b/15

Ecce advenit, 4v (1607): *BE* 7a/42

Ecce quam bonum, 4v (1605): *BE* 6b/1

Ecce virgo concipiet, 5v (1605): *BE* 5/87

Ego sum panis vivus, 4v (1607): *BE* 7a/82

Emendemus in melius, 5v (1575): *BE* 1/1

Exsurge quare obdormis, 5v (1591): *BE* 3/144

Fac cum servo tuo, 5v (1591): *BE* 3/37

Factus est repente, 5v (1607): *BE* 7b/53

Felix es sacra virgo, 5v (1605): *BE* 5/56

Felix namque es, 5v (1605): *BE* 5/113

Gaude Maria, 5v (1605): *BE* 5/127

Gaudeamus omnes (All Saints), 5v (1605): *BE* 6a/27

Gaudeamus omnes (Assumption), 5v (1605): *BE* 5/156

Haec dicit Dominus, 5v (1591): *BE* 3/97

Haec dies, 3v (1605): *BE* 6b/121

Haec dies, 5v (1607): *BE* 7a/111

Haec dies, 6v (1591): *BE* 3/251

Hodie beata Virgo, 4v (1605): *BE* 6b/77

Hodie Christus natus est, 4v (1607): *BE* 7a/20

Hodie Simon Petrus, 6v (1607): *BE* 7b/114

Iesu nostra redemptio, 4v (1607): *BE* 7a/93

In manus tuas Domine, 4v (1605): *BE* 6b/51

In resurrectione tua, 5v (1589): *BE* 2/150

Infelix ego, 6v (1591): *BE* 3/180

Iustorum animae, 5v (1605): *BE* 6a/48

Laetania, 4v (1605): *BE* 6b/56

Laetentur coeli, 5v (1589): *BE* 2/229

Laudate Dominum, 6v (1607): *BE* 7b/143

Laudate pueri, 6v (1575): *BE* 1/82

Laudibus in sanctis, 5v (1591): *BE* 3/1

Levemus corda, 5v (1591): *BE* 3/121

Libera me Domine de morte aeterna, 5v (1575): *BE* 1/213

Libera me Domine et pone me, 5v (1575): *BE* 1/8

Mass for 3 voices: *BE* 4/1

Mass for 4 voices: *BE* 4/24

Mass for 5 voices: *BE* 4/63

Memento Domine, 5v (1589): *BE* 2/62

Memento homo, 6v (1575): *BE* 1/97

Memento salutis auctor, 3v (1605): *BE* 6b/93

Miserere mei Deus, 5v (1591): *BE* 3/157

Miserere mihi Domine, 6v (1575): *BE* 1/161

Ne irascaris, 5v (1589): *BE* 2/169

Ne perdas cum impiis, 5v: *BE* 8/168

Nobis datus: see Pange lingua

Non vos relinquam orphanos, 5v (1607): *BE* 7b/73

Nunc dimittis servum tuum, 5v (1605): *BE* 5/19

Nunc scio vere, 6v (1607): *BE* 7b/80

O admirabile commercium, 4v (1607): *BE* 7a/28

O Domine adiuva me, 5v (1589): *BE* 2/32

O gloriosa Domina, 3v (1605): *BE* 6b/89

O lux beata Trinitas, 6v (1575): *BE* 1/69

O magnum mysterium, 4v (1607): *BE* 7a/34

O quam gloriosum est regnum, 5v (1589): *BE* 2/187

O quam suavis est, 4v (1607): *BE* 7a/86

O rex gloriae, 5v (1607): *BE* 7b/26

O sacrum convivium, 4v (1605): *BE* 6a/92

O salutaris hostia, 4v (1605): *BE* 6a/87

O salutaris hostia, 6v: *BE* 8/44

Oculi omnium, 4v (1605): *BE* 7a/142

Omni tempore benedic Deum, 5v: *BE* 8/178

Optimam partem elegit, 5v (1605): *BE* 5/170

Pange lingua, 4v (1605): *BE* 6a/97

Pascha nostrum, 5v (1607): *BE* 7a/132

Peccantem me quotidie, 5v (1575): *BE* 1/28

Peccavi super numerum, 5v: *BE* 9/1

Petrus beatus, 5v: *BE* 8/137

Plorans plorabit, 5v (1605): *BE* 6a/15

Post dies octo, 3v (1605): *BE* 6b/125

Post partum virgo, 5v (1605): *BE* 5/108

Precamur sancte Domine: see Christe qui lux es et dies

Psallite Domino, 5v (1607): *BE* 7b/23

Puer natus est, 4v (1607): *BE* 7a/2

Quem terra pontus, 3v (1605): *BE* 6b/83

Quis est homo, 5v (1591): *BE* 3/21

Quis me statim, 1v + 4 instruments: *BE* 15/140

Quodcunque ligaveris, 6v (1607): *BE* 7b/131

Quomodo cantabimus, 8v: *BE* 9/94

Quotiescunque manducabitis, 4v (1605): *BE* 6a/77

Recordare Domine, 5v (1591): *BE* 3/132

Reges Tharsis, 4v (1607): *BE* 7a/49

Regina coeli, 3v (1605): *BE* 6b/109

Responsum accepit Simeon, 5v (1605): *BE* 5/31

Resurrexi, 5v (1607): *BE* 7a/102

Rorate coeli, 5v (1605): *BE* 5/70

Sacerdotes Domini, 4v (1605): *BE* 6a/75

Salve regina, 4v (1605): *BE* 6b/26

Salve regina, 5v (1591): *BE* 3/47

Salve sancta parens, 5v (1605): *BE* 5/40

Salve sola Dei genetrix, 4v (1605): *BE* 6b/67

Senex puerum, 4v (1605): *BE* 6b/73
Senex puerum, 5v (1605): *BE* 5/16
Sicut audivimus, 5v (1605): *BE* 5/12
Siderum rector, 5v (1575): *BE* 1/104
Similes illis fiant, 4v: *BE* 8/4
Solve iubente Deo, 6v (1607): *BE* 7b/99
Speciosus forma, 5v (1605): *BE* 5/101
Spiritus Domini, 5v (1607): *BE* 7b/34
Surge illuminare, 4v (1607): *BE* 7a/58
Suscepimus Deus, 5v (1605): *BE* 5/2
Terra tremuit, 5v (1607): 23; *BE* 7a/129
Timete Dominum, 5v (1605): *BE* 6a/37
Tollite portas, 5v (1605): *BE* 5/78
Tribue Domine, 6v (1575): *BE* 1/167
Tribulatio proxima est, 5v (1591): *BE* 3/63
Tribulationes civitatum, 5v (1589): *BE* 2/202
Tristitia et anxietas, 5v (1589): *BE* 2/42
Tu es pastor ovium, 6v (1607): *BE* 7b/125
Tu es Petrus, 6v (1607): *BE* 7b/107
Tui sunt coeli, 4v (1607): *BE* 7a/17
Turbarum voces in passione Domini, 3v (1605): *BE* 6b/128
Unam petii a Domino, 5v (1605): *BE* 6a/4
Veni Sancte Spiritus (alleluia), 5v (1607): *BE* 7b/46
Veni Sancte Spiritus (sequence), 5v (1607): *BE* 7b/59
Venite comedite, 4v (1607): *BE* 7a/71
Venite exultemus Domino, 6v (1607): *BE* 7b/152
Victimae paschali laudes, 5v (1607): *BE* 7a/117
Vide Domine afflictionem nostram, 5v (1589): *BE* 2/73
Vide Domine quoniam tribulor, 5v: *BE* 9/185
Viderunt omnes (communion), 4v (1607): *BE* 7a/20
Viderunt omnes (gradual), 4v (1607): *BE* 7a/9
Vidimus stellam, 4v (1607): *BE* 7a/54
Vigilate, 5v (1589): *BE* 2/135
Virgo Dei genetrix, 5v (1605): *BE* 5/53
Viri Galilaei, 5v (1607): *BE* 7b/2
Visita quaesumus Domine, 4v (1605): *BE* 6b/19
Vultum tuum, 5v (1605): *BE* 5/94

English-Texted Music

1588   *Psalms, Sonnets and Songs*
1589   *Songs of Sundry Natures*
1611   *Psalms, Songs and Sonnets*
1614   *Tears or Lamentations of a Sorrowful Soul*

Great Service (Venite, Te Deum, Benedictus, Kyrie, Creed, Magnificat, Nunc Dimittis): *BE* 10b/1

Short Service (Venite, Te Deum, Benedictus, Kyrie, Creed, Magnificat, Nunc Dimittis):
  BE 10a/59
Second Service ("Verse Service"; Magnificat and Nunc Dimittis): *BE* 10a/121
Third Service ("Three Minims"; Magnificat and Nunc Dimittis): *BE* 10a/136
First Preces and Psalms 47, 54, 100: *BE* 10a/9
Second Preces and Psalms 114, 55, 119, 24: *BE* 10a/28
Preces and Responses: *BE* 10a/1
Litany: *BE* 10a/50

A feigned friend, 4v (1611): *BE* 14/30
Ah golden hairs, 5v: *BE* 15/51
Ah silly soul, 6v (1611): *BE* 14/165
Alack, when I look back, 5v: *BE* 9/93
All as a sea, 5v (1588): *BE* 12/123
Although the heathen poets, 5v (1588): *BE* 12/92
Ambitious love, 5v (1588): *BE* 12/73
An aged dame, 5v: *BE* 15/119
An earthly tree, 6v (1589): *BE* 13/113
And think ye nymphs, 5v (1589): *BE* 13/221
Arise Lord into thy rest, 5v (1611): *BE* 14/57
Arise O Lord, 5v: *BE* 11/1
As Caesar wept, 5v: *BE* 15/54
As I beheld, 5v (1588): *BE* 12/83
Attend mine humble prayer, 3v (1589): *BE* 13/18
Awake mine eyes, 4v (1611): *BE* 14/33
Be unto me O Lord, 4v (1614): *BE* 11/157
Behold how good a thing, 6v (1589): *BE* 13/200
Behold O God, 5v: *BE* 11/104
Blame I confess, 5v: *BE* 15/56
Blessed is he, 5v (1588): *BE* 12/32
Care for thy soul, 5v (1588): *BE* 12/137
Christ rising again, 6v (1589): *BE* 13/251
Come help O God, 5v (1614): *BE* 11/161
Come jolly swains, 4v (1611): *BE* 14/36
Come let us rejoice, 4v (1611): *BE* 14/47
Come pretty babe, 5v: *BE* 15/59
Come to me grief for ever, 5v (1588): *BE* 12/155
Come woeful Orpheus, 5v (1611): *BE* 14/64
Compel the hawk, 5v (1589): *BE* 13/145
Constant Penelope, 5v (1588): *BE* 12/99
Content is rich, 5v: *BE* 15/63
Crowned with flowers and lilies, 5v: *BE* 15/100
Crowned with flowers I saw fair Amaryllis, 5v (1611): *BE* 14/84
Delight is dead, 5v: *BE* 15/107
E'en as in seas, 5v: *BE* 15/66
Even from the depth, 5v (1588): *BE* 12/40
Exalt thyself O God, 6v: *BE* 11/11

Fair Britain isle, 5v: *BE* 15/124

Farewell false love, 5v (1588): *BE* 12/109

From Citheron the warlike boy, 4v (1589): *BE* 13/76

From depth of sin, 3v (1589): *BE* 13/15

From virgin's womb, 5v (1589): *BE* 13/106

Have mercy on us Lord, 5v: *BE* 15/8

Have mercy upon me O God, 6v (1611): *BE* 14/105

He that all earthly pleasure scorns, 5v: *BE* 15/128

Hear my prayer, 5v: *BE* 11/129

Help Lord for wasted, 5v (1588): *BE* 12/28

How long shall mine enemies, 5v: *BE* 11/25

How shall a young man, 5v (1588): *BE* 12/14

How vain the toils, 6v (1611): *BE* 14/171

I have been young, 3v (1611): *BE* 14/16

I joy not in no earthly bliss, 5v (1588): *BE* 12/43

I laid me down to rest, 5v (1614): *BE* 11/166

I thought that love had been a boy, 4v (1589): *BE* 13/177

I will not say, 5v: *BE* 15/68

If in thine heart, 6v (1589): *BE* 13/230

If that a sinner's sighs, 5v (1588): *BE* 12/132

If women could be fair, 5v (1588): *BE* 12/68

In angel's weed, 5v: *BE* 15/111

In crystal towers, 3v (1611): *BE* 14/18

In fields abroad, 5v (1588): *BE* 12/94

In winter cold, 3v (1611): *BE* 14/6

Is love a boy, 4v (1589): *BE* 13/51

La virginella (Italian text), 5v (1588): *BE* 12/104

Let not the sluggish sleep, 4v (1611): *BE* 14/27

Let others praise, 6v: *BE* 16/16

Look down O Lord, 4v (1614): *BE* 11/171

Lord hear my prayer, 3v (1589): *BE* 13/13

Lord in thy rage, 3v (1589): *BE* 13/1

Lord in thy wrath correct me not, 3v (1589): *BE* 13/7

Lord in thy wrath reprove me not, 5v (1588): *BE* 12/37

Lord to thee I make my moan, 5v: *BE* 15/14

Lullaby, 5v (1588): *BE* 12/142

Make ye joy to God, 5v (1611): *BE* 14/97

Mine eyes with fervency, 5v (1588): *BE* 12/6

Mount hope above the skies, 5v: *BE* 15/73

My mind to me a kingdom is, 5v (1588): *BE* 12/55

My mistress had a little dog, 5v: *BE* 15/131

My soul oppressed, 5v (1588): *BE* 12/9

O dear life, 5v (1589): *BE* 13/181

O God but God, 5v: *BE* 15/17

O God give ear, 5v (1588): *BE* 12/1

O God that guides the cheerful sun, 6v (1611): *BE* 14/136

O God the proud are risen, 6v: *BE* 11/33

O God which art most merciful, 3v (1589): *BE* 13/10
O God whom our offences, 5v: *BE* 11/42
O Lord bow down, 5v: *BE* 15/22
O Lord how long, 5v (1588): *BE* 12/20
O Lord how vain, 5v: *BE* 15/25
O Lord make thy servant Elizabeth, 6v: *BE* 11/51
O Lord my God, 4v (1589): *BE* 13/91
O Lord rebuke me not, 5v: *BE* 11/137
O Lord who in thy sacred tent, 5v (1588): *BE* 12/24
O Lord within thy tabernacle, 5v: *BE* 15/1
O sweet deceit, 5v: *BE* 16/46
O that most rare breast, 5v (1588): *BE* 12/158
O that we woeful wretches, 5v: *BE* 15/28
O you that hear this voice, 5v (1588): *BE* 12/63
Of flattering speech, 3v (1611): *BE* 14/4
Of gold all burnished, 5v (1589): *BE* 13/185
Out of the orient crystal skies, 5v: *BE* 15/31
Penelope that longed for the sight, 5v (1589): *BE* 13/134
Praise our Lord all ye Gentiles, 6v (1611): *BE* 14/144
Prevent us O Lord, 5v: *BE* 11/69
Prostrate, O Lord, I lie, 5v (1588): *BE* 12/119
Rejoice unto the Lord, 5v: *BE* 15/37
Retire my soul, 5v (1611): *BE* 14/51
Right blest are they, 3v (1589): *BE* 13/4
Save me O God, 5v: *BE* 11/75
See those sweet eyes, 5v (1589): *BE* 13/155
Sing joyfully, 6v: *BE* 11/82
Sing we merrily, 5v (1611): *BE* 14/70
Sing ye to our Lord, 3v (1611): *BE* 14/13
Sith death at length, 5v: *BE* 15/78
Sith that the tree, 5v: *BE* 15/81
Susanna fair, 3v (1589): *BE* 13/22
Susanna fair, 5v (1588): *BE* 12/127
The eagle's force, 3v (1611): *BE* 14/1
The fair young virgin (*Musica Transalpina*, 1588): see La virginella
The greedy hawk, 3v (1589): *BE* 13/47
The Lord is only my support, 5v: *BE* 15/5
The man is blest, 5v: *BE* 15/11
The match that's made, 5v (1588): *BE* 12/114
The nightingale, 3v (1589): *BE* 13/27
The noble famous queen, 5v: *BE* 15/97
This day Christ was born, 6v (1611): *BE* 14/128
This sweet and merry month of May, 4v (*Italian Madrigals Englished*, 1590, and 1611): *BE* 14/22
This sweet and merry month of May, 6v (*Italian Madrigals Englished*, 1590): *BE* 16/33
Thou God that guid'st, 5v: *BE* 11/148
Thou poets' friend, 5v: *BE* 15/84

Though Amaryllis dance in green, 5v (1588): *BE* 12/46
Though I be Brown, 5v: *BE* 15/144
Triumph with pleasant melody, 5v: *BE* 15/43
Truce for a time, 5v: *BE* 15/87
Truth at the first, 5v: *BE* 15/90
Turn our captivity, 6v (1611): *BE* 14/154
Unto the hills, 6v (1589): *BE* 13/238
Upon a summer's day, 3v (1589): *BE* 13/40
Wedded to will is witless, 5v (1611): *BE* 14/91
Weeping full sore, 5v (1589): *BE* 13/118
What is life, 4v (1611): *BE* 14/39
What pleasure have great princes, 5v (1588): *BE* 12/78
What steps of strife, 5v: *BE* 15/93
What vaileth it to rule, 5v: *BE* 16/62
When first by force, 5v (1589): *BE* 13/172
When I was otherwise, 5v (1589): *BE* 13/164
When younglings first, 3v (1589): *BE* 13/32
Where fancy fond, 5v (1588): *BE* 12/59
Where the blind, 5v: *BE* 15/146
While Phoebus used to dwell, 5v: *BE* 15/97
While that the sun, 4v (1589): *BE* 13/97
Who likes to love, 5v (1588): *BE* 12/51
Who looks may leap, 3v (1611): *BE* 14/10
Who made thee Hob, 6v (1589): *BE* 13/216
Why do I use my paper ink and pen, 5v (1588): *BE* 12/150
With lilies white, 5v: *BE*15/149
Wounded I am, 4v (1589): *BE* 13/64
Wretched Albinus, 5v: *BE* 15/152
Ye sacred Muses, 5v: *BE* 15/114

Consort Music

Browning, 5v: *BE* 17/39
Canon six in one and four in two: *BE* 16/171
Canon two in one: *BE* 16/169
Christe qui lux es, 4v, no. 1: *BE* 17/110
Christe qui lux es, 4v, no. 2: *BE* 17/114
Christe qui lux es, 4v, no. 3: *BE* 17/117
Christe Redemptor, 4v: *BE* 17/118
Fantasia in C, 3v, no. 1: *BE* 17/2
Fantasia in C, 3v, no. 2: *BE* 17/4
Fantasia in C, 3v, no. 3: *BE* 17/6
Fantasia in a, 4v: *BE* 17/11
Fantasia in G, 4v (= In manus tuas): *BE* 17/147
Fantasia in g, 4v: *BE* 17/7
Fantasia in C, 5v: *BE* 17/19
Fantasia in F, 6v (= Laudate pueri): *BE* 17/48

Fantasia in g, 6v, no. 1: *BE* 17/53
Fantasia in g, 6v, no. 2: *BE* 17/63
In Nomine, 4v, no. 1: *BE* 17/80
In Nomine, 4v, no. 2: *BE* 17/83
In Nomine, 5v, no. 1: *BE* 17/86
In Nomine, 5v, no. 2: *BE* 17/90
In Nomine, 5v, no. 3: *BE* 17/94
In Nomine, 5v, no. 4: *BE* 17/98
In Nomine, 5v, no. 5: *BE* 17/103
Miserere, 4v: *BE* 17/122
Pavan, 5v: *BE* 17/73
Pavan and Galliard, 6v: *BE* 17/75
Prelude and Ground: *BE* 17/29
Salvator mundi, 4v: *BE* 17/124
Sermone blando, 3v: *BE* 17/108
Sermone blando, 4v, no. 1: *BE* 17/127
Sermone blando, 4v, no. 2: *BE* 17/130
Te lucis ante terminum, 4v: *BE* 17/143 and 134

Keyboard Music

(Figures in parentheses refer to the sequential numbering of Byrd's works in *Musica Britannica*; these are often referred to as BK numbers.)

All in a garden green: *MB* 28/28 (BK 56)
Alman in G: *MB* 28/159 (BK 89)
Alman in g: *MB* 27/41 (BK 11)
The Barley Break: *MB* 28/163 (BK 92)
The Battle: *MB* 28/174 (BK 94)
The Bells: *MB* 27/132 (BK 38)
Callino Casturame: *MB* 27/126 (BK 35)
The Carman's Whistle: *MB* 27/127 (BK 36)
Clarifica me Pater I: *MB* 28/5 (BK 47)
Clarifica me Pater II: *MB* 28/6 (BK 48)
Clarifica me Pater III: *MB* 28/8 (BK 49)
Coranto in C: *MB* 27/168 (BK 45)
Fantasia in a: *MB* 27/42 (BK 13)
Fantasia in C, no. 1: *MB* 27/86 (BK 25)
Fantasia in C, no. 2: *MB* 27/91 (BK 26)
Fantasia in C, no. 3: *MB* 27/96 (BK 27)
Fantasia in d: *MB* 28/1 (BK 46)
Fantasia in G, no. 1 (Voluntary for my Lady Nevell): *MB* 28/51 (BK 61)
Fantasia in G, no. 2: *MB* 28/54 (BK 62)
Fantasia in G, no. 3: *MB* 28/59 (BK 63)
Fortune my foe: *MB* 27/24 (BK 6)
French Corantos I–III: *MB* 27/78 (BK 21)
Galliard in C, no. 4 (Mistress Mary Brownlow): *MB* 27/123 (BK 34)

Galliard in d, no. 2: *MB* 28/19 (BK 53)

Galliard in G, no. 9: *MB* 28/109 (BK 77)

The Galliard for the Victory: *MB* 28/186 (BK 95)

The Galliard Jig: *MB* 27/66 (BK 18)

The Ghost: *MB* 28/110 (BK 78)

Gloria tibi Trinitas: *MB* 28/10 (BK 50)

Go from my window: *MB* 28/112 (BK 79)

Ground in C: *MB* 27/164 (BK 43)

Ground in G: *MB* 28/145 (BK 86)

Ground in g: *MB* 27/35 (BK 9)

Gypsies' Round: *MB* 28/116 (BK 80)

Harding's Galliard: *MB* 28/25 (BK 55)

Hornpipe: *MB* 27/137 (BK 39)

Hugh Aston's Ground: *MB* 27/71 (BK 20)

The Hunt's Up (first version): *MB* 27/143 (BK 40)

The Hunt's Up (second version): *MB* 27/150 (BK 41)

Jig: *MB* 27/81(BK 22)

John come kiss me now: *MB* 28/121 (BK 81)

Johnson's Delight (Pavan and Galliard): *MB* 27/19 (BK 5)

La Volta: *MB* 28/162 (BK 91)

La Volta Lady Morley: *MB* 28/161 (BK 90)

Lachrymae Pavan (Dowland): *MB* 28/21 (BK 54)

The Maiden's Song: *MB* 28/126 (BK 82)

The March before the Battle, or The Earl of Oxford's March: *MB* 28/171 (BK 93)

Miserere mihi Domine I: *MB* 28/74 (BK 66)

Miserere mihi Domine II: *MB* 28/75 (BK 67)

Monsieur's Alman in C: *MB* 27/166 (BK 44)

Monsieur's Alman in G, no. 1: *MB* 28/151 (BK 87)

Monsieur's Alman in G, no. 2: *MB* 28/154 (BK 88)

My Lady Nevell's Ground: *MB* 28/32 (BK 57)

O mistress mine: *MB* 28/130 (BK 83)

Parsons' In Nomine: *MB* 28/12 (BK 51)

Passamezzo (Passing Measures) Pavan and Galliard: *MB* 27/1 (BK 2)

Pavan and Galliard in a, no. 1: *MB* 27/49 (BK 14)

Pavan and two Galliards in a, no. 2 (Earl of Salisbury): *MB* 27/57 (BK 15)

Pavan and Galliard in a, no. 3: *MB* 27/59 (BK 16)

Pavan and Galliard in B-flat: *MB* 27/81 (BK 23)

Pavan and Galliard in C, no. 1: *MB* 27/105 (BK 30)

Pavan and Galliard in C, no. 2 (Kinborough Good): *MB* 27/114 (BK 32)

Pavan and Galliard in C, no. 3: *MB* 27/118 (BK 33)

Pavan and Galliard in c, no. 1: *MB* 27/100 (BK 29)

Pavan and Galliard in c, no. 2: *MB* 27/109 (BK 31)

Pavan and Galliard in d, no. 1: *MB* 28/14 (BK 52)

Pavan and Galliard in F, no. 1 (Bray): *MB* 28/40 (BK 59)

Pavan and Galliard in F, no. 2 ("Ph. Tr."): *MB* 28/46 (BK 60)

Pavan and Galliard in G, no. 2: *MB* 28/91 (BK 71)

Pavan and Galliard in G, no. 3: *MB* 28/95 (BK 72)

Pavan and Galliard in G, no. 4: *MB* 28/99 (BK 73)
Pavan and Galliard in G, no. 5 (Echo): *MB* 28/190 (BK 114)
Pavan and Galliard in g, no. 2 (Sir William Petre): *MB* 27/11 (BK 3)
Pavan and Galliard in g, no. 3: *MB* 27/16 (BK 4)
Pavan in a, no. 4: *MB* 27/64 (BK 17)
Pavan in G, no. 6 (Canon 2 in 1): *MB* 28/102 (BK 74)
Pavan in G, no. 7 (Lady Monteagle) 28/105 (BK 75)
Pavan in G, no. 8: *MB* 28/107 (BK 76)
Prelude in a: *MB* 27/42 (BK 12)
Prelude in C: *MB* 27/85 (BK 24)
Prelude in g: *MB* 27/1 (BK 1)
Quadran Pavan and Galliard: *MB* 28/79 (BK 70)
The Queen's Alman: *MB* 27/39 (BK 10)
Qui passe for my Lady Nevell: *MB* 27/68 (BK 19)
Rowland, or Lord Willoughby's Welcome Home: *MB* 27/27 (BK 7)
Salvator mundi I: *MB* 28/76 (BK 68)
Salvator mundi II: *MB* 28/77 (BK 69)
Second Ground: *MB* 27/157 (BK 42)
Sellinger's Round: *MB* 28/135 (BK 84)
Ut mi re: *MB* 28/69 (BK 65)
Ut re mi fa sol la in F, for three hands: *MB* 28/37 (BK 58)
Ut re mi fa sol la in G: *MB* 28/64 (BK 64)
Verse: *MB* 27/99 (BK 28)
Walsingham: *MB* 27/29 (BK 8)
Wilson's Wild: *MB* 27/131 (BK 37)
The Woods so Wild: *MB* 28/141 (BK 85)

Personalia

Aylmer, John (1521–94) was archdeacon of Lincoln during the years Byrd spent there as cathedral organist. He was a strict reformer who purged the cathedral of Catholic influences; he also helped translate John Foxe's *Book of Martyrs* into Latin for an international Protestant audience. He became Bishop of London in 1577 and was the first to cite the Byrd family for failure to attend their parish church. He was also involved, as Byrd was, in the controversies over the London book trade in the 1580s.

Baldwin, John (ca. 1555–1615) was a musician and music scribe who preserved many of Byrd's unpublished works in manuscript. He spent almost twenty-five years as a tenor lay clerk at St. George's Chapel, Windsor, before his appointment to the Chapel Royal in 1598. His work at Windsor and in London gave him access to a broad range of music, some of it stylistically obsolete or no longer in political favor. We owe much of our knowledge of sixteenth-century English music to Baldwin's copying activities. In 1591 he completed *My Lady Nevell's Book*, the most important surviving collection of Byrd's keyboard works.

Bancroft, Richard (1544–1610) was Archbishop of Canterbury from 1604 until his death. He presided over the committee that translated the King James Bible, a project largely completed during his tenure as archbishop. He gave his approval for the printing of both volumes of Byrd's *Gradualia* (1605 and 1607) despite their controversial content.

Broughe, Robert (ca. 1530–1603) was a London maker of keyboard instruments who married Byrd's sister Barbara in 1555. He built and maintained various instruments for the Petre household at Thorndon Hall; he was also employed by the Paget family and by various churches, including St. Margaret's, Westminster. He died of the plague during the London epidemic of 1603.

Bull, John (ca. 1562/3–1628) was a composer and keyboard virtuoso. In 1597 he was appointed the first lecturer in music at the newly founded Gresham College. He began his inaugural lecture by referring to Byrd (who was probably present) as his master. After a lively musical career in England, shadowed by a number of controversies and scandals, he emigrated to the Netherlands in 1613 and became organist at Antwerp Cathedral. His music was featured alongside Byrd's in *Parthenia*. A contemporary portrait of Bull is still on display in the Oxford Faculty of Music.

Byrd, John (ca. 1532–1622) was the second of the composer's elder brothers. He was a chorister at St. Paul's Cathedral in the 1540s. In 1548–49 he was apprenticed to a member of the Drapers' Company, the traditional guild of cloth merchants. His father-in-law bequeathed him a number of merchant ships, which he sent as far afield as Brazil, West Africa, and Cuba. He found himself in legal difficulties during the later 1580s but was pardoned for his service in fending off the Spanish Armada with his ships. He surpassed his brother William in longevity, living to the age of about ninety.

Byrd, Julian, née Burley (died ca. 1609) was the composer's wife, born in Lincolnshire. The two probably met while Byrd was serving as organist and choirmaster at Lincoln Cathedral. They married in 1568 and had two sons and three daughters. Julian was a staunch Catholic who was regularly cited for religious nonconformity: one report accused her of "seducing" her servants to her beliefs and noted that she was unwilling to speak with the authorities.

Byrd, Simon (ca. 1530–79) was the elder of the composer's two brothers. He was a chorister at St. Paul's Cathedral alongside his brother John in the 1540s. He left music books and instruments in his will. He also appears to have been the owner of a mid-sixteenth-century collection of organ music and poetry. Much of the poetry—including a satirical lament in the voice of a young chorister and the poem "Long have I been a singing man"—is closely linked to the Tudor musical world. One of Simon's sons became an Anglican parish priest.

Byrd, Thomas (1576–after 1651) was the composer's second son and Thomas Tallis's godson. After a year spent studying law and the humanities, he emigrated to Spain at the age of twenty and entered the English College at Valladolid with the recommendation of John Gerard. He was expelled from the college three years later and came back to England, where he was described as a "professor of the science of music" and chosen in 1602 to deputize for John Bull as Gresham Lecturer in Music. His father left him a substantial inheritance, declaring it to be forfeit if Thomas should "seek by law or other ways to disturb or trouble my executors."

Campion, Edmund (1540–81) was a leading figure of Elizabethan Catholic intellectual life. After a successful academic career at Oxford and ordination as a Protestant deacon, he became a convinced Catholic and went into exile to avoid persecution. He spent many years traveling in Europe and was ordained a Jesuit priest in Prague in 1578. Shortly after he returned to England at the age of forty, he was captured and executed as a traitor. Byrd's song *Why do I use my paper, ink and pen?* is a thinly veiled elegy on his death.

Carey, Henry (1526–96), first Baron Hunsdon, was a nephew of Anne Boleyn, a cousin of Queen Elizabeth, and, according to contemporary rumor, an illegitimate child of King Henry VIII. He was a patron of the arts and founder of the Lord Chamberlain's Men, Shakespeare's theatrical company. Byrd dedicated the 1589 *Songs of Sundry Natures* to him, thanking him "for many favors to me shown."

Cecil, Robert (1563–1612), first earl of Salisbury, was one of the most powerful figures at the English Renaissance court. He served as Secretary of State to both Queen Elizabeth and King James. The cover of this book shows him presiding over a meeting of English, Spanish, and Flemish diplomats. He came to the aid of Byrd in his interminable legal battles. The composer dedicated a pavan and two galliards to him, published in *Parthenia* just after his death.

Dow, Robert (1553–88) was a scholar, calligrapher, and music copyist. He became a fellow of All Souls College, Oxford at the age of twenty-two and was still adding to his collection of music when he died thirteen years later. He preserved many of Byrd's works in one of the few sets of English Renaissance music partbooks that have survived completely intact.

Dowland, John (ca. 1563–1626) was a lutenist and composer who produced the first book of English lute songs in 1597. Although he was one of the most important figures in English Renaissance song and instrumental music, he spent much of his career abroad and complained of ill-treatment in his own country. His *Lachrimae* pavan was among the most popular musical works of its day. Byrd arranged it (as many others did) for the keyboard.

East, Thomas (1540–1608) was the printer of almost all Byrd's published vocal music. He inherited the musical font of Thomas Vautrollier at his death in 1587, and produced Byrd's *Psalms, Sonnets and Songs* in the following year. The partnership lasted through Byrd's second book of *Gradualia* in 1607. East was a keen entrepreneur and a busy printer: when he was not working on Byrd's songbooks, masses, and motet books, he kept up a lively trade in light Italianate music.

Ferrabosco, Alfonso (1543–88), the elder of two composers by that name, was an Italian musician who had become attached to the English court by 1562. He helped make the Italian madrigal popular in Elizabethan England. He also wrote a number of Latin motets, which appear to have influenced, or been influenced by, Byrd's own work. The two composers engaged in "friendly emulation" by writing numerous canons, now lost, on the plain-song *Miserere*. Ferrabosco left England under a cloud of suspicion (he had been accused—perhaps unjustly—of espionage, robbery, and murder) and died in his mid-forties in his native Bologna.

Garnet, Henry (1555–1606) was an English Jesuit who found himself implicated in the aftermath of the Gunpowder Plot and was executed for treason. The scandal and publicity surrounding his trial (presided over by Byrd's patron Henry Howard) may well have been a factor in the delayed publication of the second book of *Gradualia*. Garnet was described in his youth as "very skillful in music and in playing upon the instruments"; he kept up those interests until his death. Charles de Ligny reported having met him alongside Byrd at a musical gathering of Catholics.

Gerard, John (1564–1637) was an English Jesuit who spent nearly twenty years ministering to recusants in secret, celebrating mass and leading people through the spiritual exercises devised by Ignatius of Loyola, the founder of his order. When Byrd's son Thomas went to Valladolid to enter the English seminary there, Gerard wrote him a letter of recommendation. Unlike many of his colleagues, Gerard avoided execution and retired to the Continent. He went on to write a detailed and eminently readable memoir of recusant life.

Gibbons, Orlando (1583–1625) was the youngest of the three composers included in *Parthenia* and arguably the most musically accomplished of all Byrd's successors. He served in the Chapel Royal from 1603 until his death. Both his vocal music and his instrumental music—most notably his series of keyboard pavans and galliards—owe a great deal to Byrd's style.

Hatton, Christopher (ca. 1540–91) was Lord Chancellor of England and the patron of Byrd's first songbook, the 1588 *Psalms, Sonnets and Songs*. The title page of the book features Hatton's family crest, a golden hind—best known as the insignia of Francis Drake's ship, the first English ship to sail around the world, which was named in Hatton's honor.

Howard, Henry (1540–1614), Earl of Northampton, was the patron of Byrd's first volume of *Gradualia*. He is seated beside Robert Cecil, another Byrd patron, in the painting on the cover of this book. As a member of the inner circle of the Jacobean court, he negotiated an increase in salary for the Gentlemen of the Chapel Royal, for which Byrd thanked him in print. Despite his lifelong Catholic sympathies, Howard took part in the persecution of English recusants, including a number of Byrd's associates.

Leighton, William (ca. 1565–1622) was an amateur poet and musician who spent a number of years in prison for debt. In 1614 he published a musical anthology called *Tears or Lamentations of a Sorrowful Soul*, with settings of his own penitential poetry by twenty-one different composers, including most of the leading figures of the Jacobean musical world. The book includes four pieces by Byrd.

Lumley, John (ca. 1533–1609) was the patron of Byrd's second book of *Cantiones sacrae* (1591). He supported a number of musicians and built up an extensive library of music at the royal palace of Nonsuch, where he and his family lived for many years. He kept the words of Byrd's *Infelix ego*, the most substantial piece in the 1591 *Cantiones*, in a pocket-sized booklet in his own handwriting.

Merbecke, John (ca. 1505–85) was a professional church musician whose career, like that of Tallis and a few other musical colleagues, spanned the whole English Reformation and its aftermath. He composed music in both Latin and English, as well as a number of scholarly and controversial works. He narrowly escaped burning at the stake in 1543 on a charge of heresy. He is now best known for the 1550 *Book of Common Prayer Noted*, the first full musical setting of the new English liturgy.

Monte, Philippe de (1521–1603) was a Flemish composer who published thirty-four books of madrigals over half a century. He spent some time in England during the 1550s in the retinue of Philip of Spain, and he appears to have kept in touch with English musicians for the rest of his life. In 1583, he sent the motet *Super flumina Babylonis* to Byrd, who replied in 1584 with *Quomodo cantabimus*.

Morley, Thomas (1557/58–1602) was a composer, editor, theorist, musical entrepreneur, and pupil of Byrd, to whom he dedicated his *Plain and Easy Introduction to Practical Music* in 1597. He was one of the most versatile and ambitious musicians of the English Renaissance. His adaptations of Italian madrigals had a lasting effect on the style of English secular music.

Mundy, William (ca. 1528–91) was a London composer and, for the last twenty-five years of his life, a Gentleman of the Chapel Royal. He appears to have belonged, like Byrd and Tomkins, to a musical family spanning several generations. Robert Dow wrote a playful couplet in which he called him second only to Byrd among musicians. Mundy collaborated with Sheppard and the young Byrd on the polyphonic psalm *In exitu Israel*.

Nevell, Elizabeth (ca. 1541–1621), a half-sister of Francis Bacon, was the Lady Nevell for whom Byrd's most extensive compilation of keyboard music was named. She was a contemporary of Byrd, about fifty years old when *My Lady Nevell's Book* was finished in 1591. Morley dedicated his 1595 *First Book of Canzonets to Two Voices* to her as Lady Periam. She endowed Oxford fellowships and a charity school, and kept up an extensive correspondence.

Paget, Thomas (ca. 1544–90) was a patron and friend of Byrd, a Catholic nobleman who was an amateur composer himself and spent much of his fortune on the cultivation of music and musicians. When he fled to Europe in the mid-1580s to avoid political difficulties, he took the composer Peter Philips into his entourage. His house in Staffordshire had a guest room set aside for Byrd, furnished with a "pair of virginals."

Parsons, Robert (ca. 1535–72)—not to be confused with the Elizabethan Jesuit missionary Robert Persons—was a musician and Gentleman of the Chapel

Royal. He was an innovative and skilled composer from whom we have relatively few surviving works. His richly scored First Service is among the chief precedents for Byrd's Great Service. When Parsons drowned in the River Trent in January 1572, Byrd almost immediately took his place in the Chapel. Robert Dow's partbooks include a brief lament on his early death.

Paston, Edward (1550–ca. 1630) was a country gentleman who built up an unequalled collection of music in manuscript, including many works by Byrd that survive nowhere else. He hosted Catholic priests and had masses celebrated on his estate in Norfolk. He was fluent in Spanish and acquired a large amount of European music, both sacred and secular. His epitaph describes him as "most skillful of liberal sciences, especially music and poetry, as also strange languages."

Peacham, Henry (1578–ca. 1644) was an English author and illustrator. After an extended tour through Europe in his thirties, he published a book called *The Complete Gentleman*, offering ambitious English readers an education in the manners and refinements of courtly life. The book, written in the tradition of Castiglione's *Courtier*, includes sections on science, history, poetry, and music, the last of these praising Byrd and calling him "our Phoenix."

Petre, John (1549–1613) was a gentleman and patron of the arts who maintained two grand households within a few miles of Byrd's home in Stondon Massey. He was not a recusant himself, but he was the center of a lively Catholic community and encouraged the performance of a wide variety of vocal and instrumental music. Byrd visited Petre regularly during his later years. He dedicated the second book of *Gradualia* to him with unusual warmth and said that most of the music in it had been written at his house.

Petre, William (1575–1637) was the son of John Petre and heir to the family estates in Essex. Byrd dedicated the last pair of *Nevell* pavans and galliards to him when he was sixteen; those pieces were later revised and republished in *Parthenia*. Edmund Spenser wrote the poem *Prothalamion* ("Sweet Thames, run softly, till I end my song") in honor of William's wedding to Edward Somerset's daughter Katherine in 1596.

Philips, Peter (1560/61–1628) was a composer, organist, and student of Byrd. He was first trained under Sebastian Westcote at St. Paul's Cathedral and began his musical career in London, but he spent almost fifty years in exile abroad, most notably at the Brussels court of the Habsburg rulers Albert and Isabella. He composed Italian madrigals, instrumental works, and a vast quantity of Latin motets. He was the first English composer to publish music with a basso continuo part.

Redford, John (died 1547) was organist and master of the choristers at St. Paul's Cathedral. He was one of the first significant English keyboard composers and helped lay the groundwork for many of Byrd's innovations in keyboard style. A manuscript associated with Byrd's brother Simon, who sang under Redford at St. Paul's as a boy, includes nine of his keyboard pieces, his play *Wit and Science*, and his satirical verses on the life of a young chorister.

Rich, Penelope (1563–1607) was a renowned Elizabethan courtier, the inspiration for Sidney's sonnet sequence *Astrophel and Stella*. She appears to have been at least the implicit subject of a number of songs by Byrd, including *Penelope that longed for the sight*, *Constant Penelope*, and *Weeping full sore*. Her lover Charles Blount is seated next to Henry Howard in the painting on the cover of this book.

Shelley, Jane (died 1610) was Byrd's constant legal adversary during his mature years. She and her husband were Catholics who had been imprisoned and seen their property in Essex confiscated by the Crown in the aftermath of an unsuccessful plot to assassinate Queen Elizabeth. When Shelley's husband died in 1597, she sued to recover her property, including the house and farm where Byrd was now living. The resulting court battle with Byrd was highly acrimonious (the composer was accused of using "vile and bitter words") and dragged on for more than a decade.

Sheppard, John (ca. 1515–58) was a composer and Gentleman of the Chapel Royal. He said in his application for an Oxford degree in 1554 that he had been composing for twenty years; his surviving works include a large group of Latin cantus-firmus settings, some of them unusually complex and dissonant, and a considerable amount of English church music. He collaborated with Byrd and Mundy on the polyphonic psalm *In exitu Israel*, possibly one of the last pieces he ever wrote. He died in the London influenza epidemic of 1558, with a request (not granted) to be buried in Westminster Abbey.

Sidney, Philip (1554–86) was a poet, courtier, and literary patron whose distinguished catalogue of works included *Arcadia*, *Astrophel and Stella*, and the *Apology for Poetry*. He died of wounds received while defending the Netherlands against Spanish invasion. Although he had drifted in and out of public favor during his life, he was given a lavish funeral and immortalized as an ideal Renaissance gentleman and Protestant hero. Byrd set Sidney's poetry to music (including *O dear life* and *O you that hear this voice*, two songs from *Astrophel*) and composed elegies on his death.

Somerset, Edward (ca. 1550–1628), earl of Worcester, was the patron of Byrd's 1589 book of Latin motets. Queen Elizabeth called him "a stiff papist" but "a good subject." He was a friend and associate of the Petre family, who shared his religious sympathies. He was also an amateur musician and composer to whom Byrd offered musical advice. He and his son Charles accumulated a large library of music at their house in London, where Byrd had a private "lodging": the collection included Monteverdi's fourth and fifth books of madrigals.

Tallis, Thomas (ca. 1505–85) was the most distinguished English composer of the generation before Byrd, with a musical career lasting more than half a century. After a series of short-lived appointments during the turmoil of the Reformation years, he joined the Chapel Royal in the mid-1540s and remained there until the end of his life. Queen Elizabeth granted him and Byrd a monopoly on music printing in 1575; they responded by dedicating a joint volume of Latin motets to her later in the same year. Tallis had a deep and pervasive influence on the musical style of Byrd, who wrote the elegy *Ye sacred Muses* on his death.

Taverner, John (ca. 1490–1545) was among the last of England's great pre-Reformation composers. He dabbled in Lutheranism during his time at Oxford in the 1520s, but there is no supporting evidence for the stories told by John Foxe about his violent Protestant activities. He contributed to the final flowering of what was essentially a late medieval musical tradition. The instrumental In Nomine, a genre cultivated in England until the time of Purcell, can be traced back to a four-voice passage from one of Taverner's masses. Byrd quoted Taverner's *Mean Mass* at some length in the Sanctus of his own four-part mass.

Tomkins, Thomas (1572–1656) was a composer and organist, the longest-lived of Byrd's known students. He kept a number of Elizabethan musical practices alive through the middle of the seventeenth century. He owned and annotated a copy of Morley's *Plain and Easy Introduction*, published one of the very last English madrigal books, and (like Byrd) collected his own keyboard works in manuscript. He dedicated a madrigal to his "ancient and much reverenced master" Byrd in 1622.

Tye, Christopher (ca. 1505–73) was choirmaster of Ely Cathedral from the early 1540s onward, but he was also associated with court circles and seems to have had close ties with the Chapel Royal. His work spans nearly all the musical styles of the mid-sixteenth century, from luxurious six-part Latin polyphony to his terse, didactic, and popular *Acts of the Apostles*. A number of his instrumental pieces make use of odd titles and striking metrical irregularities.

Vautrollier, Thomas (died 1587) was a printer who came to London in 1562 as a French Huguenot refugee and soon acquired a reputation for skillful printing of difficult materials, including music. In 1570 he published an edition of French chansons by Lassus, with the texts bowdlerized to suit pious tastes. In 1575 he produced a joint volume of Latin *Cantiones* by Tallis and Byrd. His widow Jacqueline printed one of the books of political controversy acquired and signed by Byrd in the 1580s.

Verstegan, Richard (ca. 1548–1640) was an English author who fled abroad in 1581 after publishing a controversial account of the execution of Edmund Campion. He spent the remaining six decades of his long life in Europe, working first for the English Jesuit cause and later as a freelance journalist and pamphleteer. His 1599 *Primer or Office of the Blessed Virgin Mary*, a bilingual devotional book in Latin and English for recusant use, was the source for many of the texts in Byrd's 1611 *Psalms, Songs and Sonnets*.

Weelkes, Thomas (1576–1623) was perhaps the boldest and most innovative of all the English madrigalists. He spent most of his career as organist of Chichester Cathedral, where he was regularly cited for drunkenness and insubordination. He left a private manuscript collection of keyboard music, including over thirty works by Byrd.

Westcote, Sebastian (ca. 1515–82) was a London musician and theatrical director who influenced a number of Byrd's peers. He was in charge of the choristers at St. Paul's Cathedral from the late 1540s until his death. He used the time freed up by the reformed liturgical rites to cultivate his boys as a company of professional actors. Like Byrd, he was a Catholic who used his courtly connections to avoid persecution.

White, Robert (ca. 1530–74) was an older contemporary of Byrd and one of the most important cultivators of Latin-texted polyphony in post-Reformation England. His vocal works (including two large settings of the *Lamentations of Jeremiah*) and his consort music had a marked influence on Byrd's development as a composer. He married Christopher Tye's daughter and was appointed organist and master of the choristers at Westminster Abbey. Only a few years after his appointment to Westminster, he died of the plague.

Whythorne, Thomas (1528–96) was a composer, lutenist, and poet who left a colorful autobiography describing his career. His 1571 *Songs for Three, Four and Five Voices*, modeled self-consciously on Italian madrigal collections, was the first printed book of its kind to appear in sixteenth-century England. His memoirs are a unique glimpse into the social background of Elizabethan music-making.

Select Bibliography

I. Editions of Byrd's Music

The Byrd Edition. London: Stainer and Bell, 1970–2004.

1   *Cantiones sacrae (1575)*, ed. Craig Monson (1977)
2   *Cantiones sacrae I (1589)*, ed. Alan Brown (1988)
3   *Cantiones sacrae II (1591)*, ed. Alan Brown (1981)
4   *Masses*, ed. Philip Brett (1981)
5   *Gradualia I (1605): The Marian masses*, ed. Philip Brett (1989)
6a   *Gradualia I (1605): All Saints and Corpus Christi*, ed. Philip Brett (1991)
6b   *Gradualia I (1605): Other feasts and devotions*, ed. Philip Brett (1993)
7a   *Gradualia II (1607): Christmas to Easter*, ed. Philip Brett (1997)
7b   *Gradualia II (1607): Ascension, Pentecost, and feasts of Saints Peter and Paul*, ed. Philip Brett (1997)
8   *Latin motets I (from manuscript sources)*, ed. Warwick Edwards (1984)
9   *Latin motets II (from manuscript sources)*, ed. Warwick Edwards (2000)
10a *English services I*, ed. Craig Monson (1980)
10b *English services II (the Great Service)*, ed. Craig Monson (1982)
11   *English anthems*, ed. Craig Monson (1983)
12   *Psalmes, sonnets and songs (1588)*, ed. Jeremy Smith (2004)
13   *Songs of sundry natures (1589)*, ed. David Mateer (2004)
14   *Psalmes, songs, and sonnets (1611)*, ed. John Morehen (1987)
15   *Consort songs for voice and viols*, ed. Philip Brett (1970)
16   *Madrigals, songs and canons*, ed. Philip Brett (1976)
17   17 *Consort music*, ed. Kenneth Elliott (1971)

William Byrd: Keyboard Music, ed. Alan Brown. *Musica Britannica* 27–28. London: Stainer and Bell, 1969–71. 2nd ed. 1976–85. 3rd ed. 1999–2004.

II. Literature

Numerals in italics refer to annotated entries in Appendix E.

Andrews, H. K. "Printed Sources of William Byrd's 'Psalmes, Sonets and Songs.'" *Music & Letters* 44 (1963): 5–20. [*1*]

——. *The Technique of Byrd's Vocal Polyphony.* London: Oxford University Press, 1966. [*2*]

Bennett, John. "Byrd and Jacobean Consort Music: A Look at Richard Mico." In *Byrd Studies*, ed. Alan Brown and Richard Turbet, 129–40. Cambridge: Cambridge University Press, 1992. [*3*]

Bray, Roger. "The Part-Books Oxford, Christ Church, MSS 979–983: An Index and Commentary." *Musica Disciplina* 25 (1971): 179–97. [*4*]

Brennan, Michael. "Sir Charles Somerset's Music Books." *Music & Letters* 74 (1993): 501–18. [*5*]

Brett, Philip. "Editing Byrd." *Musical Times* 121 (1980): 492–95, 557–59. [*6*]

——. "Edward Paston: A Norfolk Gentleman and his Musical Collection." In *William Byrd and his Contemporaries: Essays and a Monograph*, ed. Joseph Kerman and Davitt Moroney, 31–59. Berkeley: University of California Press, 2007. [*7*]

——. "Homage to Taverner in Byrd's Masses." In *William Byrd and his Contemporaries: Essays and a Monograph*, ed. Joseph Kerman and Davitt Moroney, 8–21. Berkeley: University of California Press, 2007. [*8*]

——. "Pitch and Transposition in the Paston Manuscripts." In *Sundry Sorts of Music Books: Essays on the British Library Collections, Presented to O. W. Neighbour on his 70th Birthday*, ed. Chris Banks, Arthur Searle, and Malcolm Turner, 89–118. London: British Library, 1993. [*9*]

——. "Prefaces to *Gradualia*." In *William Byrd and his Contemporaries: Essays and a Monograph*, ed. Joseph Kerman and Davitt Moroney, 128–230. Berkeley: University of California Press, 2007. [*10*]

——. "Word Setting in the Songs of Byrd." In *William Byrd and his Contemporaries: Essays and a Monograph*, ed. Joseph Kerman and Davitt Moroney, 100–20. Berkeley: University of California Press, 2007. [*11*]

Brown, Alan. "My Lady Nevell's Book as a Source of Byrd's Keyboard Music." *Proceedings of the Royal Musical Association* 95 (1968–69): 29–39. [*12*]

——. "William Byrd (1539 or 1540–1623)." In *Keyboard Music before 1700*, ed. Alexander Silbiger, 36–47. New York: Routledge, 2004. [*13*]

——. "'The woods so wild': Notes on a Byrd Text." In *Sundry Sorts of Music Books: Essays on the British Library Collections, Presented to O. W. Neighbour on his 70th Birthday*, ed. Chris Banks, Arthur Searle, and Malcolm Turner, 54–66. London: British Library, 1993. [*14*]

——, and Richard Turbet, eds. *Byrd Studies*. Cambridge: Cambridge University Press, 1992. [*15*]

Caldwell, John. *The Oxford History of English Music.* Vol. 1: *From the Beginnings to c. 1715*. Oxford: Clarendon Press, 1991. [*16*]

The Cardinall's Musick, dir. Andrew Carwood. *The Byrd Edition*. 13 CDs. London: ASV Gaudeamus and Hyperion, 1997–2010. [*17*]

Clulow, Peter. "Publication Dates for Byrd's Latin Masses." *Music & Letters* 47 (1966): 1–9. [*18*]

Cole, Suzanne. "Who is the Father? Changing Perceptions of Tallis and Byrd in Late Nineteenth-Century England." *Music & Letters* 89 (2008): 1–14. [*19*]

Dirksen, Pieter. "Byrd and Sweelinck: Some Cursory Notes." *Annual Byrd Newsletter* 7 (2001): 11–20. Dutch version in *Het Clavecimbel* 12, no. 2 (2006), 11–16. [*20*]

Fellowes, Edmund. *William Byrd*. London: Oxford University Press, 1936, 2nd ed. 1948. [*21*]

Fenlon, Iain, and John Milsom, "'Ruled Paper Imprinted': Music Paper and Patents in Sixteenth-Century England." *Journal of the American Musicological Society* 37 (1984): 139–63. [*22*]

Fraser, David. "Sources of Texts for Byrd's 1611 *Psalmes*." *Early Music* 38 (2010): 171–72. [*23*]

Gaskin, Hilary. "Baldwin and the Nevell Hand." In *Byrd Studies*, ed. Alan Brown and Richard Turbet, 159–73. Cambridge: Cambridge University Press, 1992. [*24*]

Grimshaw, Julian. "*Fuga* in Early Byrd." *Early Music* 37 (2009): 251–65. [*25*]

Harley, John. "Merchants and Privateers: A Window on the World of William Byrd." *Musical Times* 147 (Autumn 2006): 51–66. [*26*]

———. " 'My Ladye Nevell' Revealed." *Music & Letters* 86 (2005): 1–15. [*27*]

———. "New light on William Byrd." *Music & Letters* 79 (1998): 475–88. [*28*]

———. *William Byrd: Gentleman of the Chapel Royal.* Aldershot: Ashgate, 1997, 2nd ed. 1999. [*29*]

———. *William Byrd's Modal Practice.* Aldershot: Ashgate, 2005. [*30*]

———. *The World of William Byrd: Musicians, Merchants and Magnates.* Farnham: Ashgate, 2010. [*31*]

Hunter, Desmond. "My Ladye Nevells Booke and the Art of Gracing." In *Byrd Studies*, ed. Alan Brown and Richard Turbet, 174–92. Cambridge: Cambridge University Press, 1992. [*32*]

Jackman, James. "Liturgical Aspects of Byrd's *Gradualia*." *Musical Quarterly* 49 (1963): 17–37. [*33*]

Johnstone, Andrew. " 'As it was in the beginning': Organ and Choir Pitch in Early Anglican Church Music." *Early Music* 31 (2003): 506–25. [*34*]

Kerman, Joseph. "The Byrd Edition—in Print and on Disc." *Early Music* 29 (2001): 109–18. [*35*]

———. "Byrd's Motets: Chronology and Canon." *Journal of the American Musicological Society* 14 (1961): 359–82. [*36*]

———. "Byrd's Settings of the Ordinary of the Mass." *Journal of the American Musicological Society* 32 (1979): 408–39. [*37*]

———. "Byrd, Tallis, and the Art of Imitation." In *Write All These Down: Essays on Music*, 90–105. Berkeley: University of California Press, 1994. [*38*]

———. "The Elizabethan Motet: A Study of Texts for Music." *Studies in the Renaissance* 9 (1962): 273–308. [*39*]

———. *The Masses and Motets of William Byrd.* Berkeley: University of California Press, 1981. [*40*]

———. "Music and Politics: The Case of William Byrd." *Proceedings of the American Philosophical Society* 144 (2000): 275–87. [*41*]

———. "Old and New in Byrd's *Cantiones Sacrae*." In *Essays on English Music in Honour of Sir Jack Westrup*, ed. F. W. Sternfeld, 25–43. Oxford: Blackwell, 1975. [*42*]

———. "On William Byrd's *Emendemus in melius*." In *Hearing the Motet*, ed. Dolores Pesce, 329–47. New York and Oxford: Oxford University Press, 1997. Also available in *Musical Quarterly* 49 (1963): 431–49. [*43*]

———. "William Byrd." *Grove Music Online.* An earlier version can be found in Gustave Reese *et al.*, *The New Grove High Renaissance Masters*, 229–88. New York: Norton, 1984. [*44*]

———. "Write All These Down: Notes on a Byrd Song." In *Write All These Down: Essays on Music*, 106–24. Berkeley: University of California Press, 1994. [*45*]

Kilroy, Gerald. "Paper, inke and penne: The Literary *Memoria* of the Recusant Community." *Downside Review* (April 2001), 95–124. [*46*]

Knight, Ellen E. "The praise of musicke: John Case, Thomas Watson, and William Byrd." *Current Musicology* 30 (1981): 37–51. [*47*]

Le Huray, Peter. "Some Thoughts about Cantus Firmus Composition, and a Plea for Byrd's *Christus resurgens*." In *Byrd Studies*, ed. Alan Brown and Richard Turbet, 1–23. Cambridge: Cambridge University Press, 1992. [*48*]

Mateer, David. "Oxford, Christ Church Music MSS 984–8: An Index and Commentary." *Royal Musical Association Research Chronicle* 20 (1986/87): 1–18. [*49*]

———, "William Byrd, John Petre and Oxford, Bodleian MS Mus.Sch.e.423." *Royal Musical Association Research Chronicle* 29 (1996): 21–46. [*50*]

———, "William Byrd's Middlesex Recusancy." *Music & Letters* 78 (1997): 1–14. [*51*]

McCarthy, Kerry. "'Brought to speake English with the rest': Byrd's Motet Contrafacta." *Musical Times* 148, no. 3 (Autumn 2007): 51–60. [*52*]

———. "Byrd and the Mass Proper Tradition." In *Heinrich Isaac and Polyphony for the Proper of the Mass in the Late Middle Ages and the Renaissance*, ed. David Burn and Stefan Gasch, 407–15. Turnhout: Brepols, 2011. [*53*]

———. "Byrd, Augustine, and *Tribue, Domine*." *Early Music* 32 (2004): 569–76. [*54*]

———. "Byrd's Patrons at Prayer." *Music & Letters* 89 (2008): 499–509. [*55*]

———. *Liturgy and Contemplation in Byrd's Gradualia*. New York: Routledge, 2007. [*56*]

———, with John Harley. "From the Library of William Byrd." *Musical Times* 150, no. 4 (Winter 2009): 17–30. Supplement in "More Books from the Library of William Byrd." *Musical Times* 153, no. 1 (Spring 2012): 53–60. [*57*]

Milsom, John. "Byrd on Record: An Anniversary Survey." *Early Music* 21 (1993): 446–50. [*58*]

———, "Byrd, Sidney, and the Art of Melting." *Early Music* 31 (2003): 437–50. [*59*]

———. "Caustun's Contrafacta." *Journal of the Royal Musical Association* 132 (2007): 1–31. [*60*]

———. Review of *Latin Motets II: From Manuscript Sources*, ed. Warwick Edwards. *Notes* 58 (2001): 161–64. [*61*]

———. Review of Kerman, *The Masses and Motets of William Byrd*. *Royal Musical Association Research Chronicle* 19 (1983–85): 85–95. [*62*]

———. "Sacred Songs in the Chamber." In *English Choral Practice 1400–1650*, ed. John Morehen, 161–79. Cambridge: Cambridge University Press, 1996. [*63*]

———. "Tallis, Byrd and the 'Incorrected Copy': Some Cautionary Notes for Editors of Early Music Printed from Movable Type." *Music & Letters* 77 (1996): 348–67. [*64*]

———, ed. and introduction. *The Dow Partbooks*. Oxford: DIAMM Publications, 2010. [*65*]

Monson, Craig. "Authenticity and Chronology in Byrd's Church Anthems." *Journal of the American Musicological Society* 35 (1982): 280–305. [*66*]

———. "Byrd and the 1575 *Cantiones Sacrae*." *Musical Times* 116 (1975): 1089–91; 117 (1976): 65–67. [*67*]

———. "Byrd, the Catholics and the Motet: The Hearing Reopened." In *Hearing the Motet*, ed. Dolores Pesce, 348–74. New York and Oxford: Oxford University Press, 1997. [*68*]

———. "The Preces, Psalms and Litanies of Byrd and Tallis: Another 'Virtuous Contention in Love.'" *Music Review* 40 (1979): 257–71. [*69*]

———. "Through a Glass Darkly: Byrd's Verse Service as Reflected in Manuscript Sources." *Musical Quarterly* 67 (1981): 64–81. [*70*]

———. "'Throughout All Generations': Intimations of Influence in the Short Service Styles of Tallis, Byrd and Morley." In *Byrd Studies*, ed. Alan Brown and Richard Turbet, 83–111. Cambridge: Cambridge University Press, 1992. [*71*]

Morehen, John. "Thomas Snodham and the Printing of William Byrd's *Psalmes, songs, and sonnets* (1611)." *Transactions of the Cambridge Bibliographical Society* 12 (2001): 91–131. [*72*]

Moroney, Davitt. "'Bounds and compasses': The Range of Byrd's Keyboards." In *Sundry Sorts of Music Books: Essays on the British Library Collections, Presented to O. W. Neighbour on his 70th Birthday*, ed. Chris Banks, Arthur Searle, and Malcolm Turner, 67–88. London: British Library, 1993. [*73*]

———. *William Byrd: The Complete Keyboard Works*. 7 CDs. London: Hyperion, 1999. [*74*]

Nasu, Teruhiko. "The Publication of Byrd's *Gradualia* Reconsidered." *Brio* 32 (1995): 109–20. [*75*]

Neighbour, Oliver. "Byrd's Treatment of Verse in his Partsongs." *Early Music* 31 (2003): 413–22. [*76*]

———. *The Consort and Keyboard Music of William Byrd*. London: Faber, 1978. [*77*]

———. "Music Manuscripts of George Iliffe from Stanford Hall, Leicestershire, Including a New Ascription to Byrd." *Music & Letters* 88 (2007): 420–35. [*78*]

———. Review of *Byrd Edition*, Vol. 10b: *The Great Service*. *Music & Letters* 65 (1984): 309–13. [*79*]

———. "Some Anonymous Pieces Considered in Relation to Byrd." In *Byrd Studies*, ed. Alan Brown and Richard Turbet, 193–201. Cambridge: Cambridge University Press, 1992. [*80*]

———. "Three Times Seven Songs by Byrd." In *Essays on Renaissance Music in Honour of David Fallows: Bon jour, bon mois et bonne estrenne*, ed. Fabrice Fitch and Jacobijn Kiel, 227–32. Woodbridge: Boydell, 2011. [*81*]

Olleson, Philip. " 'William Byrde's excellent antiphones': Samuel Wesley's Projected Edition of Selections from *Gradualia*." *Annual Byrd Newsletter* 9 (2003): 7–9. [*82*]

Payne, Ian. " 'The first that ever he made': Byrd's First Pavan and Galliard, and Techniques of Transcription and Reconstruction in the 'Lost' Consort Dances." *Chelys* 28 (2000): 28–58. [*83*]

Rastall, Richard. "William Byrd's String Fantasia 6/g1." in *Liber amicorum John Steele*, ed. W. Drake, 139–70. Stuyvesant, NY: Pendragon, 1997. [*84*]

Rees, Owen. "The English Background to Byrd's Motets: Textual and Stylistic Models for *Infelix ego*." In *Byrd Studies*, ed. Alan Brown and Richard Turbet, 24–50. Cambridge: Cambridge University Press, 1992. [*85*]

Schulenberg, David L. "The Keyboard Works of William Byrd: Some Questions of Attribution, Chronology, and Style." *Musica disciplina* 47 (1993): 99–121. [*86*]

Smith, Jeremy. "From 'Rights to Copy' to 'Bibliographic Ego': A New Look at the Early Edition of Byrd's *Psalmes, Sonets and Songs*." *Music & Letters* 80 (1999): 511–30. [*87*]

———. "The Hidden Editions of Thomas East." *Music Library Association Notes* 53 (1997): 1059–91. [*88*]

———. "Print Culture and the Elizabethan Composer." *Fontes artis musicae* 48 (2001): 156–70. [*89*]

———. *Thomas East and Music Publishing in Renaissance England*. New York and Oxford: Oxford University Press, 2003. [*90*]

———. "Unlawful Song: Byrd, the Babington Plot and the Paget Choir." *Early Music* 38 (2010): 497–508. [*91*]

———. "William Byrd's Fall from Grace and his First Solo Publication of 1588: A Shostakovian 'Response to Just Criticism'?" *Music and Politics* 1 (2007) <http://www.music.ucsb.edu/projects/musicandpolitics>. [*92*]

Smith, Mike. " 'Whom Music's Lore Delighteth': Words-and-Music in Byrd's *Ye sacred Muses*." *Early Music* 31 (2003): 425–35. [*93*]

Taylor, Philip. " 'O worthy queen': Byrd's Elegy for Mary I." *The Viol* 5 (2006–7): 20–24. [*94*]

Trendell, David. "Byrd's Musical Recusancy." *Musical Times* 148 (2007): 27–50. [*95*]

Turbet, Richard. "The Fall and Rise of William Byrd." In *Sundry Sorts of Music Books: Essays on the British Library Collections, Presented to O. W. Neighbour on his 70th Birthday*, ed. Chris Banks, Arthur Searle. and Malcolm Turner, 119–28. London: British Library, 1993. [*96*]

———. "Homage to Byrd in Tudor Verse Services." *Musical Times* 129 (1988): 485–90. [*97*]

———. "Horsley's 1842 Edition of Byrd and its Infamous Introduction." *British Music* 14 (1992): 36–46. [*98*]

———. "Joyful Singing: Byrd's Music at a Royal Christening." *Musical Times* 145 (Spring 2004): 85–86. [*99*]

———. "Three Glimpses of Byrd's Music during its Nadir." *The Consort* 65 (2009): 18–28. [*100*]

———. *William Byrd: A Guide to Research*. 3rd ed. New York: Routledge, 2012. [*101*]

Urquhart, Peter. "The Persistence of Exact Canon throughout the Sixteenth Century." In *Canons and Canonic Techniques*, ed. Katelijne Schiltz and Bonnie J. Blackburn, 171–96. Leuven: Peeters, 2007. [*102*]

Wulstan, David. "*Birdus tantum natus decorare magistrum*." In *Byrd Studies*, ed. Alan Brown and Richard Turbet, 63–82. Cambridge: Cambridge University Press, 1992. [*103*]

———. "Byrd, Tallis and Ferrabosco." In *English Choral Practice 1400–1650*, ed. John Morehen, 109–42. Cambridge: Cambridge University Press, 1995. [*104*]

A Reader's Guide to Byrd Literature

Byrd's music began to attract scholarly attention even in his own lifetime, and there has been a steady stream of books and articles since the tercentenary of his death in 1923. Much of the recent literature on Byrd is quite specialized. This can be daunting for the beginner, but it also guarantees that persistent readers can find detailed discussion of almost any topic or work that might interest them. What follows here is a brief introduction to the Byrd literature of recent years, along with some practical notes on finding Byrd's music in print. Numerals in italics refer to bibliographic entries in Part II of Appendix D, which are arranged alphabetically by author: *77* is Oliver Neighbour's *Consort and Keyboard Music of William Byrd*.

I. Music Editions

In the late twentieth century, Philip Brett and a group of half a dozen colleagues undertook a new *Byrd Edition* published by Stainer & Bell. This twenty-volume project encompassed all of Byrd's vocal music and consort music. When the last volume was published in 2004, the complete works of Byrd were finally available in reputable scholarly editions. Each volume in this series includes its own preface, editorial notes, list of sources, critical commentary, and other relevant materials. Some of the *Byrd Edition* prefaces, most notably those by Brett himself, are important works of scholarship in their own right.

The first complete edition of Byrd's music, the predecessor to Brett's *Byrd Edition*, was made under the supervision of Edmund Fellowes between 1937 and 1950. These older books are still widely available in libraries, but they are now obsolete and should be approached with great caution: students and performers can easily be led astray by the tangle of pitch adjustments, metrical irregularities, and other editorial interventions. The sacred pieces edited in volumes 2, 7, and 9 of *Tudor Church Music* during the 1920s are slightly harder to find but still quite usable. They also have the advantage, unlike some more recent editions, of not obscuring Byrd's original notation by transposing his music into tonal areas foreign to Renaissance England.

For those without ready access to an academic library, the online Choral Public Domain Library (cpdl.org) offers good-quality free downloadable PDF scores of all the vocal music Byrd published during his lifetime, corresponding to *Byrd Edition*, vols. 1–7b and 12–14. Each entry includes a MIDI file and, where relevant, an English translation. Complete facsimiles of all Byrd's printed works, in their original form, can also be obtained from Early English Books Online (eebo.chadwyck.com), although these must be accessed through a library subscription.

Byrd's complete keyboard music was edited by Alan Brown in *Musica Britannica* 27 and 28. The BK numbers in Appendix B of this book refer to the numbering of Byrd's keyboard works in these two volumes: they are arranged by tonal center rather than genre, starting with pieces based on G and moving up the scale to pieces based on F. The *Musica Britannica* edition includes a full account of the often contradictory sources, and Brown has continued updating it to reflect the latest scholarship. The third and most recent edition is recommended for serious students of Byrd's music.

The evergreen Dover editions of *My Lady Nevell's Book* (edited by Hilda Andrews) and the *Fitzwilliam Virginal Book* (edited by J. Fuller Maitland and W. Barclay Squire) are still in print and useful for everyday music-making. They also preserve the original musical order of the manuscripts—especially valuable in the case of Nevell, which was almost certainly compiled under Byrd's own supervision.

II. Biography and Reference

There have been rather few comprehensive studies of Byrd's life and music. Fellowes published the first serious Byrd biography (*21*) in 1936 and revised it in 1948. Much of the research is now outdated, but the book is still worth reading as a insightful account of Byrd's career and a document of twentieth-century musical scholarship. Kerman's concise and elegant article in *Grove Music Online* (*44*) should be the first port of call for most readers. Harley's *William Byrd: Gentleman of the Chapel Royal* (*29*) is a full-length life-and-works study by an accomplished archival researcher. The biographical chapters include a great deal of new information on Byrd's family, career, and non-musical preoccupations. *The World of William Byrd* (*31*) is a sequel of sorts, best read after (or alongside) the earlier book. Along with the related articles *26* and *28*, it offers further biographical insight and a more detailed glimpse into Byrd's various social circles.

A useful reference work is Turbet's *Guide to Research* (*101*), an annotated bibliography of all existing literature on Byrd. The third and most recent edition includes books and articles published through the end of 2011. The *Guide* is especially valuable for those seeking information in a particular area of Byrd studies; readers should not be discouraged by the idiosyncratic indexing system. *The Technique of Byrd's Vocal Polyphony* by H. K. Andrews

(*2*) is an analytical encyclopedia of Byrd's polyphonic style with hundreds of music examples, well suited for students of counterpoint and composition. *30* explores the pitch organization of Byrd's works in light of Renaissance modal theory. The first volume of the *Oxford History of English Music* (*16*), especially chapters 4 through 8, offers a broader musical context for Byrd's works and is recommended as background reading for non-specialists.

Most of the existing scholarship on Byrd has appeared in the form of journal articles or (much less often) individual monographs, but there are a few collected volumes that deal wholly or substantially with Byrd's music. The 1992 volume of *Byrd Studies* (*15*) is a wide-ranging collaborative project with half a dozen chapters each on Byrd's vocal and instrumental music. Much of Brett's published work on Byrd (*7, 8, 10, 11*) can be found in a posthumous collection of essays and articles, including an important 100-page account of the *Gradualia* adapted from his *Byrd Edition* prefaces. The Festschrift for Oliver Neighbour's seventieth birthday contains a good deal of work on Byrd (*9, 14, 73, 96*). The *Annual Byrd Newsletter*, published from 1995 to 2004 as a supplement to *Early Music Review*, contains a variety of short articles, reviews, and miscellanea. It can be difficult to obtain outside the UK but is well worth acquiring as a single-volume reprint from King's Music.

III. Latin-Texted Music

Byrd's Latin-texted music has enjoyed considerable attention since the middle of the twentieth century, most notably in the work of Joseph Kerman, whose *Masses and Motets of William Byrd* (*40*) is a systematic account of the whole repertory and an important study of Byrd's creative development. It includes a large selection of music examples but is best read with full scores and, if possible, recordings at hand. (The Cardinall's Musick has recorded the complete Latin works in *17*.) John Milsom's review of the book (*62*) is highly recommended, as is his related piece (*61*) on Byrd's unpublished motets. Kerman set the stage for this work with a pair of articles in the early 1960s (*36* and *39*) on Byrd's development as a composer of motets and the cultural background of the texts he chose. A companion piece to these is his close reading (*43*) of *Emendemus in melius*, the arresting motet that Byrd gave pride of place in the 1575 *Cantiones*. Kerman discussed the 1575 book in more detail in an article commemorating its 400th anniversary (*42*), as did Craig Monson (*67*) in the same year.

Byrd's motets are an unusually fruitful field for the study of imitation and other contrapuntal devices. Kerman was also a pioneering figure here (*38*), followed by Peter le Huray (*48*, focusing on Byrd's cantus-firmus compositions), Peter Urquhart (*102*, focusing on his use of canon), and Julian Grimshaw (*25*, focusing on his monumental early works). *95* revisits the style of the motets with reference to possible Continental models and older English precedents. *98* recalls the meddlesome Victorian editor who first published the 1589 *Cantiones* with cautionary notes on their "awkward and unmelodious" part-writing and "vague and timid" harmonies. Other studies of the motets take on textual issues (*54, 85*) and contemporary adaptations of these works into English (*52*; precedents and parallels from Byrd's early years are discussed in *60*).

Although Byrd's three masses may well be his best-known works, the existing literature on them is rather sparse. Kerman's musical exploration (*37*, most of which is also available in chapter 4 of *40*) is recommended, as is Brett's preface to volume 4 of the

Stainer & Bell *Byrd Edition*. Brett traces the distinctively English background of the masses in *8*, while Peter Clulow (*18*) offers perhaps the most crucial discovery of all, their precise dates and order of publication. Byrd's later and more complex Catholic liturgical works, the two books of *Gradualia*, were not fully understood until the 1960s, when James Jackman (*33*) unraveled their correct liturgical order. The most useful account of the *Gradualia* is Brett's extensive essay (*10*); *56* and *53* offer some additional cultural and musical background. *75* discusses the patronage of this music (most notably a surprising endorsement by the Archbishop of Canterbury in 1605), and *82* recalls a pioneering nineteenth-century attempt to edit and publish it.

IV. English-Texted Music

Philip Brett died in 2002 without completing his long-promised book on Byrd's English-texted music. We can gain some idea of its projected scope from *11*, a pioneering study on Byrd's consort songs and how they differ from the aesthetic ideals of the more familiar Elizabethan madrigal. The August 2003 issue of *Early Music* is a tribute to Brett that includes several essays (*93, 76, 59*) on Byrd's settings of English poetry: topics include his lament on the death of Tallis and a close reading of his song *O dear life*, a setting of an erotic poem by Sidney published (with the latter verses discreetly left unprinted) in *Songs of Sundrie Natures*. Such close readings of the English-texted works are still rather rare. One distinguished exception is *45*, on the beautiful late song *Retire my soul*. In *92*, Jeremy Smith (whose book on Byrd's earlier songs is due to appear with Boydell and Brewer in 2014) searches for political subtexts in Byrd's first songbook, with reference to the more recent and equally ambiguous career of Shostakovich. *81* offers a long-overdue discussion of Byrd's second and more eclectic songbook. *46* deals with Byrd's controversial elegy for Campion, *94* with his elegy for Queen Mary Tudor, and *47* with his encomium "in praise of Music." *23* reveals that most of the *Psalmes* of the outwardly respectable 1611 book were in fact drawn from a contraband Catholic source.

Much of the existing work on Byrd's English church music was done by Monson, who edited this repertory for the new *Byrd Edition*. He has written about the anthems (*66*), the Verse Service (*70*; see also *97*), the Short Service (*71*), and the smaller liturgical works (*69*). Neighbour's review (*79*) of his modern edition of the Great Service offers some valuable stylistic and historical perspective on Byrd's greatest Anglican work. There are also a handful of smaller investigations, among them *99*, which reveals that the famous anthem *Sing joyfully* was performed at the christening of King James's infant daughter. Andrew Johnstone's systematic study of the English church works is currently in press and due to appear in 2014.

V. Instrumental Music

Byrd's keyboard music has enjoyed considerable popularity since the publication of the complete works in *Musica Britannica* and, more recently, the outstanding set of recordings (*74*) by Davitt Moroney, whose detailed booklet is an ideal introduction to this music. Novices might also choose to start by consulting Alan Brown's chapter in *13*. Neighbour's book (*77*) is the most complex and searching account of Byrd's keyboard style. Like Kerman's volume on the Latin-texted works, it is best read with the music at hand; in fact it is best of all read at the keyboard. *80* is a useful supplement to the book. David Schulenberg contends in *86* with some of Neighbour's arguments and questions the authenticity of a number of the pieces published in *Musica Britannica*. *32* and *73* deal with performing matters and will be of special interest to keyboard players. A considerable amount of research has been done on *My Lady Nevell's Book*, the most important source of Byrd's keyboard music: those materials are discussed below under *Sources*.

Free-standing studies of individual instrumental pieces are still somewhat rare. One exception is Alan Brown's article (*14*) on the much-copied *Woods so Wild*, the only one of Byrd's keyboard works given an exact date by a scribe. Pieter Dirksen's important study of the connections between Byrd and Sweelinck (*20*; worth obtaining even in Dutch if necessary) includes a European version of the Petre pavan and galliard. Neighbour (*77*) offers the most thorough treatment of the music for viols. More recent scholarship tends either to build on it or to challenge it, as *84* does on issues of chronology (concentrating on the two great G minor fantasias) and *3* on matters of musical influence. Ian Payne discusses the underappreciated links between Byrd's consort and keyboard styles in *83*. The viol consorts Fretwork and Phantasm have both made excellent complete recordings of the repertory.

VI. Sources

There is much to be learned from the material sources, both print and manuscript, in which Byrd's music has been preserved. Some of the best work on published sources has been done by Smith in his book on Thomas East (*90*), who was Byrd's printer and collaborator for more than two decades, and in a series (*87, 88, 89*) of associated articles. *1* deals with Byrd's first solo publication, and *72* with his last. Readers interested in the printing process and the physical details of music production will also want to consult *64*, which takes the 1575 *Cantiones* as a case study, and *22*, which examines a lesser-known aspect of the Tallis–Byrd music patent, the production of ruled music paper.

The numerous surviving manuscripts of Byrd's music are equally important windows into the musical culture of their day. Detailed studies include *49* and *65* (on the Dow partbooks), *4* (on the Baldwin partbooks), *7* and *9* (on the music copied by the Catholic Paston scriptorium), and *5* and *50* (on books compiled or collected in the houses of Byrd's other patrons). Harley informs us (*27*) of the real identity of the mysterious Lady Nevell; *12* and *24* deal with the contents and production of her famous book of keyboard music.

VII. Historical and Political Context

The study of Byrd extends well beyond his music to the complex historical and political circumstances in which he lived. A good deal of new evidence in this area has been discovered in recent years. *41* is a helpful introduction to the issues. Byrd's activities as a Catholic dissenter are treated in *51* (a detailed account of his legal travails), *68* (an especially useful contextual study by Monson), and *91* (dealing with one of the rare occasions when Byrd's music was cited as evidence in anti-Catholic persecutions.) David Trendell focuses in *95* on the rich Catholic resonances of the Latin motets. There are increasing signs that Byrd's political situation was even more complex than we may have suspected. *57* announces the discovery of a dozen books owned and signed by the composer, most of which are works of Protestant polemic; *55* studies the ambiguous loyalties of his major patrons; and *78*, most surprisingly, reveals a new

English anthem credibly attributed to Byrd in which the singers pray for protection from "Turk and Pope."

VIII. Reception and Performance

Byrd's works have been adapted, disputed, rejected, and rediscovered in the four centuries since his death. Milsom makes the crucial point in *63* that his motets were originally conceived and performed as private chamber music rather than what we would now consider "Tudor church music." *52* traces the partial assimilation of these motets into the Anglican church tradition, and Turbet follows their subsequent fate in *96* and *100* with some colorful anecdotes. Suzanne Cole continues to do important new work on the nineteenth-century revival of Byrd's works, notably in *19*, her study of evolving Victorian attitudes toward his cultural and musical importance. There is still a lively debate about some aspects of how his music should be performed, especially about the issue of performing pitch. David Wulstan weighs in on the side of substantial upward transposition in *103* and *104*—a practice familiar to many singers from performing editions in unusual keys—while Johnstone uses new physical evidence from English Renaissance organs to argue in *34* that church pitch in Byrd's day was approximately a semitone above modern concert pitch. There have been a few detailed reviews of notable Byrd recordings. *35* is a searching discussion of the new Cardinall's Musick motet series (*17*) and some insights gained from it. *58* reviews the state of things at the close of the twentieth century, what was considered at the time to be the 350th anniversary of the composer's birth, and calls for systematic and thoughtful performance of a wider range of works. (As this book goes to press, many English-texted pieces by Byrd still remain unrecorded.)

General Index

Index of Byrd's Works

Note: This index does not include the systematic listing in Appendix B of all extant pieces by Byrd.